Everyman, I will go with thee,
and be thy guide

THE EPICUREAN PHILOSOPHERS

Edited by
JOHN GASKIN
Trinity College Dublin

Translated by
C. BAILEY, R. D. HICKS
AND J. C. A. GASKIN

EVERYMAN
J. M. DENT · LONDON
CHARLES E. TUTTLE
VERMONT

Introduction, critical apparatus,
translations of Epicurus' Letter to Menoeceus and
translations from Cicero and Seneca
copyright © J. C. A. Gaskin, 1995

First published in Everyman in 1995

J. M. Dent
Orion Publishing Group
Orion House, 5 Upper St Martin's Lane,
London WC2H 9EA
and
Charles E. Tuttle Co., Inc.
28 South Main Street,
Rutland, Vermont 05701, USA

Typeset in Sabon by CentraCet Ltd
Printed in Great Britain by
The Guernsey Press Co. Ltd,
Guernsey, Channel Islands

British Library Cataloguing-in-Publication Data
is available upon request.

ISBN 0 460 87607 4

CONTENTS

Note on the Authors and Editor   vii
Preface   ix
Chronologies of the Epicureans and their Times   xii
Introduction   xxiii
Sources, Translations and Acknowledgements   li

Epicurus

1 THE PRINCIPAL DOCTRINES   5

2 ON PHYSICS, OR THE NATURE OF THINGS
  'Letter to Herodotus'   12

3 ON TERRESTRIAL AND CELESTIAL PHENOMENA
  'Letter to Pythocles'   30

4 THE HAPPY LIFE
  'Letter to Menoeceus'   42

5 EPICURUS' EXHORTATION
  'Vatican Sayings'   47

6 FRAGMENTS FROM EPICURUS QUOTED IN
  GREEK LITERATURE   54

7 QUOTATIONS FROM EPICURUS IN CICERO'S
  PHILOSOPHICAL WORKS   65

8 SAYINGS OF EPICURUS IN SENECA'S WORKS   68

9 EPICURUS' LAST WILL AND TESTAMENT   72

Philodemus

THE FOURFOLD REMEDY   77

Lucretius

ON THE NATURE OF THE UNIVERSE: *De Rerum Natura* 81

BOOK I: PHYSICAL AND METAPHYSICAL PRINCIPLES 83

BOOK II: THE ATOMIC THEORY 117

BOOK III: MIND, LIFE AND DEATH 153

BOOK IV: SENSATION AND SEXUALITY 189

BOOK V: THE NATURAL ORIGINS OF THE WORLD,
LIFE AND SOCIETY 227

BOOK VI: ERRATIC ATMOSPHERIC AND
TERRESTRIAL EVENTS 269

Diogenes of Oenoanda

THE LAST APPEAL 307

Suggestions for Further Reading 309

NOTE ON THE AUTHORS AND EDITOR

EPICURUS, an Athenian citizen, was born on the island of Samos in the eastern Aegean in 341 BC. At the age of about fifteen he may have received instruction from a pupil of Democritus, the famous early exponent of atomist physics. In 323 Epicurus went to Athens to enlist for the obligatory two years' military service. Having taught philosophy inconspicuously in several Aegean cities between 321 and 308, he moved to Athens and, in 306, established a school of philosophy known as 'The Garden'. He died in about 270, bequeathing his property in trust 'to preserve the common life of the Garden in whatever way is best'. The devout dissemination of his ideas by his friends was to make Epicurean Philosophy – often called the Philosophy of the Garden – known throughout the civilized world.

LUCRETIUS, a well-connected Roman citizen, was born c. 95 BC. Almost nothing is known about him except that he was the author of *De Rerum Natura*, 'On the Nature of the Universe', the definitive account of Epicurean Philosophy in Latin. An internal reference in the text shows him to have heard about the dreadful weather in Britain (Julius Caesar conducted campaigns in south Britain in 55 and 54 BC), and Cicero commends his poetry in a letter of February 54 BC. It is probable that Lucretius died at this time or a bit later. Apart from being a faithful exposition of Epicureanism as a systematic philosophy, Lucretius' work is a passionate quest for natural explanations of the world and a rejection of religious fears.

JOHN GASKIN is a Fellow of Trinity College Dublin, and a Professor in the Department of Philosophy in Dublin University. He was educated at Oxford University and has spent most of his academic career in Dublin. His publications include *Hume's Philosophy of Religion, The Quest for Eternity* and *Varieties of Unbelief*. He has edited a collection of Hume's works on religion and Hobbes's *Element of Law* for World's Classics.

Consultant editor for this volume:
David Berman, Trinity College, Dublin.

PREFACE

*Only this I ask of you, do not be
a passer-by to these words:
they are for all people*
OLD EPICUREAN

It must be emphasized that this book is not addressed to classical
scholars or specialists. Its aim is to bring together in English, in
a readily available form, the writings and sayings of Epicurus
together with the complete and vivid account of his system
provided by Lucretius. In this way I hope the real ideas of the
Epicureans – not merely Stoic, Christian or popular caricatures
of them – will become better known through their own words,
better understood, more accessible to philosophers and, above
all, better known for their own intrinsic worth and interest.

Epicurean ideas were never intended to be difficult or esoteric
or the preserve of the learned. They were addressed to mankind
almost as widely as St Paul addressed his letters on Christianity.
Indeed, in some ways the content of the Epicurean Philosophy –
'the Philosophy of the Garden' as it was often called – has a
more apparent relevance to the world we now know than
Christianity itself. The Epicurean idea of an infinite universe of
matter and space, indifferent to human hopes and concerns but
whose workings can be understood, is the predominant scientific
idea with which we now live. We have fellow feeling with the
importance Epicurus attaches to happiness in *this* life, with his
desire to diminish pain and overcome irrational fears, and with
his attempt to understand and come to terms with death, the
frontier we shall all reach but not cross as the individuals we
now are.

Although this book is not aimed at specialists, it could not
have existed at all without their immense labours in times past.
In the immediate present I would like to record my thanks,
among other colleagues, to Kathleen Coleman for her patient

correction of some of the infelicities in my translations from the Latin of Cicero and Seneca, and to John Luce for the time he devoted to my Chronologies and Introduction. I must thank them both for errors avoided. Those that remain are entirely my own. I am also pleased to record my indebtedness to the support of the Arts and Social Sciences Benefactions Fund of Trinity College, and to Leona Coady for transforming the antique simplicity of handwriting in accordance with the approved complexity of floppy disks and print-outs.

                                                    JOHN GASKIN

CHRONOLOGY OF THE EPICUREANS

Greek philosophical questioning began in the eastern Ionian states in the sixth century BC: Is there a common stuff from which all things could be made? What is the origin of the world? How does change take place? Is anything permanent? It is not until the second half of the fifth century that philosophy – now including ethics and politics – becomes the jewel in the crown of Athenian culture.

Year (BC)	*Philosophical Events*
c. 460	Birth of Democritus of Abdera
430s	Leucippus, reputed originator of Atomism, may have flourished in this decade
420s	Democritus, widely known exponent of Atomist Philosophy, flourished
c. 370	Democritus dies at some very advanced age

CHRONOLOGY OF THEIR TIMES

In 510 BC the first significant democratic government was established at Athens. In 490 the Athenians defeated, at the battle of Marathon, the first Persian attempt to occupy mainland Greece. In 480–79 united Greek forces totally destroyed a vast Persian invasion force, thus securing the freedom in which their philosophy and culture could flourish.

Year (BC)	Historical Events
479–48	Continued expansion of Athenian power in hostilities with Persia and other Greek states
456	Death of Aeschylus, writer of tragedies
c. 450	Birth of Aristophanes, writer of comedies
448	Peace concluded between Athens and Persia. The Greek allies remain subject to Athens, and the Delian League becomes the Athenian Empire
445–31	Age of Pericles
447	Construction of Parthenon began, completed in 431
431–04	Peloponnesian war (between Athenian Empire and Sparta)
429	Death of Pericles
c. 429	Plato born
415–13	Disastrous Athenian expedition to Sicily (chronicled by Thucydides)
c. 406	Euripides and Sophocles die
404	Fall of Athens to Sparta followed by a short-lived oligarchic coup. Over the next decade a restored democracy re-established Athenian naval power and rebuilt the Empire in a modified form
399	Socrates condemned to death and executed
c. 385	Death of Aristophanes
384	Birth of Aristotle

Year (BC)	*Philosophical Events*
341	EPICURUS born on Samos as an Athenian citizen
326	Possible visit to Teos, on coast of Asia Minor, to study under Nausiphanes, a pupil of Democritus
323	Goes to Athens to undertake obligatory two years' military service. The dramatist Menander in same draft
321–06	Epicurus lives successively at Colophon, Mytilene and Lampsacus teaching philosophy
308	Moves to Athens
306	Establishes 'The Garden', the first School of Epicurean Philosophy, situated outside the walls of Athens
c. 277	METRODORUS (born c.330), close colleague of Epicurus and exponent of his system, dies
c. 270	EPICURUS dies; succeeded by HERMARCHUS (born c.325) as Leader of the School
c. 250	HERMARCHUS dies; succeeded by POLYSTRATUS
250–100	Gradual establishment of Epicurean centres in cities on eastern half of Mediterranean. Apollodorus of Tyre, Zeno of Sidon, Diogenes of Tarsus, Ptolemy the White and Ptolemy the Black all recorded as distinguished Epicureans

Year (BC)	Historical Events
347	Death of Plato
344	Birth of Zeno of Citium, founder of Stoicism
c. 342	Birth of Menander, writer of Greek comedies
338	Battle of Chaeronea: all of Hellas falls under suzerainty of Philip of Macedon
336–23	Alexander the Great, son of Philip, conquers Persian Empire from Egypt to Indus
323	Death of Alexander
323–31	Hellenistic Age in which Greek culture and ideas were widely established in the three large empires established by the successors of Alexander, particularly by the Ptolemys in Alexandria (Egypt)
322	Death of Aristotle
c. 300	Euclid (the geometer) flourished
c. 290	Death of Menander
c. 287	Birth of Archimedes, mathematician and scientist
c. 280	Birth of Chrysippus, systematic Stoic
270s	Aristarchus of Samos flourished in Alexandria in this decade and proposed heliocentric account of universe
262	Death of Zeno of Citium, founder of Stoic philosophy
218	Hannibal crosses Pyrenees and Alps to attack Rome with Carthaginian army; Italy laid waste
212	Archimedes killed in the Roman sack of Syracuse
207	Death of Chrysippus
202	Battle of Zama ends Carthaginian threat to Rome
190s	Plautus writing domestic Roman comedies

Year (BC)	Philosophical Events
c. 155	Birth of Zeno of Sidon in Syria
90s	Titus LUCRETIUS Carus, presumed by some, on the evidence of his name, to be a well-connected Roman citizen, born early in this decade
c. 75–c. 35	PHILODEMUS of Gadara (in Syria) established as house philosopher and Epicurean writer in residence with a substantial library at home of Calpurnius Piso in Herculaneum, near Naples. SIRO the Greek (died 42 BC) establishes sophisticated Epicurean community and school at Naples; much patronized by cultured Romans including Virgil. AMAFINIUS and others publish in Latin popular over-simplifications of Epicurean philosophy
c. 75	Death of Zeno of Sidon
c. 55	LUCRETIUS dies having all but completed the definitive Latin account of Epicureanism in *The Nature of the Universe*
54 (February)	Cicero mentions Lucretius' Latin poems in a letter. *The Nature of the Universe* was probably published about this time under Cicero's supervision with the aid of the copying service provided by his friend Atticus, who was an Epicurean
45–4	Cicero composes accounts of Greek philosophy for Latin audiences including (unsympathetic) outlines of Epicureanism, mainly in *De Finibus* and *De Natura Deorum*

Year (BC)   *Historical Events*

148   Macedonia becomes a Roman province
146   Demolition of city of Carthage by Rome
            Sack of Corinth; Greece becomes a Roman province
c. 135   Birth of Posidonius, great Stoic philosopher and polymath
106   Birth of Cicero, great Roman politician, philosopher and writer

88–30   Period of intermittent civil wars that eventually brought
            Roman Republic to an end

70   Virgil, author of *The Aeneid*, born
65   Birth of Horace, Latin poet
63   Syria becomes a Roman province
58–49   Julius Caesar's campaigns in Gaul
55–4   Caesar's expeditions to Britain

51   Death of Posidonius
49–8   Civil war between Pompey and Caesar

44   Murder of Caesar
43   Cicero obliged by Mark Antony to kill himself
            Birth of Ovid, Latin poet

Year   Philosophical Events

c. 40 BC–*c.* AD 60   Epicureanism slowly overtaken by Stoicism as the
                    major philosophy in the Roman Empire

c. AD130 (?)   DIOGENES, a wealthy citizen of Oenoanda, causes last
                    known extensive exposition of the Epicurean system in
                    antiquity to be inscribed in Greek on the walls of a
                    stone colonnade in Oenoanda (in south-west Asia
                    Minor). Considerable fragments of the inscription
                    survive

Year	Historical Events
42 BC	Battle of Philippi: death of Brutus leaves Antony and Octavius (later Augustus) masters of the Roman world
31	Battle of Actium between Antony (with Cleopatra) and Octavius leaves Octavius with absolute power and establishes Egypt as a Roman province
29	Augustus Caesar (Octavius) becomes in effect first Roman Emperor
19	Death of Virgil
6	Death of Horace
c. 4	Birth of Seneca, Roman imperial administrator and eloquent advocate of Stoicism
AD 14	Death of Augustus; Tiberius becomes Emperor
17	Death of Ovid
c. 29	Jesus executed in Jerusalem
37	Caligula becomes Emperor
41	Claudius becomes Emperor
43	Claudius initiates annexation of southern Britain
c. 50	Birth of Plutarch, polymath and voluminous writer
54	Nero becomes Emperor (murdered AD 68)
c. 56	Birth of Tacitus, greatest Roman historian (died c. 115)
65	Seneca obliged by Nero to kill himself
70	Destruction of Jerusalem ends Jewish Rebellion
79	Eruption of Mt Vesuvius entombs Pompei and Herculaneum
c. 90	Birth of Ptolemy of Alexandria, geographer, mathematician and astronomer
96	Nerva becomes Emperor and initiates long succession of highly competent emperors who secured 'Pax Romana' in second century
98	Trajan becomes Emperor
117	Hadrian becomes Emperor
c. 120	Death of Plutarch
c. 129	Birth of Galen, brilliant anatomist and physician
138	Antoninus Pius becomes Emperor
161	Marcus Aurelius, the Stoic, becomes Emperor
c. 168	Death of Ptolemy of Alexandria

Year	Philosophical Events
c. 180	Lucian, the satirist (c. 120–after 180), appeals to the rational humanism of the Epicureans in combating religious charlatanism in his *Alexander the False Prophet*
c. 200	'The Garden' still in existence as the Epicurean School in Athens
c. 220–50	DIOGENES LAERTIUS incorporates anecdotal life of Epicurus, and the only four authentic works of Epicurus that now survive, in his *Lives of Eminent Philosophers* written in Greek.

In the remaining two centuries of the Roman Empire in the West, and in the Dark Ages that followed, the Epicureans were extinguished by barbarian violence and Christian hostility. Lucretius' poem, and the book of Diogenes Laertius, survived only in one or two manuscripts to be republished in the sixteenth and seventeenth centuries when Atomism became the foundation theory of modern science.

Year	Historical Events
180	Death of Marcus Aurelius; succeeded by his son Commodus
180–93	Period of bad government and confusion
193	Septimius Severus becomes Emperor (dies 211)
c. 199	Death of Galen
c. 260?	Sextus Empiricus, compiler of influential works on sceptical philosophy, flourished

The Empire in the West gradually became more and more difficult to sustain in the face of barbarian attacks, economic instability and religious dissent. In 410 Rome was sacked, for the first time since 387 BC, by the Goths. In 476 the Western Empire formally ended when Odovacar became king of Italy. The Eastern Empire, centred on Constantinople, survived until the capture of the city by the Ottoman Turks in 1453.

INTRODUCTION

Vain is the word of a philosopher which healeth not the sufferings of man.

PORPHYRY, AFTER EPICURUS

All that is real in the universe is an infinity of void space, and an infinity of primary particles in random and everlasting motion. Such is the physics of Epicurus.

The ethics have a like simplicity: all that is needed for human happiness is a life among friends, a body free from pain, and a mind free from fear and anxiety.

The working out in detail of these two great themes in an argued, evidenced and coherent philosophy, and the founding of a community in Athens (generally known as 'The Garden') that would live according to such a philosophy, was the business of Epicurus in the years 306–270 BC. His followers were to spread his works and the Epicurean way of life throughout the Hellenistic world, then to Rome itself in whose empire both were to survive as an active influence until well into the third century AD. Then there is silence for more than a thousand years, broken only by hideously distorted caricatures of the way of life. Finally, in seventeenth-century Europe, Epicurean physics are rediscovered and become the foundation of modern science.

The way of life – the Epicurean ethic – was and is attractive in itself. It was gentle, tolerant and open to all people regardless of race or sex or social standing. It spoke to the emotional and physical needs of ordinary human beings, and it did so in ways which evidently had practical and long-term success. But since the ethic was always commended, not merely and only because human beings are the creatures they are, but also and primarily because it was an appropriate response to the true nature of the universe, it is essential to begin as Lucretius begins – with Epicurean physics.

A convenient summary of these can be given by listing some of the main principles in the order in which they are identifiable in Lucretius' *On the Nature of the Universe*, completed in about 54 BC. Most can also be given clear textual illustration from Epicurus' own somewhat meagre surviving writings. But Lucretius, although his tone is more fervent and his intentions more anti-religious, is a faithful reporter, and his exposition is more complete and systematic than anything to be found elsewhere. They are 'principles' in the sense that each is essential to the structure of the system, and each either has to be established independently because it does not follow from the others, or is so important that an attempt is in fact made to establish it independently. Principles XIV (A)–(C) are vestiges of the largely lost Epicurean 'canonic', the theory of knowledge and perception that lay between the physics and the ethics. It is, however, not misleading to include them under 'physics' since Epicurus himself appears to have treated them in this way. His system is founded on the reliability of sensation, and sensation cannot be explained without recourse to physics. Each principle can be located by consulting the synopsis of Lucretius which precedes Books I, II and IV in this edition of his poem. Principles I to IX are in Book I, X to XIV (B) in Book II.

THE PHYSICAL PRINCIPLES

I. No thing is ever created out of nothing by divine will: everything happens according to natural laws without the aid of gods.

II. No thing is ever put out of existence: natural laws resolve each thing again into its primary parts.

III. Primary particles or 'first beginnings' cannot be discerned with the eye but exist.

IV. Nothing can touch or be touched unless it is body.

V. Void – mere space, untouchable and empty – exists.

VI. Nothing other than body and void is real.

VII. Bodies are primary particles ('primordia'), or the union of these: primary particles are solid (contain no void) and everlasting.

VIII. The universe has no limit.

IX. The quantity of matter (i.e., primordia viewed collectively) is fixed (see I and II) but infinite.

X. Primary particles move of themselves.

XI. Primary particles move 'down', and uniformly, irrespective of weight, except for random swerves which set up multiple collisions, groupings and rebounds.

XII. The totality of matter and the totality of movements are both constant.

XIII. Primary particles vary finitely in shape and size.

XIV (A). Things with sensation are composed of primordia which have no sensation.

XIV (B). Living things with sensation are just primordia grouped in an appropriate way.

XIV (C). Sensation is reliable because it cannot be gainsaid by anything more reliable than itself.

ONE WORLD REALISM

The foundation principle of the system, principle VI, is that the universe, the all viewed as one, has two real constituents: body and void. In the 'Letter to Herodotus' Epicurus puts it thus: 'the whole of being consists of bodies and space.' The existence of body is proved to us by sensation: if we cannot know that there are bodies, we cannot know anything at all (Lucretius, I, 418–25). But bodies have location, and they move. That is to say the universe is not as it might have been – solid, packed tight, immobile. 'There is then void, mere space untouchable and empty' (I, 334). In brief, 'All nature . . . as it is of itself, is built of those two things: for there are bodies, and there is the void in which they are *placed* and where they *move*' (I, 419–20). Nothing else is real: 'There is nothing which you could say is distinct from body and sundered from void, which could be discovered, as it were a third nature in the list' (I, 430). All other entities – things, events, memories, the gods, time, I myself and life – are, or are in the final analysis a property or accident[1] of body and void.

---

[1] As Lucretius explains (I, 449–58), a property (*coniunctum*: that which is connected) is that which cannot be separated from a thing without the 'fatal disunion' of the thing, e.g. you cannot remove (all) heat from a fire and still have a fire. An accident (*eventum*: a chance happening) is something which can come and go without the thing ceasing to be what it is, e.g. a man may become rich or poor without ceasing to be a man.

It will be noticed that the foundation principle is defended, not merely asserted. We sense bodies by touch (IV), and that they move. This is perhaps our most basic sense experience; so basic that no one using words with their common significations is likely to deny it. And sense experience is the ultimate standard for any information we can have about the world (see XIV (C)[2]). We also have some conception of space because we move in it and we sense other things moving, and movement is not even conceptually possible unless there is space which allows more than one location. What is more, the Epicureans claimed that the foundation principle has vast explanatory powers when worked out in detail with the other principles. Even apparently recalcitrant phenomena – life itself and human minds for example – can be included within its scope (as Lucretius argues with such vigour in Book III.).

The outcome of the foundation principle is a world view shared by Epicureans and Stoics, and *de facto* adopted by all actual investigations and explanations in modern science. It is a view rejected by Plato, Descartes and all traditional Christian philosophy and worship. It is the view that reality is of one and only one sort. There is no 'other' world of spirits, gods, human minds and eternal objects. If these in any way exist, then they are of this physical world, a part, property or accident of it, not beings of some totally different order of reality. Indeed, the word 'physical' is wholly redundant. There is simply nothing else from which this world can or cannot be distinguished as 'physical'. There is *one* world, this world, and all that is real is of it.

---

[2] Epicurus asserts his crucial rejection of scepticism with regard to the senses thus, 'If you fight against all your sensations, you will have no standard to which to refer, and thus no means of judging even those judgements which you pronounce false' ('Principal doctrines' 23; see also 24). The arguments are complicated in themselves and Epicurus' deployment of them is in lost works. This means that any discussion has to be uncertainly reconstructed from a tangle of ancient comments, hostile critiques and terminology which shifts its meaning from one author to another. Such discussion, important as it is, is beyond the scope of the present volume. It should be followed in R. M. Rist, *Epicurus: an Introduction* (Cambridge, 1972), pp. 17–25 and 80–88, and in A. A. Long, *Hellenistic Philosophy* (London, 1974), pp. 21–30. More advanced discussions can be found in Stephen Everson's article 'Epicurus on the Truth of the Senses' in *Epistemology*, ed. S. Everson (Cambridge, 1990) and in C. C. W. Taylor's article 'All Perceptions are True' in *Doubt and Dogmatism*, eds. M. Schofield et al. (Oxford, 1980).

The one-world realism of Epicurus is made sharper by principles I and II. These have a double function. They assert that no divine intervention (from within or without this world) brings into being, or puts out of being, any primary body of matter.[3] They also assert what is virtually another unspoken presupposition of the natural sciences, namely that sensible events and things do not occur randomly. Pigs' ears don't grow suddenly on trees, nor do healthy women suddenly turn into pillars of salt. On the scale of what is large enough to be sensible, nature works regularly. It is not chaotic, nor does it function according to the caprice of divine beings. When it appears to do either of these things, the business of the Epicurean (like the modern scientist) is to understand *how* the apparently irregular phenomenon fits into the natural patterns of things.

So how does nature work? Epicurus' first steps largely follow the atomism of his predecessor Democritus (much revered by Lucretius). The steps are principles VII, X, and XI.

THE FUNDAMENTAL BUILDING BLOCKS

The Democritan-Epicurean claim is that the workings of the world of sensible bodies in space can be accounted for by the existence of an infinite number of tiny particles, the 'first-beginnings' of things. These may be of different sizes, but all are too small to be sensed. They are everlasting, contain no void within themselves, and have a large but finite set of shape variations.

Epicurus and the Greeks called these particles *atomoi* (uncutables). No similar Latin word was available for Lucretius, and the term he most commonly uses is *primordia* (first-beginnings). For very understandable reasons the Greek word was employed

---

[3] This would commonly be taken as a contradiction of the Genesis story which forms the foundation of Jewish, Christian and Islamic credos about God creating *ex nihilo*, out of nothing. But there is an ambiguity. The first two verses of the Book of Genesis may mean either (a) 'In the beginning God created [out of nothing] the heavens and the earth and [when he had done this] the earth was without form and void . . .' or (b) 'In the beginning the earth was without form and void and [from the pre-existing condition] God created the heavens and the earth . . .'. The first time that meaning (a) appears unequivocally in the Hebrew canon is in 2 Maccabees 7:28. Generally Christians have preferred (a), and Muslims (b).

by John Dalton and others at the beginnings of modern chemistry to name particles which, it transpired after a hundred and thirty years, do not in fact have the indestructibility of *atomoi*. Perhaps no entity exists that is an *atomos* as understood by Epicurus, but what we call 'atoms' is certainly not what he intended. Unless this is noted, one is liable to the curious error perpetrated by, for example, R. E. Latham in the Introduction to his much-used and much-modernized translation of Lucretius, where he indicates that Lucretius is no longer reconcilable with modern science because 'the atom has been well and truly split' (p. 9). But atoms are not *atomoi*. To avoid confusions of this sort, throughout the present volume the ultimate building blocks of composite bodies as identified by the Epicureans will be referred to as 'primary particles' or 'primordia'.

But, as I was once asked by a scientific colleague, 'how on earth did they ever come to think of things as made up of invisible particles in the first place?' Part of the answer is that Epicurus (and even Democritus) came comparatively late in the long Greek adventure of asking about the nature of things. But some of the more immediate reasons are reported by Lucretius in Book II. One is by intelligent questioning of common observations. For example: how is it that two objects of identical size, say a cube of gold and a cube of marble, weigh differently? It could be that one has more particles packed into its apparent solidity than the other. Or again, we may notice motes in a sunbeam (II, 112–41), and infer from this that minute bodies may well also exist below the level of the visible. Another reason for the atomist hypothesis is that it provides a way of explaining other phenomena. For example, solids could be composed of primordia clogged together in some way, fluids of smoother or less densely packed primordia, air of even finer particles, and so on. Or the attrition of hard objects by soft, e.g., coins by fingers, might be explained by the loss of imperceptible primordia.

What cannot be intelligibly asked is *why* there are primordia. Their existence, on the Epicurean view, is an ultimate fact about the nature of the universe (like the operation of gravity in modern physics). And to ask why this fact is so, is misguided because the question looks outside all that really exists for an explanation of what exists, and nothing exists outside all that is. What is more, according to the Epicureans, the misguided question leads us to imagine that natural things are somehow dependent upon the will, or perhaps the caprice, of divine beings not of this world, and this is a fantasy that can carry fear with it.

So the existence of primordia is an irreducibly ultimate fact about the nature of things. But they do not merely exist. Primordia, in Lucretius' words, 'wander through the void' (II, 83 and II, 105). They 'move of themselves' (II, 133). They 'of their own accord fly on, spurred by everlasting motion' (IV, 47). But Epicurus has a suggestion concerning the *way* primordia move which is not to be found in his atomist precursors. According to Epicurus, particles move uniformly 'down' – not the 'down' of common experience for 'we must not assert "up" or "down" of that which is unlimited, as if there were a top or bottom' ('Letter to Herodotus', p. 21). There is a 'rain' of primordia throughout the universe (principle XI). But this cannot be the whole story. If it were, no collisions or bonding would ever take place. Every primary particle would eternally retain the same fixed spatial relations with every other particle, and this total immobility relative to each other would not explain what happens; because on that hypothesis nothing would happen. So the primordia must 'swerve' or alter direction randomly, that is to say in such a way that no prior knowledge of the particles and their movements could ever give knowledge of when and in what manner any given particle would change direction. The outcome of such swerves would then be particle chaos: an infinite number of random collisions taking place for eternity.

Two questions immediately arise. What is the status of the supposed 'downward' movement of particles? How does the chaos of primary particles result in the ordered cosmos we sense all the time?

The short answer to the first question is that the supposition of 'downward' movement by particles is both meaningless and redundant, and on examination turns out to be no more than an assertion that primordia move 'of themselves' as Lucretius puts it. It had already been established (principle VIII) that the universe is unlimited, and has no frame of reference or fixed axis independent of itself. The total uniform movement of everything in any one 'direction' – down, up, or in any way –

has thus no meaning since 'direction' has to be relative to something other than the things directed. So, one might conclude, all Epicurus really needed for the primary chaos of particles was the swerve, and the resulting collisions. But that would not do either. The swerve had been introduced as a random change of direction for a supposedly *already moving* particle. Without prior movement, each swerve would be a new beginning of motion. The appeal to 'downward' movement is thus no more than a confused attempt to assert the ultimate and universal fact *that primordia move* (principle X) but to assert it in terms of our familiar experience of downward movements on earth. What we actually have in the Epicurean system is two ultimate and universal facts: that there are primordia, *and* that primordia move randomly. To put it another way – matter and its random movement are together at the ultimate limit of explanation of how the universe operates and why it is as it is.

So given that principle X, and a principle XI modified to refer only to the random swerve, would together give a primary chaos of impacting particles, how does cosmic order result? 'Regular and rhythmical motion is impossible without design' says Cicero's Stoic (anticipating two millennia of Christian appeals to the design argument for God's existence) in *On the Nature of the Gods* (II, 43), and the anti-Epicurean argument is later made explicit:

> At this point must I not marvel that there should be anyone who can persuade himself that there are certain solid and indivisible particles of matter born along by the force of gravity, and that the fortuitous collision of those particles produces this elaborate and beautiful world?
> (II, 93–4)

But despite Stoic derision and Christian condemnation, Epicurus does have some sort of mechanism to bridge the gap between particle chaos and cosmic order without appealing to an external designer. Particles come in a large but finite set of categories defined by shape (modern usage of the word 'element' might almost convey the idea), and the shapes set limits to the possibilities of linking up with other particles when collisions take place. Thus it becomes possible to think of a certain category of primordia as the 'seed' of a limited, or even a very specific type of thing. Primordial collisions and movements are chaotic, but their successful unions in things are not.

FROM PHYSICS TO ETHICS

To sum up so far: for the Epicureans, the whole universe is comprehended within the two natures void space, and primordia in random motion, both existing eternally. The motions of primary particles account for all that happens, and all sensible bodies that exist. They also account for sensation itself.[4]

But before the appropriateness of the way of life – the Epicurean ethic – can be satisfactorily grasped, three consequences of the physics which touch very closely upon human life and hopes have to be made clear. I shall call them the purposeless existence consequence, the deity consequence and the mortality consequence.

THE PURPOSELESS EXISTENCE CONSEQUENCE

In the 'Letter to Herodotus', principles VIII and IX appear together in the form 'the sum of things is unlimited both by reason of the multitude of the primordia and the extent of the void'. This is a position defended by vivid arguments (of the sort Lucretius sets out in I, 958–1007) to display what we might now call the 'logical impossibility' of supposing that the universe could be limited. However, what the arguments do not establish is that matter itself is infinite in quantity, or that it will be uniformly distributed throughout space rather than peter out at some extremity leaving only the void. Once these assumptions are granted (or merely that the physical universe is almost inconceivably vast), we have no reason to suppose that mankind or our world is unique. The same conditions which produced

---

[4] Epicurus' account of sensation can be found in the 'Letter to Herodotus', pp. 16–18, and in Lucretius IV, 54–721. The matter is important to Epicurus because it is sensation that connects us with the universe and gives us all the information we can ultimately rely on (see note 2). His account is essentially that particles emitted by bodies from their surfaces encounter the bodies which are our sense organs. In the case of sight, the emitted particles are to be called *eidola*. The conventional English translation is 'idols'. But this sounds so odd that I have employed Lucretius' term *simulacra* throughout the translations in this volume. It has at least the desirable overtone of 'similar to' which is entirely missing in 'idols'.

us, and it, will, very probably, exist elsewhere many times over. In particular, other earths with other or the same creatures on them, in the same or different stages of development, will exist.[5] Mankind is not alone; but neither are we the result of a purposeful evolution of primordia (I, 1021–54); nor is this, or any world, made by God or gods for our convenience (II, 1048–143). In short, we have no significance beyond that which we give ourselves; no final purpose, no metaphysical or religious objective. We and our world are like all other things: we form, we grow, we decay and return to the primordial store of the universe.

This conclusion is brought out again and again by Lucretius, and is developed at length in V, 91–508. It was a conclusion which led to disputes with Stoic philosophers, and set the Epicureans on a collision course with all the coming theistic religions of the world – Judaism, Christianity and Islam. It is also a foretaste of what has been called the 'bleak materialism' of modern science. But it is not bleak. Having accepted that life has no meaning beyond itself, the Epicureans set about arguing that happiness in life is actually enhanced by such an acceptance: that there is no *ultimate* tomorrow for anyone or anything does not mean that there can be no happy today.

THE DEITY CONSEQUENCE

The deity consequence is that the existence of gods is either ruled out at the start by one-world realism *or* what gods are has to be described in a highly unusual and, for Christian purposes, a rebarbatively unacceptable way.

Epicurus in the 'Letter to Herodotus' and Lucretius in Books I and II go most of the way towards saying in general terms

---

[5] Hippolytus, a Christian bishop who flourished about AD 220, in his remarks on Democritus in Book I of his *Refutation of All Heresies*, gives a fascinating account of this theory as maintained by Epicurus' predecessor: 'He said also that the ordered worlds are boundless and differ in size, and that in some there is neither sun nor moon, but that in others both are greater than with us, and in yet others more in number. And that the intervals between the ordered worlds are unequal, here more and there less, and that some increase, others flourish and others decay, and here they come into being and there they are eclipsed. But that they are destroyed by colliding with one another. And that some ordered worlds are bare of animals and plants and of all water.' See J. M. Rist, *Epicurus: An Introduction* (London, 1972), pp. 90–99.

what they set out in detail for particular events in the 'Letter to Pythocles' and Books V and VI respectively. Namely, that all the phenomena of the universe have natural explanations. There are no grand designs, no divine interventions, no miracles, no acts of a vengeful or loving or just god. There are only natural phenomena that challenge us to find explanations within the world.

The obvious conclusion to all this is that there is no God or gods. But it is not a necessary conclusion from one-world realism, and Epicurus does not take it. How and why does he avoid it? A succinct and probably reliable paraphrase of how he avoided denying the existence of gods is to be found in Cicero's *On the Nature of the Gods*, I, 43–5:

> that the gods exist, because nature herself has imprinted a conception of them on the minds of all mankind ... the word is *prolepsis*, that is, a sort of preconceived mental picture of a thing, without which nothing can be understood or investigated or discussed.

And in the 'Letter to Menoeceus' Epicurus observes: 'For indeed gods exist. Our perception of them is clear.' But we do not perceive the gods with our senses. They are directly 'seen' in our minds by a form of analogy with what has been perceived by sense. We might well be inclined to reply that this is how the concept of a god acquires *meaning*, not evidence that any gods exist. But Epicurus does indeed take the prevalence of the mental concept as evidence that it is caused by that which it is a concept of.[6]

But why does Epicurus bother with the existence of gods? An element in any answer must be that in Greek cities and under the Roman *imperium* gods were politically important as the focus for civic and imperial ceremony, loyalty and identity. Hence, if at all possible, they should not be denied. A further element may well have been that Epicurus himself felt a real piety towards the multitude of immortals with which his culture surrounded him. What is more, the gods had a use. They

---

[6] The Epicurean account of gods is complex. See A. J. Festugière, *Epicurus and his Gods* (Oxford, 1955) and B. Farrington, *The Faith of Epicurus* (London, 1967). See also the more recent interpretation argued by A. A. Long and D. N. Sedley in their *The Hellenistic Philosophers* (Cambridge, 1987) vol. I, pp. 144–9.

provided an ideal towards which our lives would be directed by the Epicurean way.

So we know that gods exist. But since all that exists must be of this world, gods can only exist as natural bodies of some unobservably fine primordia located in inter-mundane space. This must mean, as Cicero observes, that they are not eternal: 'For what is made of atoms came into existence at some time; but if the gods came into existence, before they came into existence there were no gods; and if the gods had a beginning, they must also perish . . .' (op. cit., I, 68). But what is even worse from any religious point of view is that the gods do nothing. The point is made in the first 'Principal Doctrine': the gods are blessed, inactive, self-sufficient, totally without concern for, or knowledge of us. The account could be illustrated often enough from Lucretius, but W. H. Mallock's verse paraphrase says it all:

> Visions divine! Far off in crystal air,
> What forms are these? The immortal gods are there.
> > Ay – but what gods? Not those that trembling men
> Would bribe with offerings, and appease with prayer.
>
> At ease they dream, and make perpetual cheer
> Far off. From them we nothing have to fear
> > And nothing hope. How should the calm ones hate?
> The tearless, know the meaning of a tear?

So there are gods, blessed beings in and of the universe, who somehow escape the deaths to which we are subject. But they do not create or design the universe, or stand as guardians of good and evil, or at the gateways of life and death. Above all we are no concern of theirs, and we are as free to live our lives according to our own values as if there were no gods at all.

THE MORTALITY CONSEQUENCE

The mortality consequence of Epicureanism is that no individual human being can survive bodily death since there are no categories of existence that might comprehend such survival.

The two crucial terms for Epicurus are – a word he seldom used – *dianoia*, which readily translates 'mind' in most contexts, and – the much more used – *psychē*, which is conventionally (and misleadingly) translated 'soul'. The (almost) corresponding terms in Lucretius are *animus* and *anima*. I shall concentrate discussion upon the Latin terms since Lucretius is very careful about the way they are introduced and used. What is more, Book III of *On the Nature of the Universe* far exceeds in sophistication, thoroughness and ardour anything which survives of Epicurus' writings on the question whether individual human beings survive death. So at least on this matter it is Lucretius, not his master, who must be the focus of philosophical attention.

Lucretius used the word *animus* for the physical part of us which thinks, feels and directs the rest of the body. Conservative even for 55 BC, he is inclined to say the physical part is, or rather is something too tiny to be observed but located in, the heart. We would of course say that this part is the brain. And Cicero, writing at almost exactly the same time as Lucretius, might have been inclined to agree: 'some say the seat of the *animus* is in the brain [*cerebellum*].' But Lucretius also uses *animus* for whatever it is that is the central 'me' and gives me identity and memory. There is no word in classical Latin for 'consciousness' as in 'he lost consciousness' or 'the nature of my consciousness is . . .', but Lucretius clearly tries to pack something of this concept into *animus*, for example, in III, 145: '[*animus*] alone by itself, has understanding for itself, it rejoices for itself.' The combination of that which thinks, feels, directs, understands itself and is the core of 'me' makes the conventional translation 'mind' reasonably satisfactory for *animus* (as it was for Epicurus' *dianoia*). The word 'mind' also commonly translates Lucretius' *mens* (intellect), which he substitutes for *animus* when he is making particular reference to the mind's function as intelligence, understanding or intellect; and *cor* (heart) when he is giving particular attention to mind's function as a centre of feeling.

But it is *anima* which is the real problem word. It has a complex of overlapping usages in Latin (and the Greek word *psychē* is similarly complex) which include, for example: the last breath of a dying person; wind; a ghost or bodyless person; the vital principle in plants; and whatever it is that characterizes life as opposed to death in an animal. In general, and particularly in Lucretius, the conventional translation 'soul' is thus very misleading. Whatever 'soul' now conveys to the scholarly few familiar with the original Latin, or whatever it conveyed to seventeenth- and eighteenth-century Englishmen who argued about 'the natural immortality of the soul', the word 'soul' in ordinary present-day English usage has strong connotations of an actually or potentially disembodied entity, the *me that is not my body*. Thus the *OED* gives as primary senses: 'principle of thought and action in a person, regarded as an entity distinct from body'; 'disembodied spirit of a dead person'; 'a person's spiritual as opposed to corporeal nature'. None of these senses of 'soul' are really suitable for Lucretius' *anima* or Epicurus' *psychē*; and indeed they work against both writers, since a major element in their argument is that *anima* is indeed a part, and nothing other than a part, albeit a necessary part, of the living, embodied *me*. I shall thus leave the word *anima* as an untranslated cypher that gains its meaning in use, always remembering that the whole force of Lucretius' argument is that *anima* has a physiological reference to life rather than a spiritual reference to we know not what. I shall also use the Latin *anima* to translate *psychē* in Epicurus' works.

According to Lucretius, *anima* is composed of very minute *primordia* dispersed throughout a living body. Their presence gives the body and its separate parts life. *Anima* is a continuation of the same sort of stuff as the *animus*; but unlike the *animus*, it is dispersed rather than gathered in the heart/brain as the director etc. of the body. So there is a physical continuum between *animus*, with its specific bodily location, and *anima*. And there is a functional continuum: *animus* is me, the bodily core of my life, *anima* is the life of my body by possession of which the *animus* itself is kept in place and active. I and the life of my body are one, not two entities. (For this reason, at III, 417–24, Lucretius is able to say that when the distinction between *animus* and *anima* is of no importance, both may be referred to by the latter word alone.[7])

---

[7] All this has some parallel in modern physiology. The brain is the director of the body, and it directs through the nerves which are indeed a continuation of the same type of stuff as the brain itself. What is more, life in any part of the human body, although depending upon the continuation of a complex of systems, can, in the final analysis, be identified with the movement of ions (molecules with positive or negative electric charges). If they disperse or cease to be in dynamic equilibrium, the part of the body (or the whole body if the dispersal is general) is dead.

Having already established principles XIII(A) and XIII(B) to show that individually and in themselves primordia have no sensation, and that sensation depends upon an appropriate grouping of primordia, Lucretius in Book III argues in three clear stages.

The first stage, lines 94–416, maintains that mind and *anima* exist like everything else as primordia. Mind and *anima* are parts of the human body, and the mind functions as it does because its primordia are held together in an appropriate way by the structure of the rest of the body just as it, the mind, directs and controls much of what the rest of the animated body can do. This is of course essentially an application of principle VI, the fundamental principle of one-world realism, backed up with principle IV. Since the mind moves the rest of the body (we experience this), it must in some sense be touching it, connected with it as part of the same physical thing, not as a ghost or other entity whose nature precludes it from being of this world. If mind touches this world and moves bodies, then it must be primordia (appropriately structured). If it is not of this world then it cannot touch body or move things. Hence the mind is primordia. Hence at death it will be subject to the same dissolution and loss of structure as the rest of the body, and will become again uncombined, or otherwise combined primary particles. In A. E. Housman's lines, surely influenced by Lucretius:

> From far, from eve and morning
>   And yon twelve-winded sky,
> The stuff of life to knit me
>   Blew hither, here am I.

And then the process reverses and the stuff returns to the primordial store of the universe. This is the forthright articulation of what Antony Flew calls 'the enormous initial obstacle' to claims about personal survival of one's own death. Namely, that a dead body simply is not, and everyone knows it is not, a living person any more: no more than a dead fly is a living fly, or a broken vessel is a whole vessel. Nor is anyone seriously going to suggest that the particles of smoke and the tiny casket of bones ejected by the crematorium are identical with the former person, or could be the self-knowing mind of the former person, or that the memories of the former person could be carried by the dispersed primordia any more than the unassembled primordia that were to be the person before he or she was assembled could in any meaningful sense be the person who is not yet in existence. So one-world realism implies the mortality of individual men and women.

But the second stage of Lucretius' argument, lines 417–829, goes far beyond merely affirming human mortality as the obvious consequence of the bodily nature of mind and *anima*. He provides a welter of supporting arguments, most of which are independent of the main Epicurean principles and have ever since been the quarry from which mortalist arguments have been cut. (Look, for example, at David Hume's little essay 'Of the Immortality of the Soul', 1757.) Why does Lucretius go so far beyond Epicurus' principles in his arguments?

The reason surely is that belief in some sort of immortality was deeply dug into the society of which Lucretius was a member (and has remained deeply dug in) and it needed (and still needs) more argument than a mere general consequence of one-world realism to dislodge this cherished (though contrary to simple apparent fact) belief. For example, it is all too obvious that Lucretius is right, independently of Epicurean principles, when he argues that there is a general concomitant variation between the state of my mind and the state of the rest of my body. We experience this variation in ourselves. We can observe it in others. Mind and body grow and commonly decline together. Health and disease enhance or depress both. Medicine and drugs have similar access to both. Hence it might be predicted that the final dissolution of the body will produce a like alteration in the mind. Again, Lucretius has an interesting independent argument for mortality when he points out that because mind has a special, particular and ascertainable place in the body, it looks as if it must be located in, or be physically identical with, or be an activity of, a bodily organ such as the heart or brain which is itself as much dependent on the biological organization we call 'life' for its continuation as a hand or foot is dependent.

Again, the argument in III, 624–33 is near to the archetype of a very sophisticated philosophical position: since eyes, ears and the other sense organs are the extensions of the *animus*, which enables me to encounter other bodies; without these extensions, i.e. without any body, the mind could have no experiences. Thus

Cicero's Epicurean (*op. cit.* II, 11) remarks 'mind naked and simple, without any material adjunct to serve as an organ of sensation seems to elude the capacity of our understanding'. (Contrast the remark about God in Cicero's *Tusculan Disputations*, I, 23.)

Or again, since memory, even if interrupted by intervals of sleep or in other ways, is a necessary condition for me to know my own continuity, (a) the complete lack of pre-natal memories implies my pre-natal non-existence, and (b) the conceivable reconstruction of a body like mine, of the same primordia that made me, but at some remote time or region of the universe, does not concern me when (III, 851) 'once the recollection of our former selves is broken'. (Of course, Lucretius assumes that the re-assembling of the primordia would not carry the recollection of me since primordia as such do not have or carry recollection of sensation.) Or yet again, III 359–69, Lucretius has an embryonic argument against ghost-in-the-machine dualism: the mind does not look out of the eyes as a man looks through doors. The mind and the senses are a unity, not a duality, and the unity is body.

At line 830 Lucretius reaches the triumphant goal of his argument, *Nil igitur mors est ad nos*, 'Death therefore is nothing to us' (compare Epicurus' 'Principal Doctrine' 2, and Lucretius lines 845, 850, 852, 926 and 972). It is followed by one of the most concentrated passages of inspired poetry in any language, lines 830–1094. This, the third stage in Lucretius' argument, achieves the extraordinary feat of confronting fear of death at two levels. The first level is fear of what will happen – nothing will happen. There will be no you to experience either the fictitious horrors of hell, or anything real that will ever happen in the universe. Again Housman has it all in the cold economy of his verse:

> When earth's foundations flee,
> Nor sky nor land nor sea
>   At all is found.
> Content you; let them burn,
> It is not your concern:
>   Sleep on, sleep sound.

But Lucretius also confronts an even deeper level of fear: fear of loss of self and of non-being or sheer vacuity. His remedy is –

grasp the reality with your imagination. You will *not* be in a vacuity of non-existence. You will *not* be longing for life from the void spaces of the universe. You will *not* be any thing, and, what is more, the nature of life makes it fit and just that you will become again as though you had never been born. Unlimited life would become limitlessly weary. Individual lives need to end in eternal sleep. If it were otherwise, we would destroy the value of our lives, and we would destroy what is achieved by passing on the torch of life to others.

THE WAY OF LIFE

So the nature of the universe in which we live and move and have all the being that is ours to have, is an endless unity of space and primordial particles in motion. It has no destiny or purpose that is given by anything outside itself. Our own world is one of many. It was not made for us by divine or any other foresight. It is a thing that will grow, change and perish like all other things. There are no gods watching over us or concerned with us. Out of matter that was not us we came, and we shall again be dissolved into our component particles without past or future. How then shall we conduct our lives?

Epicurus' answer is simple. We shall make the very best of the life we have by seeking happiness and avoiding pain. The first necessity is that we live without fears and worries which we can avoid. The two great fears that we can avoid are religious fears of what gods or God may bring upon us now or in an after-life, and fear of death itself. A right understanding of the nature of the universe rids us of both these fears.

The rest, in Epicurus' prescription, is a wise and careful application of the maxim 'seek pleasure and avoid pain'. But the very use of the word 'pleasure' sounds like an invitation to self-indulgence and sensual excess, and it was the sound of the invitation rather than the reality of the way that tended to attract voluptuaries and sybarites. But, Epicurus contends, they err badly if they think that genuine, life-long, happiness does consist or ever could have consisted in an unrestrained indulgence of sex, food, wine, drugs, fine possessions and luxury. And they err even more if they think that such a way of life is appropriate because life has no 'meaning', and no one will be

called to account for what they do.[8] They err because such a life
of indulgence would destroy the only life we have. It would be
to invite sickness, wretched satiation, ill health and probably a
short life. It would deprive you of friends and the real affection
of other people, and, above all, it would make your pleasure
and its continuance depend upon what is difficult to acquire and
difficult to sustain. It is certainly true that no form of pleasure is
absolutely prohibited by Epicurus, but the repeated injunction is
to attend to the full consequence of what you want. 'No pleasure
is in itself evil, but the things which produce certain pleasures
entail annoyances many times greater than the pleasure itself'
('Principal Doctrines', 8). And again: 'Every desire must be
confronted with this question: what will happen to me, if the
object of my desire is accomplished and what if it is not?'
('Vatican Sayings', LXXI. See also LI with particular reference
to sexual desires.)

Given then that no desire as such should be regarded as guilty
or wrong, and that conduct should be tested by its consequences,
how should we live? Epicurus' answer can be found in the
'Letter to Menoeceus', in the 'Vatican Sayings', the 'Principal
Doctrines' and in various collected fragments.

Live among friends, with kindness towards them. Live simply,
letting your happiness depend upon common things that are
easy to find. Live quietly, so that you are not troubled by high
office or undue responsibilities. Live with few possessions so
that you do not attract the attentions of robbers or the envy of
officials. Above all, as Aristotle has already convincingly argued,
live with moderation in all things and avoid excesses – even the
excesses of frugality and simplicity.

Such injunctions may require understanding and wisdom for
their application, but they do not require learned annotation.
They are what makes Epicurus' teaching so immediately attractive in any world where there are great opportunities for
indulgence and wealth, but where there is also insecurity with

---

[8] Hippolytus (q.v. note 5) concludes his remarks on Epicurus: 'so that whatever any
one may do in this life and escape notice, he is in no way called to account for it.'
Epicurus would of course have replied (see 'Principal Doctrines', 35 and Seneca's
quotation xcvii, 13) that human beings are called to account throughout their lives by
fear of being found out. A more judicious version of Hippolytus' criticism can be
found in Epictetus' *Discourses*, III, vii.

regard to possessions, scepticism with regard to gods, where vast and remote state organizations diminish personal autonomy, and where science or other factors cause us to see ourselves as insignificant beings in a vast but ultimately purposeless system.

THE GENESIS OF EPICUREANISM

When Epicurus established his school in Athens in 306 BC (it was nicknamed 'the Garden' from its secluded grounds, and Epicureanism has ever since been known as the Philosophy of the Garden) and began to teach a distinctive species of philosophy there, it must not be assumed, as he would rather have liked us to assume, that his ideas were entirely original. What Epicurus added to previous theory was the conception of a random swerve by the primary particles, and an ethic or way of life that was rooted in, and appropriate to, the physical theory. Atomism, a particle theory of the physical universe, had been in existence for well over a hundred years.[9] Its original proponent, himself following upon a long history of Ionian Greek speculation about the possible hidden nature of things and the origins of life and the whole, was, by ancient repute, Leucippus.

Leucippus is a name associated with Abdera (a somewhat unimportant Ionian colony in northern Greece) or possibly with Miletus (the great Ionian trading city in south-western Asia Minor where scientific and philosophical speculation originated in the sixth century BC). His theories are briefly summarized by Diogenes Laertius in Book IX, ch. 6, and again, even more briefly, by Simplicus (c. AD 500–40) in his commentaries on Aristotle's *Physics*. He is overshadowed by, and not readily distinguished from, his presumed pupil, more certainly from Abdera, Democritus (? 460-? 370 BC)

Democritus was an immensely prolific writer – we have a catalogue of his works – and it is one of the calamities of history that no single book of his was allowed to survive the destruction of classical civilization. All we can put together is ancient

---

[9] A very succinct but masterful account of the movement of Greek Philosophy from Presocratic physicalism to Epicureanism and beyond can be found in *An Introduction to Greek Philosophy* by J. V. Luce (London, 1992), ch. 6. More detailed information is in C. Bailey, *The Greek Atomists and Epicurus* (Oxford, 1928).

summaries and numerous short quotations (see J. Barnes', *Early Greek Philosophy*, Harmondsworth, 1987, pp. 244–88). From these we have strong evidence of a man of real wisdom, humour, literary flair and quotable good sense. We also have from him the origins of the atomic theory. In Diogenes Laertius' summary:

> His opinions are these. The first principles of the universe are atoms and empty space; everything else is merely thought to exist. Worlds are unlimited; they come into being and perish. Nothing can come into being from that which is not nor pass away into that which is not. Further, the atoms are unlimited in size and number, and they are borne along in the whole universe in a vortex, and thereby generate all composite things – fire, water, air, earth; for even these are conglomerations of given atoms. And it is because of their solidity that these atoms are impassive and unalterable. The sun and the moon have been composed of such smooth and spherical masses [i.e. atoms], and so also the soul, which is identical with reason. We see by virtue of the impact of images upon our eyes.
>
> All things happen by virtue of necessity, the vortex being the cause of the creation of all things, and this he calls necessity. The end of action is tranquillity, which is not identical with pleasure, as some by a false interpretation have understood, but a state in which the soul continues calm and strong, undisturbed by any fear or superstition or any other emotion. This he calls well-being and many other names. The qualities of things exist merely by convention; in nature there is nothing but atoms and void space. (Loeb edn., vol. II, p. 455)

The similarity to Epicurus is immediately evident. Differences are focused mainly upon the processes of world-formation. In Democritus the process is an immense vortex of atoms. In Epicurus it is an infinite chaos of randomly moving particles building up accumulations and types of things by the different connectability of particles. Even Democritus' ethic has suggestive hints of what Epicurus was to propose, but without the emphasis on happiness and on a community of like-minded people held together by friendship.

THE CONFLICT WITH STOICS AND CHRISTIANS

The teachings of Epicurus were not confined to a select club in Athens. It was a philosophy in active competition with other philosophies for the minds of men and women, and its disciples – the word is not inappropriate for the followers of Epicurus – went out into the great cities of the eastern Mediterranean to found communities on the model of the Garden. Such communities were to be found in Tyre, Sidon, Tarsus, Alexandria, Gadara in Syria, and in many other places. (Indeed the Gadarene swine, 'about two thousand', Mark 5:13 and Luke 8:33, may well be a very early Christian denigration of their Epicurean arch-enemies from the Hellenized city of Gadara.)

In the first century BC the Epicureans had so established themselves in Italy and elsewhere that Cicero wrote, with some irritation, 'Here is a famous philosopher, whose influence has spread not only over Greece and Italy but throughout all barbarian lands as well . . .' (*De Finibus*, II, 49). The influence at the heart of the Roman Empire probably reached its height in the three decades 60–30 BC. In that period not only had Lucretius written his great poem, but Philodemus was living and teaching in Herculaneum, Amafinius had published popularized Latin accounts of Epicureanism at Rome, and Epicurean influences were strong in the cultured 'salon' sustained at Naples by the Greek teacher Siro – a community that later included Virgil.

Lucretius himself is favourably mentioned by Cicero in a letter to his brother dated 10 or 11 February, 54 BC: 'The poems of Lucretius are just as you write – with flashes of genius, and yet exceedingly artistic.' There is a trace of evidence from badly carbonized papyrus rolls found in Herculaneum that a copy of Lucretius' poem was in the library there, and the young Ovid, writing in about 20 BC, observes that 'The verses of the sublime Lucretius, shall perish only when the last day gives the earth to destruction' (*The Amores*, I, xv, 23).

So by the end of the first century BC the Epicureans were widely known, influential, and quite possibly numerous. In the middle of the second century AD, the emperor Marcus Aurelius and his tutor Fronto are quoting Lucretius to each other in letters, and there is much evidence that the Epicureans were still active late in that century. But in AD 363 the emperor Julianus,[10]

---

[10] Julian, a very learned and industrious administrator, was educated as a Christian, but in disgust at the new religion and its intolerance, became a devout follower of the ancient religion. He was emperor 361–3.

in a letter to a pagan priest, wrote 'Let us not admit [as reading matter] discourses by Epicurus or Pyrrho; but indeed the gods have already in their wisdom destroyed their works, so that most of their books have ceased to be' (Loeb edn., vol. II, p. 327). What had happened?

1. One of Epicurus' maxims was 'Live unnoticed', implying among other things, that 'The wise man will not be involved in public affairs unless something prevents him'. The Epicureans, somewhat as the Christians were to do a little later, tended to live as self-isolating communities within the State. They were not for public activity. As a consequence they were looked upon as poor citizens, lacking in the civic and imperial enthusiasms which were the bonds of the Greek city and the Roman State. The disapproval is particularly evident in Cicero, and neither Plutarch (the pagan conservative) nor Epictetus (the Stoic advocate) make any effort to disguise it. The emperor Marcus Aurelius was doubtless wise and liberal when in AD 176 he sanctioned the payment of professorial salaries to heads of the philosophical schools at Athens, including the Epicureans. But he was also unique. The Epicureans were officially disliked and politically unpopular.

2. Ancient philosophies were the bread and butter of their professors. There was quite literally competition for students and student fees, and the competition was both personal and intellectual. In such conditions the Stoics and Epicureans were natural rivals. They shared one common principle – that the universe was all one; there was no 'other' world of spirits or supernatural beings – after that they disagreed at every point. The disagreements can be seen in Lucretius. When he opposes the views of unnamed others, the others almost always turn out to be Stoics. But the Stoics were better equipped for a long-term intellectual fight because (a) unlike the Epicureans, who generally cherished and defended the exact views of their Master, the Stoics were intellectually agile and adaptable. They could and did reformulate their basic positions in the light of Sceptical and Academic criticisms, and their principal advocates – Cleanthes, Chrysippus, Panaetius, Posidonius and many others – were gifted philosophers. In short, the Stoics usually got the better of any *argument*. Also, (b) the Stoics, for all their apparent fatalism of the sort 'Seek not to have things happen as you choose them,

but rather choose them to happen as they do' (Epictetus, see also the opening of his *Encheiridion*) were men of action – at their best, great public servants like Cicero, Seneca and Marcus Aurelius. Perhaps for this reason as much as any other, Stoicism superseded Epicureanism as the preferred philosophy of the Roman governing class.

3. But more than political unacceptability and Stoic success was amiss with the Epicureans and contributed to their decline. Like other 'dogmatic' philosophies (that is to say philosophies – including Stoicism – which were not merely critical and sceptical but affirmed a positive account of nature, and/or a particular way of life), the Epicureans were vulnerable to common-sense objections levelled at the narrow and occasionally silly emphasis they gave to some of their doctrines. Admirable compendiums of such objections can be found in Plutarch's *Moralia*, particularly in the essay written somewhere about AD 100 entitled 'That Epicurus actually Makes a Pleasant Life Impossible' (Loeb edn., vol. XIV, pp. 15–149) and, with Stoic bias, in Cicero's *De Finibus*, Book II.

Plutarch's objections were directed, for instance, at the view of the Epicureans that happiness consisted in the mere absence of pain and fear (an objection which of course takes no account of their concern with friendship and community): 'it does not follow that if pain, fear of the supernatural and terror about the hereafter are evil, escape from them is godlike and bliss beyond compare' (*op. cit.*, p. 51). There is, he urges, more to happiness than release from ills. Happiness includes positive intellectual delights, aesthetic pleasures, activity and the pleasing hope of an after-life: 'For the "nothing to us" [of death], when achieved by the extinction of everything that is ours, is already "something to us" in our thoughts. And lack of sensation is no hardship to those who when the time comes no longer are, but it is to those who are, because it plunges them into non-being, from which they are never to emerge' (p. 147). There can be no doubt that Plutarch's argument occupies strong ground in any society in which an after-life is still in itself credible – ground shortly to be triumphantly colonized by Christianity at the expense of pagan and Epicurean alike. Again, Plutarch attacks the *inertia* of the Epicurean gods and the somewhat depressing consequences of this for human hopes: 'the attitude toward God that we find in the ignorant but not greatly wicked majority of mankind contains ... [some superstition but] ... outweighing this a thousand times is the element of cheerful hope, of exultant joy ...' (p. 113). And the catalogue of such common-sense objections to certain features of Epicureanism, when they are dogmatically defended, or considered in isolation, can be continued.

4. But perhaps the most persistent damage to the Epicureans was done by their reputation for, as Plutarch put it, 'absence of activity, irreligion, sensuality and indifference – and such is the reputation of their sect among all mankind except for themselves' (p. 107). In a perceptive passage in one of the *Moral Essays*, Seneca puts the matter very judiciously:

> Personally I hold the opinion ... that the teachings of Epicurus are upright and holy and, if you consider them closely, austere; for the famous doctrine of pleasure is reduced to small and narrow proportions ... he bids that it obey nature. But it takes a very little luxury to satisfy nature! What then is the case? Whoever applies the term 'happiness' to slothful idleness and the alternate indulgence in gluttony and lust, looks for a good sponsor for his evil course, and when, led on by an attractive name, he has found [Epicureanism], the pleasure he pursues is not the form that he is taught, but the form that he has brought [with him] and when he begins to think that his vices accord with the teacher's maxims ... he riots in them ... And so I shall not say, as do most of our sect [the Stoics], that the school of Epicurus is an academy of vice, but this is what I say – it has a bad name, is of ill repute, and yet undeservedly. (Loeb edn., vol. II, p. 131)

But it was the name, not the undeserving, that stuck and made the Epicureans an easy target for moral condemnation by Stoics, Christians and pagan conservatives. As Plutarch remarks with disarming honesty – 'we are considering reputation, not truth' (*op. cit.* p. 107).

Sixteen hundred years after Seneca, the English essayist Sir William Temple, writing in 1685 (three years after Lucretius' poem had first – and very successfully – been published in English), remarks somewhat similarly, but with the benefit of greater hindsight:

> I have often wondered how such sharp and violent invectives came to be made so generally against Epicurus, by the ages that followed

him, whose admirable wit, felicity of expression, excellence of nature, sweetness of conversation, temperance of life, and constancy of death, made him so beloved by his friends, admired by his scholars, and honoured by the Athenians. But this injustice may be fastened chiefly upon the envy and malignity of the Stoics at first, then upon the mistakes of some gross pretenders to his sect (who took pleasure only to be sensual), and afterwards, upon the piety of the primitive Christians . . .

5. It is the final clause that says most, for it was upon the rocks of religion – particularly and ultimately the Christian – that ancient Epicureanism foundered. At almost every point the Epicureans were the loathly opposite of Christians – and the one point of similarity was a cause for rivalry. The Epicureans affirmed a scientifically explainable natural world which had no supernatural and spiritual objective, no creator, no director. They affirmed the existence of uncaring and inactive gods. They systematically and comprehensively argued against any form of after-life, or resurrection for any living thing. They had gone out of their way, over many hundreds of years, to find fault with pagan superstition and with any religion that disturbed human tranquillity and humanistic values. It is thus not difficult to see, for example, why Lucian, writing in about AD 180 should enlist the Epicureans in his satire *Alexander the False Prophet*, or why the said Alexander should have reacted as Lucian reports: 'Upon whom else would a quack who loved humbug, and bitterly hated truth, more fittingly make war than upon Epicurus, who discerned the nature of things and alone knew the truth in them?' (Loeb edn., vol. IV, p. 209). At the time, the Christians applauded the discomforture of Alexander. Soon they were reacting like him. For not only were the Epicureans direct philosophical and moral opponents of Christianity, they were also its earthly rivals. They offered a community-based way of life which depended upon friendship (*philia*), perhaps a more psychologically realistc alternative to the Christian communities' bond of spiritual love (*agape*), and certainly in practical competition with it.

The outcome of this collision of word and way was inevitable. The Christian promise of an eternal tomorrow overwhelmed the Epicurean assurance of a tranquil today, and the virtually deliberate self-separation of the Epicureans from the mainstreams of public life facilitated their defeat. They were too quiet in a world that was becoming dangerous from barbarian incursions, and noisy with the shouting of many faiths – as if men were craving for the deceptive religious certainties against which the Epicureans had always resolutely turned their face. As Diogenes of Oenoanda put it towards the end, 'the majority are sick as with a disease, and the tale of them increases, for they take the disease from one another like sheep' – a disease of increasing virulence that no quietness could resist. By the mid-fourth century AD not only was the Epicurean way all but abandoned, but as Julianus Caesar observed (himself waging a hopeless pagan crusade against tomorrow) their words were all but extinct. And yet the story was far from concluded.

THE TRAVESTY AND THE TRIUMPH

The chronicle of 'The Mediaeval Interlude' (considerably in excess of a thousand years!) is well told by Howard Jones in ch. 5 of *The Epicurean Tradition* (London and New York, 1989). Epicurus is now cast as the Antichrist of Sensuality. The quotation from John of Salisbury (*c.* 1115–80) which Jones reproduces is the symptom of a more lurid sickness than Diogenes could ever have foreseen:

> ... the garden of the Epicureans has as its source lust, which also produces rivers which irrigate the whole of this vale of tears ... One stream is, as it were, the love of possession, by which wealth is sought for sufficiency and in which avarice labours to possess or to know more than is lawful; a second spreads the enticements of self-indulgence and flows down into a variety of delights as it strives to attain the joys of tranquillity and pleasure; the third gathers strength with which to protect natural liberty and to ward off the injury of any discomfort whatsoever, and after it has acquired abounding strength it bursts forth into the odious stream of tyranny; the fourth, as a result of its striving for celebrity and respect, in the struggle for eminence becomes swollen with trickery. These are the four rivers which pour out upon and surround the whole world and gush forth from the spring of ill will which has its origin from the slime of vanity.

The picture is a travesty, and the colourings those of a religion which, at least in the mediaeval 'interlude', had successfully taught men to worship suffering, fear knowledge and hate happiness. Seneca, closer to the original, also a critic, but kinder and less contorted by hostile dogma, painted a somewhat different picture:

> Go to his Garden and read the motto carved there: STRANGER, HERE YOU WILL DO WELL TO TARRY; HERE OUR HIGHEST GOOD IS PLEASURE. The care-taker of that abode, a kindly host, will be ready for you. He will welcome you with barley-meal and serve you water also in abundance, with these words: 'Have you not been well entertained?' 'This garden' he says, 'does not whet your appetite; it quenches it. Nor does it make you more thirsty with every drink. It slakes the thirst by a natural cure, – a cure that demands no fee. This is the "pleasure" in which I have grown old.' (Loeb edn., vol. I, p. 147)

In whatever way one may now respond to the original kindly simplicity and tolerant welcome of the Epicurean ethic, their physics and their desire to understand the natural world are with us whether we like them or not. And if Epicurus and John of Salisbury would both, in their different ways, deplore the relentless pursuit of wealth, the ruthless marketing of goods, and the frenetic activity we now substitute for Epicurean happiness and Christian hopes, Epicurus would stand alone, astonished, vindicated, and perhaps rejoicing, at the understanding of nature that we now have; an understanding which comes ultimately from his principles, and from those of his atomist predecessor Democritus, and not from the religions that reviled him.

SOURCES, TRANSLATIONS AND
ACKNOWLEDGEMENTS

The 'Principal Doctrines', 'Letter to Herodotus', 'Letter to Pythocles' and 'Epicurus' Last Will and Testament' are reprinted by permission of the publishers of the Loeb Classical Library from Diogenes Laertius, *Lives of the Eminent Philosophers*, vol. II, translated by R. D. Hicks, Cambridge, Mass.: Harvard University Press, 1925. The following small alterations have been made. Sub-headings have been interpolated to guide the reader to particular topics or changes of subject matter. A handful of archaisms have been modernized. The words 'atom', 'soul' and 'idol' have been rendered in accordance with the principles explained in the Introduction, and ancient scholia (comments not by Epicurus) have been removed from the text.

The manuscript sources from which the Greek text of Diogenes Laertius has been established are exceedingly complex. A brief account of them can be found in H. S. Long's introduction to vol. I of the 1972 edition of the Loeb translation, pp. xxv–vi. But although these matters are interesting in their own right, they do not impinge upon and need not impinge upon the general reader's or the philosopher's understanding of Epicurus' ideas and arguments.

'The Vatican Sayings' and the 'Fragments from Greek Literature' are reprinted from *Epicurus: The Extant Remains*, translated by Cyril Bailey (1926), by permission of Oxford University Press.

Translation of Epicurus' Greek is not easy. He wrote in an unstylish and sometimes careless way, sometimes ambiguously, and, except in the simpler moral aphorisms, in a manner much prone to technical terms and what we would now call 'jargon'. But at least translation can follow the tone of the original as utilitarian prose. Lucretius, on the other hand, has left us one of the greatest *poems* in the Latin language, and translation has to confront the choice between a verse paraphrase with inevitable loss of philosophical precision, or a prose translation with inevitable loss of poetic fire. In this conflict I have felt obliged to choose a prose translation since the modern reader will almost certainly be turning to Lucretius as an exposition of the physics and philosophy of the Epicureans. If he or she is then confronted with the slow, contemplative and imprecise progress dictated by seven or eight thousand lines of verse, impatience is likely to result.

Nevertheless, I have risked reminding the reader that the original is a poem by employing a variety of verse translations for the invocations or addresses with which Lucretius commences each book. In Books I, III, V and VI these are from a very little known translation of parts of the Latin poem by the Revd Charles Foxley, which was published by W. Heffer & Sons, Cambridge, in 1933. I have been unable to trace Mr Foxley via his publishers or in any other way, but am happy to acknowledge Heffer as the source, and to commend the work. The proem to Book II is from W. H. Mallock's remarkable attempt to render sections of Lucretius in the metre of Omar Khayyám (1900). His design is a poem in its own right taking themes from Lucretius, and some of it is very fine indeed, but the opening of Book II is one of only a few sections which continuously paraphrase the original. Finally, the opening to Book IV gives a sample of the very first complete translation into English. It was done by Thomas Creech, a Fellow of Wadham College, and published at Oxford in 1682. It is of consistently high quality, but the late seventeenth-century verse style, together with Creech's tendency to loose paraphrase, makes it as a whole unattractive to the modern reader.

Among prose translations the choice is between literal versions and versions in modernized English which may depart quite far from Lucretius' Latin. The former is best represented by H. A. J. Munro's exact attention to the Latin wording and syntax (and to Lucretius' own sometimes archaic vocabulary) in his translation of 1860; the latter by R. E. Latham's avowed rejection of the grammatical structure of the Latin and his adoption of colloquial English and modern scientific terms in his translation (Harmondsworth, 1951). After some hesitation I have opted for a slightly modified version of Cyril Bailey's translation of 1921. This is closer to Munro's literalism than Latham's modernization.

There are disadvantages. The more literal version slows down one's reading, and it makes Lucretius sound more like the far away voice that he is, and less like a somewhat quaintly phrased but essentially modern philosopher-scientist prone to odd illustrations and dotty errors. But there are significant advantages. One is that anyone even faintly familiar with Latin can see what Bailey is doing and where his clauses relate to the original. Another is that the very slowing down of our reading forces us to think more about what we read, and Lucretius requires thought. Again, the voice of the original – its poetic fervour, its consciously archaic style, its organization into blocks of sense amounting to between seven and nine lines of verse, its singularity as a combination of great poetry *and* philosophical argument – can still be heard to some extent in Bailey. But most important of all, the near literal translation makes far fewer decisions for the reader about what Lucretius meant and how he will sound. One is *closer* to the original.

The text of Lucretius is reprinted from *Lucretius on the Nature of Things*, translated by Cyril Bailey (1921), by permission of Oxford University Press. The following small adjustments have been made:

1. Long paragraphs, which have no decisive warrant from the Latin text, have been broken up in order to facilitate ease of reading and the separation of arguments and subject matter.

2. Bailey usually preserves Lucretius' units of sense in the punctuation of his translation. This results in many sentences of inordinate length for normal English. Accordingly, such sentences have been sub-divided wherever this can be done without undue intrusion into the syntax.

3. Archaisms of vocabulary such as 'thee' or 'I trow', 'verily', 'rare' (for 'porous') have been replaced by their modern English equivalents. Such archaisms now sound like affectation, and are no longer needed to give a 'poetic' feel to what is written (despite Lucretius' own occasional recourse to them).

4. The words Bailey conventionally renders as 'first beginnings', 'soul' and 'idols' have been uniformly replaced in accordance with the principles explained in the Introduction.

5. Finally, a small number of actual changes have been made in the translation. Two of these are in Book IV and one in Book VI where Bailey must have found the Latin too uninhibited for early twentieth-century publication. The changes are signalled in a footnote. Other changes are few and trivial. They are confined to silently adjusting the word order if it seemed excessively difficult to follow in English.

All footnotes, unless otherwise indicated, are by the present Editor, as are the sub-headings interpolated in the text. I have also added the line number with which each paragraph of translation commences.

A full account of the manuscript tradition from which the Latin text of Lucretius has been established can be found in *De Rerum Natura*, ed. Cyril Bailey (Oxford, 1947), vol. I, pp. 37–44, or in *Texts and Transmission: a Survey of the Latin Classics*, ed. L. D. Reynolds (Oxford, 1983), pp. 218–22 or, more briefly, in the 1992 Introduction to the Loeb edition of *Lucretius*, pp. liv–lvii. In a few words: all extant manuscripts can be traced back to two ninth-century manuscripts now in Leiden. Both of these are copies from some common original now lost. Thus one of the world's greatest poems, and the most vivid and complete account of Epicureanism that exists, survived the Dark Ages on the precarious thread of a single written copy.

The text was first printed *c.* 1473 at Brescia. An account of all known printed editions and translations to date can be found in C. A. Gordon, *A Bibliography of Lucretius* (London, 1962; 2nd edn., 1985). But even Gordon missed the admirable versification of Charles Foxley that is in small part utilized in the present volume.

Brief notes on Philodemus and Diogenes of Oenoanda can be found on pp. 77 and 307 respectively. Both authors are included as tokens of material which may one day be more completely available. See 'Suggestions for Further Reading'.

THE EPICUREAN
PHILOSOPHERS

EPICURUS

1 The Principal Doctrines[1]

1. A blessed and eternal being has no trouble himself and brings no trouble upon any other being; hence he is exempt from movements of anger and partiality, for every such movement implies weakness.

2. Death is nothing to us; for the body, when it has been resolved into its elements, has no feeling, and that which has no feeling is nothing to us.

3. The magnitude of pleasure reaches its limit in the removal of all pain. When pleasure is present, so long as it is uninterrupted, there is no pain either of body or of mind or of both together.

4. Continuous pain does not last long in the flesh; on the contrary, pain, if extreme, is present a very short time [because it kills], and even that degree of pain which barely outweighs pleasure in the flesh does not last for many days together. Illnesses of long duration even permit of an excess of pleasure over pain in the flesh.

5. It is impossible to live a pleasant life without living wisely and well and justly, and it is impossible to live wisely and well and justly without living pleasantly. Whenever any one of these is lacking, when, for instance, the man is not able to live wisely, though he lives well and justly, it is impossible for him to live a pleasant life.

[1] A collection of forty easily understood aphorisms (the numbering is traditional) preserved by Diogenes Laertius and dealing mainly with the way of life which Epicurus recommended for happiness. The collection was widely known and quoted in antiquity. It could have been made up from sayings remembered by his followers, or cardinal items gleaned from his voluminous writings. But it is now generally considered to be a work actually constructed by Epicurus himself as a straightforward list of main guiding principles. With the exception of the sequence of sayings 31 to 40 on guilt and justice, there is only a loose order to the sayings, and a few of the entries are near repetitions of others. Words enclosed in square brackets are not in the original Greek as it has survived, but are required for the sense in English.

6. In order to obtain security from other men any means whatsoever of procuring this is a natural good.

7. Some men have sought to become famous and renowned, thinking that thus they would make themselves secure against their fellow-men. If, then, the life of such persons really was secure, they attained natural good; if, however, it was insecure, they have not attained the end which by nature's own prompting they originally sought.

8. No pleasure is in itself evil, but the things which produce certain pleasures entail annoyances many times greater than the pleasures themselves.

9. If all pleasure had been capable of accumulation – if this had gone on not only by recurrence in time, but all over the frame or, at any rate, over the principal parts of man's nature, there would never have been any difference between one pleasure and another, as in fact there is.

10. If the objects which are productive of pleasures to profligate persons really freed them from fears of the mind, – the fears, I mean, inspired by celestial and atmospheric phenomena, the fear of death, the fear of pain; if, further, they taught them to limit their desires, we should never have any fault to find with such persons, for they would then be filled with pleasures to overflowing on all sides and would be exempt from all pain, whether of body or mind, that is, from all evil.

11. If we had never been molested by alarms at celestial and atmospheric phenomena, nor by the misgiving that death somehow affects us, nor by neglect of the proper limits of pains and desires, we should have had no need to study natural sciences.

12. It would be impossible to banish fear on matters of the highest importance, if a man did not know the nature of the whole universe, but lived in dread of what the legends tell us. Hence without the study of nature there was no enjoyment of unmixed pleasures.

13. There would be no advantage in providing security against our fellow-men, so long as we were alarmed by occurrences over our heads or beneath the earth or in general by whatever happens in the boundless universe.

14. When tolerable security against our fellow-men is attained, then (on a basis of power sufficient to afford support and of material prosperity) arises in most genuine form the security of a quiet private life withdrawn from the multitude.

15. Nature's wealth at once had its bounds and is easy to procure; but the wealth of vain fancies recedes to an infinite distance.

16. Fortune but seldom interferes with the wise man; his greatest and highest interests have been, are, and will be, directed by reason throughout the course of his life.

17. The just man enjoys the greatest peace of mind, while the unjust is full of the utmost disquietude.

18. Pleasure in the flesh admits no increase when once the pain of want has been removed; after that it only admits of variation. The limit of pleasure in the mind, however, is reached when we understand the pleasures themselves and their consequences – which cause the mind the greatest alarms.

19. Unlimited time and limited time afford an equal amount of pleasure, if we measure the limits of that pleasure by reason.

20. The flesh receives as unlimited the limits of pleasure; and to provide it requires unlimited time. But the mind, grasping in thought what the end and limit of the flesh is, and banishing the terrors of futurity, procures a complete and perfect life, and has no longer any need of unlimited time. Nevertheless it does not shun pleasure, and even in the hour of death, when ushered out of existence by circumstances, the mind does not lack enjoyment of the best life.

21. He who understands the limits of life knows how easy it is to procure enough to remove the pain of want and make the whole life complete and perfect. Hence he has no longer any need of things which are not to be won save by labour and conflict.

22. We must take into account as the end all that really exists and all clear evidence of sense to which we refer our opinions; for otherwise everything will be full of uncertainty and confusion.

23. If you fight against all your sensations, you will have no standard to which to refer, and thus no means of judging even those judgements which you pronounce false.

24. If you reject absolutely any single sensation without stopping to discriminate with respect to that which awaits confirmation between matter of opinion and that which is already present, whether in sensation or in feeling or in any presentative perception of the mind, you will throw into confusion even the rest of your sensations by your groundless belief, and so you will be rejecting the standard of truth altogether. If in your ideas based upon opinion you hastily affirm as true all that awaits confirmation as well as that which does not, you will not escape error, as you will be maintaining complete ambiguity whenever it is a case of judging between right and wrong opinion.

25. If you do not on every separate occasion refer each of your actions to the end prescribed by nature, but instead of this in the act of choice or avoidance swerve aside to some other end, your acts will not be consistent with your theories.

26. All such desires as lead to no pain when they remain ungratified are unnecessary, and the longing is easily got rid of, when the thing desired is difficult to procure or when the desires seem likely to produce harm.

27. Of all the means which are procured by wisdom to ensure happiness throughout the whole of life, by far the most important is the acquisition of friends.

28. The same conviction which inspires confidence that nothing we have to fear is eternal or even of long duration, also enables us to see that even in our limited conditions of life nothing enhances our security so much as friendship.

29. Of our desires some are natural and necessary; others are natural, but not necessary; others, again, are neither natural nor necessary, but are due to illusory opinion. [Epicurus regards as natural and necessary desires which bring relief from pain, as e.g. drink when we are thirsty; while by natural and not necessary he means those which merely diversify the pleasure without removing the pain, as e.g. costly viands; by the neither natural nor necessary he means desires for crowns and the erection of statues in one's honour.][2]

30. Those natural desires which entail no pain when not gratified, though their objects are vehemently pursued, are also due to illusory opinion; and when they are not got rid of, it is not because of their own nature, but because of the man's illusory opinion.

31. Natural justice is a symbol or expression of expediency, to prevent one man from harming or being harmed by another.

32. Those animals which are incapable of making covenants with one another, to the end that they may neither inflict nor suffer harm, are without either justice or injustice. And those tribes which either could not or would not form mutual covenants to the same end are in like case.

33. There never was an absolute justice, but only an agreement made in reciprocal intercourse in whatever localities now and again from time to time, providing against the infliction or suffering of harm.

---

[2] The words in square brackets in this instance are a scholium, or ancient comment, added to the text.

34. Injustice is not in itself an evil, but only in its consequence, viz. the terror which is excited by apprehension that those appointed to punish such offences will discover the injustice.

35. It is impossible for the man who secretly violates any article of the social compact to feel confident that he will remain undiscovered, even if he has already escaped ten thousand times; for right on to the end of his life he is never sure he will not be detected.

36. Taken generally, justice is the same for all, to wit, something found expedient in mutual intercourse; but in its application to particular cases of locality or conditions of whatever kind, it varies under different circumstances.

37. Among the things accounted just by conventional law, whatever in the needs of mutual intercourse is attested to be expedient, is thereby stamped as just, whether or not it be the same for all; and in case any law is made and does not prove suitable to the expediencies of mutual intercourse, then this is no longer just. And should the expediency which is expressed with the prior conception, nevertheless for the time being it was just, so long as we do not trouble ourselves about empty words, but look simply at the facts.

38. Where without any change in circumstances, the conventional laws, when judged by their consequences, were seen not to correspond with the notion of justice, such laws were not really just; but wherever the laws have ceased to be expedient in consequence of a change in circumstances, in that case the laws were for the time being just when they were expedient for the mutual intercourse of the citizens, and subsequently ceased to be just when they ceased to be expedient.

39. He who best knew how to meet fear of external foes made into one family all the creatures he could; and those he could not, he at any rate did not treat as aliens; and where he found even this impossible, he avoided all encounters, and, so far as was expedient, kept them at a distance.

40. Those who are best able to provide themselves with the means of security against their neighbours, being thus in possession of the surest guarantee, passed the most agreeable life in each other's society; and their enjoyment of the fullest intimacy was such that, if one of them died before his time, the survivors did not lament his death as if it called for commiseration.

2 On Physics, or the Nature of Things
'Letter to Herodotus'[3]

INTRODUCTION

Epicurus to Herodotus, greeting.

For those who are unable to study carefully all my physical writings or to go into the longer treatises at all, I have myself prepared an epitome of the whole system, Herodotus, to preserve in the memory enough of the principal doctrines, to the end that on every occasion they may be able to aid themselves on the most important points, so far as they take up the study of Physics. Those who have made some advance in the survey of the entire system ought to fix in their minds under the principal headings an elementary outline of the whole treatment of the subject. For a comprehensive view is often required, the details but seldom.

To the former, then – the main heads – we must continually return, and must memorize them so far as to get a valid conception of the facts, as well as the means of discovering all the details exactly when once the general outlines are rightly understood and remembered; since it is the privilege of the

[3] This is the first, longest and most important of the three letters preserved by Diogenes Laertius. It is also, as the great Epicurean scholar Cyril Bailey observes in his commentary (see Suggestions for Further Reading, p. 309), because of its long sentences, its badly preserved text and its technical terms, 'one of the most difficult and obscure pieces of writing in the Greek language'. Its purpose, as Epicurus explains in the Introduction and Conclusion, is to provide a useful summary of the main points of his philosophy for those already familiar with the details. But it also serves as a short but difficult summary for those who have not had an opportunity to think their way into the details of the system. It is sometimes known as the Lesser Epitome to distinguish it from the Greater Epitome (now lost) referred to in its first sentence. Lucretius' exposition, particularly in Books I–III, picks up in a systematic and much more extensive way many of the principles touched upon in this letter, and it is conjectured that he may have been using the Greater Epitome, (or possibly Epicurus' vast work *On Nature*, also now lost) as his source. But the 'Letter to Herodotus' is now the fundamental text, however difficult, for Epicurus' physics and metaphysics as expressed in his own words. Concerning the Herodotus addressed, nothing is known except that he is reputed to have written a work *On the Youth of Epicurus*. In the 'Letter to Herodotus', as elsewhere in the present volume, the sub-heading in the text are interpolated by the Editor as a guide to the subject matter.

mature student to make a ready use of his conceptions by referring every one of them to elementary facts and simple terms. For it is impossible to gather up the results of continuous diligent study of the entirety of things, unless we can embrace in short formulas and hold in mind all that might have been accurately expressed even to the minutest detail.

Hence, since such a course is of service to all who take up natural science, I, who devote to the subject my continuous energy and reap the calm enjoyment of a life like this, have prepared for you just such an epitome and manual of the doctrines as a whole.

WORDS MUST CLEARLY SIGNIFY AND THE SENSES BE TAKEN AS RELIABLE

In the first place, Herodotus, you must understand what it is that words denote, in order that by reference to this we may be in a position to test opinions, inquiries, or problems, so that our proofs may not run on untested *ad infinitum*, nor the terms we use be empty of meaning. For the primary signification of every term employed must be clearly seen, and ought to need no proving; this being necessary, if we are to have something to which the point at issue or the problem or the opinion before us can be referred.

Next, we must by all means stick to our sensations, that is, simply to the present impressions whether of the mind or of any criterion whatever, and similarly to our actual feelings, in order that we may have the means of determining that which needs confirmation and that which is obscure.

PHYSICAL PRINCIPLES[4]

When this is clearly understood, it is time to consider generally things which are obscure. To begin with, [I] *nothing comes into being out of what is non-existent*. For in that case anything

---

[4] The interpolated Roman numerals in this section relate Epicurus' principles to some of those identified in the summaries of Lucretius' argument which I have placed before each book in *The Nature of the Universe*. See also, Introduction, p. xxivf. In general the first third of the 'Letter to Herodotus' is much amplified in the first two books of Lucretius.

would have arisen out of anything, standing as it would in no need of its proper germs. And [II] *if that which disappears had been destroyed and become non-existent, everything would have perished*, that into which the things were dissolved being non-existent. Moreover, [IX] *the sum total of things was always such as it is now*, and such it will ever remain. For there is nothing into which it can change. For outside the sum of things there is nothing which could enter into it and bring about the change.

Further, [VI] *the whole of being consists of bodies and space.* For the existence of bodies is everywhere attested by sense itself, and it is upon sensation that reason must rely when it attempts to infer the unknown from the known. And if there were no space (which we call also void and place and intangible nature), bodies would have nothing in which to be and through which to move, as they are plainly seen to move. Beyond bodies and space there is nothing which by mental apprehension or on its analogy we can conceive to exist. When we speak of bodies and space, both are regarded as wholes or separate things, not as the properties or accidents of separate things.

Again, [VII] *of bodies some are composite, others the fundamental particles*[5] *of which these composite bodies are made.* These *particles are indivisible and unchangeable*, and necessarily so, if things are not all to be destroyed and pass into non-existence, but are to be strong enough to endure when the composite bodies are broken up, because they possess a solid nature and are incapable of being anywhere or anyhow dissolved. It follows that the first beginnings must be indivisible, corporeal entities.

Again, [VIII] *the sum of things is infinite*. For what is finite has an extremity, and the extremity of anything is discerned only by comparison with something else. [Now the sum of things is not discerned by comparison with anything else]: hence,

---

[5] The Greek word here is *atomoi*, usually translated by its modern derivative 'atoms'. For reasons explained in the Introduction, p. xxvii, this translation is now misleading. (Atoms can be split; atomoi cannot.) Hence I am using the phrase 'fundamental particles' to indicate the ultimate, unsplitable building-blocks of matter that Epicurus intended by the word *atomoi*. Lucretius generally uses the word *primordia* in his Latin text for the same concept. In all translations in this volume, 'fundamental particles', 'primary particles', 'particles' and 'primordia' (the last usually in Lucretius) will all be understood as synonyms for Epicurus' *atomoi*.

since it has no extremity, it has no limit; and, since it has no limit, it must be unlimited or infinite.

Moreover, [IX] the sum of things is unlimited both by reason of the multitude of the primordia and the extent of the void. For if the void were infinite and bodies finite, the bodies would not have stayed anywhere but would have been dispersed in their course through the infinite void, not having any supports or counterchecks to send them back on their upward rebound. Again, if the void were finite, the infinity of bodies would not have anywhere to be.

Furthermore, the primary particles which have no void in them – out of which composite bodies arise and into which they are dissolved – vary indefinitely in their shapes; for so many varieties of things as we see could never have arisen out of a recurrence of a definite number of the same shapes. [XIII] *The like particles of each shape are absolutely infinite; but the variety of shapes though indefinitely large, is not absolutely infinite.*

[X] *Primary particles are in continual motion through all eternity.* Some of them rebound to a considerable distance from each other, while others merely oscillate in one place when they chance to have got entangled or to be enclosed by a mass of other particles shaped for entangling.

This is because each primary particle is separated from the rest by void, which is incapable of offering any resistance to the rebound; while it is the solidity of the particle which makes it rebound after a collision, however short the distance to which it rebounds, when it finds itself imprisoned in a mass of entangling atoms. Of all this there is no beginning, since both primary particles and void exist from everlasting.

The repetition at such length of all that we are now recalling to mind furnishes an adequate outline for our conception of the nature of things.

THE INFINITY OF WORLDS

Moreover, there is an infinite number of worlds, some like this world, others unlike it. For the fundamental particles being infinite in number, as has just been proved, are borne ever further in their course. For the particles out of which a world might arise, or by which a world might be formed, have not all been expended on one world or a finite number of worlds, whether like or unlike this one. Hence there will be nothing to hinder an infinity of worlds.

THE SENSATION OF SIGHT[6]

Again, there are outlines or films, which are of the same shape as solid bodies, but of a thinness far exceeding that of any object that we see. For it is not impossible that there should be found in the surrounding air combinations of this kind, materials adapted for expressing the hollowness and thinness of surfaces, and effluxes preserving the same relative position and motion which they had in the solid objects from which they come. To these films we give the name of 'images' or 'simulacra'. Furthermore, so long as nothing comes in the way to offer resistance, motion through the void accomplishes any imaginable distance in an inconceivably short time. For resistance encountered is the equivalent of slowness, its absence the equivalent of speed.

Not that, if we consider the minute times perceptible by reason alone, the moving body itself arrives at more than one place simultaneously (for this too is inconceivable), although in time perceptible to sense it does arrive simultaneously, however different the point of departure from that conceived by us. For if it changed its direction, that would be equivalent to its meeting with resistance, even if up to that point we allow nothing to impede the rate of its flight. This is an elementary fact which in itself is well worth bearing in mind. In the next place the exceeding thinness of the images is contradicted by none of the facts under our observation. Hence also their velocities are enormous, since they always find a void passage to fit them. Besides, their incessant effluence meets with no resistance, or very little, although many fundamental particles, not to say an unlimited number, do at once encounter resistance.

Besides this, remember that the production of the images is as quick as thought. For particles are continually streaming off from the surface of bodies, though no diminution of the bodies

[6] This and the following section on hearing and smell are much amplified in Lucretius, IV, 54–1036. For the word 'simulacra' see p. xxxi, note 4.

is observed, because other particles take their place. And those given off for a long time retain the position and arrangement which their particles had when they formed part of the solid bodies, although occasionally they are thrown into confusion. Sometimes such films are formed very rapidly in the air, because they need not have any solid content; and there are other modes in which they may be formed. For there is nothing in all this which is contradicted by sensation, if we in some sort look at the clear evidence of sense, to which we should also refer the continuity of particles in the objects external to ourselves.

We must also consider that it is by the entrance of something coming from external objects that we see their shapes and think of them. For external things would not stamp on us their own nature of colour and form through the medium of the air which is between them and us, or by means of rays of light or currents of any sort going from us to them, so well as by the entrance into our eyes or minds, to whichever their size is suitable, of certain films coming from the things themselves, these films or outlines being of the same colour and shape as the external things themselves. They move with rapid motion; and this again explains why they present the appearance of the single continuous object, and retain the mutual interconnexion which they had in the object, when they impinge upon the sense, such impact being due to the oscillation of the particles in the interior of the solid object from which they come. And whatever presentation we derive by direct contact, whether it be with the mind or with the sense-organs, be it shape that is presented or other properties, this shape as presented is the shape of the solid thing, and it is due either to a close coherence of the image as a whole or to a mere remnant of its parts. Falsehood and error always depend upon the intrusion of opinion [when a fact awaits], confirmation or the absence of contradiction, which fact is afterwards frequently not confirmed [or even contradicted].

For the presentations which, e.g., are received in a picture or arise in dreams, or from any other form of apprehension by the mind or by the other criteria of truth, would never have resembled what we call the real and true things, had it not been for certain actual things of the kind with which we come in contact. Error would not have occurred, if we had not experienced some other movement in ourselves, conjoined with, but distinct from, the perception of what is presented. And from this movement, if it be not confirmed or be contradicted, falsehood results; while, if it be confirmed or not contradicted, truth results.

And to this view we must closely adhere, if we are not to repudiate the criteria founded on the clear evidence of sense, nor again to throw all these things into confusion by maintaining falsehood as if it were truth.

SENSATIONS OF HEARING AND SMELL

Again, hearing takes place when a current passes from the object, whether person or thing, which emits voice or sound or noise, or produces the sensation of hearing in any way whatever. This current is broken up into homogeneous particles, which at the same time preserves a certain mutual connexion and a distinctive unity extending to the object which emitted them, and thus, for the most part, cause the perception in that case or, if not, merely indicate the presence of the external object. For without the transmission from the object of a certain interconnexion of the parts no such sensation could arise. Therefore we must not suppose that the air itself is moulded into shape by the voice emitted or something similar; for it is very far from being the case that the air is acted upon by it in this way. The blow which is struck in us when we utter a sound causes such a displacement of the particles as serves to produce a current resembling breath, and this displacement gives rise to the sensation of hearing.

Again, we must believe that smelling, like hearing, would produce no sensation, were there not particles conveyed from the object which are of the proper sort for exciting the organ of smelling, some of one sort, some of another, some exciting it confusedly and strangely, others quietly and agreeably.

PARTICLES HAVE ONLY PRIMARY QUALITIES

Moreover, we must hold that fundamental particles in fact possess none of the qualities belonging to things which come under our observation, except shape, weight, and size, and the properties necessarily conjoined with shape. For every quality changes, but the primary particles do not change, since, when the composite bodies are dissolved, there must needs be a permanent something, solid and indissoluble, left behind, which makes change possible: not changes into or from the non-existent, but often through differences of arrangement, and sometimes through additions and subtractions of the particles. Hence these somethings capable of being diversely arranged must be indestructible, exempt from change, but possessed each of its own distinctive bulk and configuration. This must remain.

For in the case of changes of configuration within our experience the figure is supposed to be inherent when other qualities are stripped off, but the qualities are not supposed, like the shape which is left behind, to inhere in the subject of change, but to vanish altogether from the body. Thus, then, what is left behind is sufficient to account for the differences in composite bodies, since something at least must necessarily be left remaining and be immune from annihilation.

OF THE SIZE OF PARTICLES

Again, you should not suppose that the primary particles have any and every size, lest you be contradicted by facts; but differences of size must be admitted; for this addition renders the facts of feeling and sensation easier of explanation. But to attribute any and every magnitude to the particles does not help to explain the differences of quality in things; moreover, in that case particles large enough to be seen ought to have reached us, which is never observed to occur; [III] *nor can we conceive* how its occurrence should be possible, i.e. *that a primary particle should become visible.*

Besides, you must not suppose that there are parts unlimited in number, be they ever so small, in any finite body. Hence not only must we reject as impossible subdivision *ad infinitum* into smaller and smaller parts, lest we make all things too weak and, in our conceptions of the aggregates, be driven to pulverize the things that exist, i.e. the primary particles, and annihilate them; but in dealing with finite things we must also reject as impossible the progression *ad infinitum* by less and less increments.

For when once we have said that an infinite number of particles, however small, are contained in anything, it is not possible to conceive how it could any longer be limited or finite in size. For clearly our infinite number of particles must have some size; and, then, of whatever size they were, the aggregate they made would be infinite. And, in the next place, since what is finite has an extremity which is distinguishable, even if it is not by itself observable, it is not possible to avoid thinking of another such extremity next to this. Nor can we help thinking that in this way, by proceeding forward from one to the next in order, it is possible by such a progression to arrive in thought at infinity.

We must consider the minimum perceptible by sense as not corresponding to that which is capable of being traversed, i.e. is extended, nor again as utterly unlike it, but as having something in common with the things capable of being traversed, though it is without distinction of parts. But when from the illusion created by this common property we think we shall distinguish something in the minimum, one part on one side and another part on the other side, it must be another minimum equal to the first which catches our eye. In fact, we see these minima one after another, beginning with the first, and not as occupying the same space; nor do we see them touch one another's parts with their parts, but we see that by virtue of their own peculiar character (i.e. as being unit indivisibles) they afford a means of measuring magnitudes: there are more of them, if the magnitude measured is greater; fewer of them, if the magnitude measured is less.

We must recognize that this analogy also holds of the minimum in the primary particle; it is only in minuteness that it differs from that which is observed by sense, but it follows the same analogy. On the analogy of things within our experience we have declared that the particle has magnitude; and this, small as it is, we have merely reproduced on a larger scale. And further, these least and simplest points must be regarded as extremities of lengths, furnishing from themselves as units the means of measuring lengths, whether greater or less, the mental vision being employed since direct observation is impossible. For the community which exists between them and the unchangeable parts (i.e. the minimal parts of area or surface) is sufficient to justify the conclusion so far as this goes. But it is not possible that these minima of the primary particle should group themselves together through the possession of motion.

OF THE DIRECTION AND SPEED OF PARTICLES

Further, we must not assert 'up' or 'down' of that which is unlimited, as if there were a top or bottom. As to the space overhead, however, if it be possible to draw a line to infinity from the point where we stand, we know that never will this space – or, for that matter, the space below the supposed standpoint if produced to infinity – appear to us to be at the same time 'up' and 'down' with reference to the same point; for this is inconceivable. Hence it is possible to assume one direction of motion, which we conceive as extending upwards *ad infinitum*, and another downwards, even if it should happen ten thousand times that what moves from us to the spaces above our heads reaches the feet of those above us, or that which moves downwards from us the heads of those below us. None the less is it true that the whole of the motion in the respective cases is conceived as extending in opposite directions *ad infinitum*.

When they are travelling through the void and meet with no resistance, primary particles must move with equal speed. Neither will heavy particles travel more quickly than small and light ones, so long as nothing meets them, nor will small particles travel more quickly than large ones, provided they always find a passage suitable to their size, and provided also that they meet with no obstruction. Nor will their upward or their lateral motion, which is due to collisions, nor again their downward motion, due to weight, affect their velocity. As long as either motion obtains, it must continue, quick as the speed of thought, provided there is no obstruction, whether due to external collision or to the particles' own weight counteracting the force of the blow.

Moreover, when we come to deal with composite bodies, one of them will travel faster than another, although their particles have equal speed. This is because the particles in the aggregates are travelling in one direction during the shortest continuous time, albeit they move in different directions in times so short as to be appreciable only by the reason, but frequently collide until the continuity of their motion is appreciated by sense. For the assumption that beyond the range of direct observation even the minute times conceivable by reason will present continuity of motion is not true in the case before us. Our rule is that direct observation by sense and direct apprehension by the mind are alone invariably true.

CONCERNING MIND AND ANIMA[7]

Next, keeping in view our perceptions and feelings (for so shall we have the surest ground for belief), we must recognize generally that the anima is a corporeal thing, composed of fine particles, dispersed all over the frame, most nearly resembling wind with an admixture of heat, in some respects like wind, in others like heat. But, again, there is the third part which exceeds the other two in the fineness of its particles and thereby keeps in closer touch with the rest of the frame. And this is shown by the mental faculties and feelings, by the ease with which the mind moves, and by thoughts, and by all those things the loss of which causes death. Further, we must keep in mind that anima has the greatest share in causing sensation. Still, it would not have had sensation, had it not been somehow confined within the rest of the frame. But the rest of the frame, though it provides this indispensable condition for the anima, itself also has a share, derived from the anima, of the said quality; and yet does not possess all the qualities of anima. Hence on the departure of the anima it loses sentience. For it had not this power in itself; but something else, congenital with the body, supplied it to body: which other thing, through the potentiality actualized in it by means of motion, at once acquired for itself a quality of senti-

---

[7] The Greek word is *psychē*, roughly corresponding with the Latin *anima*, both of which are conventionally translated 'soul'. For reasons explained on pp. xxxiv–vi above, this translation is now misleading, mainly because in modern English 'soul' carries the implication of a something (we know not what) independent of our animal bodies. For Epicurus, 'soul' is emphatically not something independent of, or other than, the body. It *is* body in the sense of being some kind of primary particles of some very minute sort dispersed throughout whatever body can be said to live. *Psychē* can almost be understood as 'physical life force' or 'physical animation'. To avoid the misleading implication of 'soul', the word used throughout this volume is Lucretius' technical term '*anima*'. In general, this section of Epicurus' 'Letter' is much amplified in Book III of Lucretius.

ence, and, in virtue of the neighbourhood and interconnexion between them, imparted it (as I said) to the body also.

Hence, so long as the anima is in the body, it never loses sentience through the removal of some other part. The containing sheath may be dislocated in whole or in part, and portions of the anima may thereby be lost; yet in spite of this the anima, if it manage to survive, will have sentience. But the rest of the frame, whether the whole of it survives or only a part, no longer has sensation, when once those particles have departed, which, however few in number, are required to constitute the nature of anima. Moreover, when the whole frame is broken up, the anima is scattered and has no longer the same powers as before, nor the same motions; hence it does not possess sentience either.

For we cannot think of it as sentient, except it be in this composite whole and moving with these movements; nor can we so think of it when the sheaths which enclose and surround it are not the same as those in which the anima is now located and in which it performs these movements.

NO INCORPOREAL ENTITY CAN EXIST

There is the further point to be considered, what the incorporeal can be, if, I mean, according to current usage the term is applied to what can be conceived as self-existent. But it is impossible to conceive anything that is incorporeal as self-existent except empty space. And empty space cannot itself either act or be acted upon, but simply allows body to move through it. Hence those who call anima incorporeal speak foolishly. For if it were so, it could neither act nor be acted upon. But, as it is, both these properties, you see, plainly belong to anima.

If, then, we bring all these arguments concerning anima to the criterion of our feelings and perceptions, and if we keep in mind the proposition stated at the outset, we shall see that the subject has been adequately comprehended in outline: which will enable us to determine the details with accuracy and confidence.

THE PROPERTIES AND ACCIDENTS OF BODIES

Moreover, shapes and colours, magnitudes and weights, and in short all those qualities which are predicated of body, in so far as they are perpetual properties either of all bodies or of visible bodies, are knowable by sensation of these very properties: these, I say, must not be supposed to exist independently by themselves (for that is inconceivable), nor yet to be non-existent, nor to be some other and incorporeal entities cleaving to body, nor again to be parts of body. We must consider the whole body in a general way to derive its permanent nature from all of them, though it is not, as it were, formed by grouping them together in the same way as when from the particles themselves a larger aggregate is made up, whether these particles be primary or any magnitudes whatsoever less than the particular whole. All these qualities, I repeat, merely give the body its own permanent nature. They all have their own characteristic modes of being perceived and distinguished, but always along with the whole body in which they inhere and never in separation from it; and it is in virtue of this complete conception of the body as a whole that it is so designated.

Again, qualities often attach to bodies without being permanent concomitants. They are not to be classed among invisible entities nor are they incorporeal. Hence, using the term 'accidents' in the commonest sense, we say plainly that 'accidents' have not the nature of the whole thing to which they belong and to which, conceiving it as a whole, we give the name of body, nor that of the permanent properties without which body cannot be thought of. And in virtue of certain peculiar modes of apprehension into which the complete body always enters, each of them can be called an accident. But only as often as they are seen actually to belong to it, since such accidents are not perpetual concomitants. There is no need to banish from reality this clear evidence that the accident has not the nature of that whole – by us called body – to which it belongs, nor of the permanent properties which accompany the whole. Nor, on the other hand, must we suppose the accident to have independent existence (for this is just as inconceivable in the case of accidents as in that of the permanent properties); but, as is manifest, they should all be regarded as accidents, not as permanent concomitants of bodies, nor yet as having the rank of independent existence. Rather they are seen to be exactly as and what sensation itself makes them individually claim to be.

THE NATURE OF TIME

There is another thing which we must consider carefully. We must not investigate time as we do the other accidents which we investigate in a subject, namely, by referring them to the preconceptions envisaged in our minds; but we must take into account the plain fact itself, in virtue of which we speak of time as long or short, linking to it in intimate connexion this attribute of duration. We need not adopt any fresh terms as preferable, but should employ the usual expressions about it. Nor need we predicate anything else of time, as if this something else contained the same essence as is contained in the proper meaning of the word 'time' (for this also is done by some). We must chiefly reflect upon that to which we attach this peculiar character of time, and by which we measure it. No further proof is required: we have only to reflect that we attach the attribute of time to days and nights and their parts, and likewise to feelings of pleasure and pain and to neutral states, to states of movement and states of rest, conceiving a peculiar accident of these to be this very characteristic which we express by the word 'time'.

OF OTHER WORLDS

After the foregoing we have next to consider that the worlds and every finite aggregate which bears a strong resemblance to things we commonly see have arisen out of the infinite. For all these, whether small or great, have been separated off from special conglomerations of particles; and all things are again dissolved, some faster, some slower, some through the action of one set of causes, others through the action of another.

And further, we must not suppose that the worlds have necessarily one and the same shape. For nobody can prove that in one sort of world there might not be contained, whereas in another sort of world there could not possibly be, the seeds out of which animals and plants arise and all the rest of the things we see.

OF LEARNING AND THE ORIGIN OF LANGUAGE

Again, we must suppose that nature too has been taught and forced to learn many various lessons by the facts themselves, that reason subsequently develops what it has thus received and makes fresh discoveries, among some tribes more quickly, among others more slowly, the progress thus made being at certain times and seasons greater, at others less.

Hence even the names of things were not originally due to convention, but in the several tribes under the impulse of special feelings and special presentations of sense primitive man uttered special cries. The air thus emitted was moulded by their invidi-dual feelings or sense-presentations, and differently according to the difference of the regions which the tribes inhabited. Sub-sequently whole tribes adopted their own special names, in order that their communications might be less ambiguous to each other and more briefly expressed. And as for things not visible, so far as those who were conscious of them tried to introduce any such notion, they put in circulation certain names for them, either sounds which they were instinctively compelled to utter or which they selected by reason on analogy according to the most general cause there can be for expressing oneself in such a way.

GODS TAKE NO PART IN THE WORLD: PHENOMENA HAVE NATURAL EXPLANATIONS

Nay more: we are bound to believe that in the sky, revolutions, solstices, eclipses, risings and settings, and the like, take place without the ministration or command, either now or in the future, of any being who at the same time enjoys perfect bliss along with immortality. For troubles and anxieties and feelings of anger and partiality do not accord with bliss, but always imply weakness and fear and dependence upon one's neigh-bours. Nor, again, must we hold that things which are no more than globular masses of fire, being at the same time endowed with bliss, assume these motions at will. Nay, in every term we use we must hold fast to all the majesty which attaches to such notions as bliss and immortality, lest the terms should generate opinions inconsistent with this majesty. Otherwise such incon-sistency will of itself suffice to produce the worst disturbance in our minds. Hence, where we find phenomena invariably recur-ring, the invariableness of the recurrence must be ascribed to the original interception and conglomeration of primary particles whereby the world was formed.

Further, we must hold that to arrive at accurate knowledge of the cause of things of most moment is the business of natural science, and that happiness depends on this (viz. on the knowledge of celestial and atmospheric phenomena), and upon knowing what heavenly bodies really are, and any kindred facts contributing to exact knowledge in this respect.

Further, we must recognize on such points as this no plurality of causes or contingency, but must hold that nothing suggestive of conflict or disquiet is compatible with an immortal and blessed nature. And the mind can grasp the absolute truth of this.

OF REGULAR CELESTIAL PHENOMENA

But when we come to subjects for special inquiry, there is nothing in the knowledge of risings and settings and solstices and eclipses and all kindred subjects that contributes to our happiness; but those who are well-informed about such matters and yet are ignorant what the heavenly bodies really are, and what are the most important causes of phenomena, feel quite as much fear as those who have no such special information – nay, perhaps even greater fear, when the curiosity excited by this additional knowledge cannot find a solution or understand the subordination of these phenomena to the highest causes.

Hence, if we discover more than one cause that may account for solstices, settings and risings, eclipses and the like, as we did also in particular matters of detail, we must not suppose that our treatment of these matters fails of accuracy, so far as it is needful to ensure our tranquility and happiness. When, therefore, we investigate the causes of celestial and atmospheric phenomena, as of all that is unknown, we must take into account the variety of ways in which analogous occurrences happen within our experience; while as for those who do not recognize the difference between what is or comes about from a single cause and that which may be the effect of any one of several causes, overlooking the fact that the objects are only seen at a distance, and are moreover ignorant of the conditions that render, or do not render, peace of mind impossible – all such persons we must treat with contempt. If then we think that an event could happen in one or other particular way out of several, we shall be as tranquil when we recognize that it actually comes about in more ways than one as if we knew that it happens in this particular way.

HEAVENLY BODIES ARE NOT GODS: SCIENCE BANISHES SUCH FEARS

There is yet one more point to seize, namely, that the greatest anxiety of the human mind arises through the belief that the heavenly bodies are blessed and indestructible, and that at the same time they have volitions and actions and causality inconsistent with this belief; and through expecting or apprehending some everlasting evil, either because of the myths, or because we are in dread of the mere insensibility of death, as if it had to do with us; and through being reduced to this state not by conviction but by a certain irrational perversity, so that, if men do not set bounds to their terror, they endure as much or even more intense anxiety than the man whose views on these matters are quite vague. But mental tranquility means being released from all these troubles and cherishing a continual remembrance of the highest and most important truths.

Hence we must attend to present feelings and sense perceptions, whether those of mankind in general or those peculiar to the individual, and also attend to all the clear evidence available, as given by each of the standards of truth. For by studying them we shall rightly trace to its cause and banish the source of disturbance and dread, accounting for celestial phenomena and for all other things which from time to time befall us and cause the utmost alarm to the rest of mankind.

CONCLUSION

Here then, Herodotus, you have the chief doctrines of Physics in the form of a summary. So that, if this statement be accurately retained and take effect, a man will, I make no doubt, be incomparably better equipped than his fellows, even if he should never go into all the exact details. For he will clear up for himself many of the points which I have worked out in detail in my complete exposition; and the summary itself, if borne in mind, will be of constant service to him.

It is of such a sort that those who are already tolerably, or even perfectly, well acquainted with the details can, by analysis of what they know into such elementary perceptions as these, best prosecute their researches in physical science as a whole; while those, on the other hand, who are not altogether entitled to rank as mature students can in silent fashion and as quick as thought run over the doctrines most important for their peace of mind.

3 On Terrestrial and Celestial Phenomena

Letter to Pythocles[8]

INTRODUCTION

Epicurus to Pythocles, greeting.

In your letter to me, of which Cleon was the bearer, you continue to show me affection which I have merited by my devotion to you, and you try, not without success, to recall the considerations which make for a happy life. To aid your memory you ask me for a clear and concise statement respecting celestial phenomena; for what we have written on this subject elsewhere is, you tell me, hard to remember, although you have my books constantly with you. I was glad to receive your request and am full of pleasant expectations. We will then complete our writing and grant all you ask. Many others besides you will find these

---

[8] This is the second of the three letters preserved by Diogenes Laertius. As Epicurus himself points out at the start, its conclusions are not as decisive as 'when we discuss human life [the 'Letter to Menoeceus'] or explain the principles of physics in general [the 'Letter to Herodotus']. Many types of phenomena – for example death – may arise from more than one cause; or more than one explanation may account for the phenomena and leave us with no grounds in experience for preferring one explanation to another. But, and this is perhaps the most important general lesson urged in the 'Letter', natural explanations can be found. The phenomena of the world, however strange or apparently malevolent or benevolent, are not the results of divine interventions. In the variety of explanations Epicurus offers (typically 'it may be thus . . . or perhaps it is thus'), he is often wildly wrong from the vantage point of modern knowledge. But the significant thing is that Epicurus could welcome almost all modern scientific explanations within the structure of his philosophy by simply noting that further experience of just the sort he would have approved of has been able to get at the true descriptions of natural phenomena which eluded him. Scientific progress is welcome to his philosophy not (as for so long with Christianity) alien to it.

From the somewhat *ad hoc* sequence of topics, and the occurrence of material on the stars in two unrelated chunks, it is suspected that the 'Letter to Pythocles' may have been an ancient amalgam of two or more letters, or an abridgement of some longer work. The same *ad hoc* development is evident in Lucretius, V, 509–779, and VI, 96–607, which deal with similar topics.

Pythocles was a beautiful young man of whom Epicurus was very fond ('Fragments' 33 and 34). That does not imply that Epicurus was a homosexual in the sense the concept has acquired in the 1990s. Account must be taken of the well-established Greek social convention under which it was perfectly common and normal for an older man to patronize a youth with advantage to both and stigma to neither.

reasonings useful, and especially those who have but recently made acquaintance with the true story of nature and those who are attached to pursuits which go deeper than any part of ordinary education. So you will do well to take and learn them and get them up quickly along with the short epitome in my letter to Herodotus.

THE PURPOSE OF EXPLANATION AND ITS METHODS

In the first place, remember that, like everything else, knowledge of celestial phenomena, whether taken along with other things or in isolation, has no other end in view than peace of mind and firm conviction. We must not try to force an impossible explanation, nor to understand all matters equally well, nor make our treatment always as clear as when we discuss human life or explain the principles of physics in general – for instance, that the whole of being consists of bodies and intangible nature, or that the ultimate elements of things are indivisible, or any other proposition which admits only one explanation of the phenomena to be possible. But this is not the case with celestial phenomena: these at any rate admit of manifold causes for their occurrence and manifold accounts, none of them contradictory of sensation.

For in the study of nature we must not conform to empty assumptions and arbitrary laws, but follow the promptings of the facts; for our life has no need now of unreason and false opinion; our one need is untroubled existence. All things go on uninterruptedly, if all be explained by the method of plurality of causes in conformity with the facts, so soon as we duly understand what may be plausibly alleged respecting them. But when we pick and choose among them, rejecting one equally consistent with the phenomena, we clearly fall away from the study of nature altogether and tumble into myth. Some phenomena within our experience afford evidence by which we may interpret what goes on in the heavens. We see how the former really take place, but not how the celestial phenomena take place, for their occurrence may possibly be due to a variety of causes. However, we must observe each fact as presented, and further separate from it all the facts presented along with it, the occurrence of which from various causes is not contradicted by facts within our experience.

WHAT A WORLD IS

A world is a circumscribed portion of the universe, which contains stars and earth and all other visible things, cut off from the infinite, [whose dissolution will cause all within to fall into confusion, and which ends] in an exterior which may either revolve or be at rest, and be round or triangular or of any shape whatever. All these alternatves are possible: they are contradicted by none of the facts in this world, in which an extremity can nowhere be discerned.

THE FORMATION OF WORLDS

That there is an infinite number of such worlds can be perceived, and that such a world may arise in a world or in one of the *intermundia* (by which term we mean the spaces between worlds) in a tolerably empty space and not, as some maintain, in a vast space perfectly clear and void. It arises when certain suitable seeds rush in from a single world or *intermundium*, or from several, and undergo gradual additions or articulations or changes of place, it may be, and waterings from appropriate sources, until they are matured and firmly settled in so far as the foundations laid can receive them. For it is not enough that there should be an aggregation or a vortex in the empty space in which a world may arise, as the necessitarians hold, and may grow until it collide with another, as one of the so-called physicists says.[9] For this is in conflict with facts.

SUN, MOON AND STARS

The sun and moon and the stars generally were not of independent origin and later absorbed within our world, [such parts of it at least as serve at all for its defence]; but they at once began

---

[9] The 'necessitarians' may refer to Leucippus, who appears to have held that worlds are mere agglomerates of particles in the void. Epicurus wants to say that the right kinds of particle must be brought together in a suitable way. The 'so-called physicists' very probably refers to Democritus and his followers, who thought that worlds were brought about by a chaotic whirl of particles in a vortex whose size increased until it entangled with another vortex. See D. J. Furley, *The Greek Cosmologists*, vol. I (Cambridge, 1987).

to take form and grow [and so too did earth and sea] by the accretions and whirling motions of certain substances of finest texture, of the nature either of wind or fire, or of both; for thus sense itself suggests.

The size of the sun and the remaining stars relatively to us is just as great as it appears. But in itself and actually it may be a little larger or a little smaller, or precisely as great as it is seen to be. For so too fires of which we have experience are seen by sense when we see them at a distance. And every objection brought against this part of the theory will easily be met by anyone who attends to plain facts, as I show in my work *On Nature*.[10] And the rising and setting of the sun, moon and stars may be due to kindling and quenching, provided that the circumstances are such as to produce this result in each of the two regions, east and west: for no fact testifies against this. Or the result might be produced by their coming forward above the earth and again by its intervention to hide them: for no fact testifies against this either. And their motions may be due to the rotation of the whole heaven, or the heaven may be at rest and they alone rotate according to some necessary impulse to rise, implanted at first when the world was made . . . and this through excessive heat, due to a certain extension of the fire which always encroaches upon that which is near it.

The turnings of the sun and moon in their course may be due to the obliquity of the heaven, whereby it is forced back at these times. Again, they may equally be due to the contrary pressure of the air or, it may be, to the fact that either the fuel from time to time necessary has been consumed in the vicinity or there is a dearth of it. Or even because such a whirling motion was from the first inherent in these stars so that they move in a sort of spiral. For all such explanations and the like do not conflict with any clear evidence, if only in such details we hold fast to what is

---

[10] The 'theory' that the sun is about as big as it appears to be is superficially silly and question-begging. At best it is Epicurus affirming the reliability of sensation as a source of knowledge *and* saying that since we cannot get near to the sun, all we have is the appearance, and we are left with a problem awaiting further data. See also Lucretius, V, 564–84. *On Nature*, reputedly Epicurus' most substantial and important work, was, according to Diogenes Laertius, thirty-seven books long. No copy survives from antiquity except small parts – largely unread and possibly unreadable – recovered from the Epicurean library entombed at Herculaneum.

possible, and can bring each of these explanations into accord with the facts, unmoved by the servile artifices of the astronomers.

THE PHASES OF THE MOON

The waning of the moon and again her waxing might be due to the rotation of the moon's body, and equally well to configurations which the air assumes; further, it may be due to the interposition of certain bodies. In short, it may happen in any of the ways in which the facts within our experience suggest such an appearance to be explicable. But one must not be so much in love with the explanation by a single way as wrongly to reject all the others from ignorance of what can, and what cannot, be within human knowledge, and consequent longing to discover the indiscoverable. Further, the moon may possibly shine by her own light, just as possibly she may derive her light from the sun; for in our own experience we see many things which shine by their own light and many also whch shine by borrowed light. And none of the celestial phenomena stand in the way, if only we always keep in mind the method of plural explanation and the several consistent assumptions and causes, instead of dwelling on what is inconsistent and giving it a false importance so as always to fall back in one way or another upon the single explanation. The appearance of the face in the moon may equally well arise from interchange of parts, or from interposition of something, or in any other of the ways which might be seen to accord with the facts. For in all the celestial phenomena such a line of research is not to be abandoned; for, if you fight against clear evidence, you never can enjoy genuine peace of mind.

ECLIPSES

An eclipse of the sun or moon may be due to the extinction of their light, just as within our own experience this is observed to happen; and again by interposition of something else – whether it be the earth or some other invisible body like it. And thus we must take in conjunction the explanations which agree with one another, and remember that the concurrence of more than one at the same time may not impossibly happen.

And further, let the regularity of their orbits be explained in the same way as certain ordinary incidents within our own experience; the divine nature must not on any account be adduced to explain this, but must be kept free from the task and in perfect bliss. Unless this be done, the whole study of celestial phenomena will be in vain, as indeed it has proved to be with some who did not lay hold of a possible method, but fell into the folly of supposing that these events happen in one single way only and of rejecting all the others which are possible, suffering themselves to be carried into the realm of the unintelligible, and being unable to take a comprehensive view of the facts which must be taken as clues to the rest.

DAY AND NIGHT

The variations in the length of nights and days may be due to the swiftness and again to the slowness of the sun's motion in the sky, owing to the variations in the length of spaces traversed and to his accomplishing some distances more swiftly or more slowly, as happens sometimes within our own experience; and with these facts our explanation of celestial phenomena must agree; whereas those who adopt only one explanation are in conflict with the facts and are utterly mistaken as to the way in which man can attain knowledge.

The signs in the sky which betoken the weather may be due to mere coincidence of the seasons, as is the case with signs from animals seen on earth, or they may be caused by changes and alterations in the air. For neither the one explanation nor the other is in conflict with facts, and it is not easy to see in which cases the effect is due to one cause or to the other.

CLOUDS, RAIN AND THUNDER

Clouds may form and gather either because the air is condensed under the pressure of winds, or because particles which hold together and are suitable to produce this result become mutually entangled, or because currents collect from the earth and the waters; and there are several other ways in which it is not impossible for the aggregations of such bodies into clouds to be brought about. And that being so, rain may be produced from them sometimes by their compression, sometimes by their transformation; or again may be caused by exhalations of moisture rising from suitable places through the air, while a more violent inundation is due to certain accumulations suitable for such discharge. Thunder may be due to the rolling of wind in the hollow parts of the clouds, as it is sometimes imprisoned in vessels which we use; or to the roaring of fire in them when blown by a wind, or to the rending and disruption of clouds, or to the friction and splitting up of clouds when they have become as firm as ice. As in the whole survey, so in this particular point, the facts invite us to give a plurality of explanations.

LIGHTNING AND THUNDERBOLTS

Lightnings too happen in a variety of ways. For when the clouds rub against each other and collide, that collocation of particles which is the cause of fire generates lightning; or it may be due to the flashing forth from the clouds, by reason of winds, of particles capable of producing this brightness; or else it is squeezed out of the clouds when they have been condensed either by their own action or by that of the winds; or again, the light diffused from the stars may be enclosed in the clouds, then driven about by their motion and by that of the winds, and finally make its escape from the clouds; or light of the finest texture may be filtered through the clouds (whereby the clouds may be set on fire and thunder produced), and the motion of this light may make lightning; or it may arise from the combustion of wind brought about by the violence of its motion and the intensity of its compression; or, when the clouds are rent asunder by winds, and the atoms which generate fire are expelled, these likewise cause lightning to appear. And it may easily be seen that its occurrence is possible in many other ways, so long as we hold fast to facts and take a general view of what is analogous to them. Lightning precedes thunder, when the clouds are constituted as mentioned above and the configuration which produces lightning is expelled at the moment when the wind falls upon the cloud, and the wind being rolled up afterwards produces the roar of thunder; or, if both are simultaneous, the lightning moves with a greater velocity towards us and the thunder lags behind, exactly as when persons who are striking blows are observed from a distance.

A thunderbolt is caused when winds are repeatedly collected, imprisoned, and violently ignited; or when a part is torn asunder and is more violently expelled downwards, the rending being due to the fact that the compression of the clouds has made the neighbouring parts more dense; or again it may due like thunder merely to the expulsion of the imprisoned fire, when this has accumulated and been more violently inflated with wind and has torn the cloud, being unable to withdraw to the adjacent parts because it is continually more and more closely compressed [generally by some high mountain where thunderbolts mostly fall]. And there are several other ways in which thunderbolts may possibly be produced. Exclusion of myth is the sole condition necessary; and it will be excluded, if one properly attends to the facts and hence draws inferences to interpret what is obscure.

WHIRLWINDS

Fiery whirlwinds are due to the descent of a cloud forced downwards like a pillar by the wind in full force and carried by a gale round and round, while at the same time the outside wind gives the cloud a lateral thrust; or it may be due to a change of the wind which veers to all points of the compass as a current of air from above helps to force it to move; or it may be that a strong eddy of winds has been started and is unable to burst through laterally because the air around is closely condensed. And when they descend upon land, they cause what are called tornadoes, in accordance with the various ways in which they are produced through the force of the wind; and when let down upon the sea, they cause waterspouts.

EARTHQUAKES

Earthquakes may be due to the imprisonment of wind underground, and to its being interspersed with small masses of earth and then set in continuous motion, thus causing the earth to tremble. And the earth either takes in this wind from without or from the falling in of foundations, when undermined, into subterranean caverns, thus raising a wind in the imprisoned air. Or they may be due to the propagation of movement arising from the fall of many foundations and to its being again checked when it encounters the more solid resistance of earth. And there are many other causes to which these oscillations of the earth may be due.

WIND, HAIL AND OTHER ATMOSPHERIC PHENOMENA

Winds arise from time to time when foreign matter continually and gradually finds its way into the air; also through the gathering of a great store of water. The rest of the winds arise when a few of them fall into the many hollows and they are thus divided and multiplied.

Hail is caused by the firmer congelation and complete transformation, and subsequent distribution into drops, of certain particles resembling wind: also by the slighter congelation of certain particles of moisture and the vicinity of certain particles of wind which at one and the same time forces them together and makes them burst, so that they become frozen in parts and in the whole mass. The round shape of hailstones is not impossibly due to the extremities on all sides being melted and to the fact that, as explained, particles either of moisture or of wind surround them evenly on all sides and in every quarter, when they freeze.

Snow may be formed when a fine rain issues from the clouds because the pores are symmetrical and because of the continuous and violent pressure of the winds upon clouds which are suitable; and then this rain has been frozen on its way because of some violent change to coldness in the regions below the clouds. Or again, by congelation in clouds which have uniform density a fall of snow might occur through the clouds which contain moisture being densely packed in close proximity to each other; and these clouds produce a sort of compression and cause hail, and this happens mostly in spring. And when frozen clouds rub against each other, this accumulation of snow might be thrown off. And there are other ways in which snow might be formed.

Dew is formed when such particles as are capable of producing this sort of moisture meet each other from the air: again by their rising from moist and damp places, the sort of place where dew is chiefly formed, and their subsequent coalescence, so as to create moisture and fall downwards, just as in several cases something similar is observed to take place under our eyes. And the formation of hoar-frost is not different from that of dew, certain particles of such a nature becoming in some such way congealed owing to a certain condition of cold air.

Ice is formed by the expulsion from the water of the circular, and the compression of the scalene and acute-angled primary particles contained in it; further by the accretion of such particles from without, which being driven together cause the water to solidify after the expulsion of a certain number of round particles.

The rainbow arises when the sun shines upon humid air; or again by a certain peculiar blending of light with air, which will cause either all the distinctive qualities of these colours or else some of them belonging to a single kind, and from the reflection of this light the air all around will be coloured as we see it to be, as the sun shines upon its parts. The circular shape which it assumes is due to the fact that the distance of every point is perceived by our sight to be equal; or it may be because, particles in the air or in the clouds and deriving from the sun having been thus united, the aggregate of them presents a sort of roundness.

A halo round the moon arises because the air on all sides extends to the moon; or because it equably raises upwards the currents from the moon so high as to impress a circle upon the cloudy mass and not to separate it altogether; or because it raises the air which immediately surrounds the moon symmetrically from all sides up to a circumference round her and there forms a thick ring. And this happens at certain parts either because a current has forced its way in from without or because the heat has gained possession of certain passages in order to effect this.

COMETS AND STARS

Comets arise either because fire is nourished in certain places at certain intervals in the heavens, if circumstances are favourable;

or because at times the heaven has a particular motion above us so that such stars appear; or because the stars themselves are set in motion under certain conditions and come to our neighbourhood and show themselves. And their disappearance is due to the causes which are the opposite of these.

Certain stars may revolve without setting not only for the reason alleged by some, because this is the part of the world round which, itself unmoved, the rest revolves, but it may also be because a circular eddy of air surrounds this part, which prevents them from travelling out of sight like other stars; or because there is a dearth of necessary fuel farther on, while there is an abundance in that part where they are seen to be. Moreover there are several other ways in which this might be brought about, as may be seen by anyone capable of reasoning in accordance with the facts. The wanderings of certain stars,[11] if such wandering is their actual motion, and the regular movement of certain other stars, may be accounted for by saying that they originally moved in a circle and were constrained, some of them to be whirled round with the same uniform rotation and others with a whirling motion which varied; but it may also be that according to the diversity of the regions traversed in some places there are uniform tracts of air, forcing them forward in one direction and burning uniformly, in others these tracts present such irregularities as cause the motions observed.

To assign a single cause for these effects when the facts suggest several causes is madness and a strange inconsistency; yet it is done by adherents of rash astrology, who assign meaningless causes for the stars whenever they persist in saddling the divinity with burdensome tasks. That certain stars are seen to be left behind by others may be because they travel more slowly, though they go the same round as the others; or it may be that they are drawn back by the same whirling motion and move in the opposite direction; or again it may be that some travel over a larger and others over a smaller space in making the same revolution. But to lay down as assured a single explanation of these phenomena is worthy of those who seek to dazzle the multitude with marvels.

[11] Wandering stars are the planets, which appear to follow an erratic course about the sky in comparison with the regular constellations.

Falling stars, as they are called, may in some cases be due to the mutual friction of the stars themselves, in other cases to the expulsion of certain parts when that mixture of fire and air takes place which was mentioned when we were discussing lightning; or it may be due to the meeting of particles capable of generating fire, which accord so well as to produce this result, and their subsequent motion wherever the impulse which brought them together at first leads them; or it may be that wind collects in certain dense mist-like masses and, since it is imprisoned, ignites and then bursts forth upon whatever is round about it, and is carried to that place to which its motion impels it. And there are other ways in which this can be brought about without recourse to myths.

ANIMAL BEHAVIOUR HAS NO REAL INFLUENCE ON WEATHER

The fact that the weather is sometimes foretold from the behaviour of certain animals is a mere coincidence in time. For the animals offer no necessary reason why a storm should be produced; and no divine being sits observing when these animals go out and afterwards fulfilling the signs which they have given. For such folly as this would not possess the most ordinary being if ever so little enlightened, much less one who enjoys perfect felicity.

CONCLUSION

All this, Pythocles, you should keep in mind; for then you will escape a long way from myth, and you will be able to view in their connexion the instances which are similar to these. But above all give yourself up to the study of first principles and of infinity and of kindred subjects, and further of the standards and of the feelings and of the end for which we choose between them. For to study these subjects together will easily enable you to understand the causes of the particular phenomena. And those who have not fully accepted this, in proportion as they have not done so, will be ill acquainted with these very subjects, nor have they secured the end for which they ought to be studied.

4 *The Happy Life*
Letter to Menoeceus[12]

INTRODUCTION

Epicurus to Menoeceus, greeting.

No one should hold back from thinking about philosophy when young, nor in old age grow weary of the search for wisdom. It is never too soon or too late to secure the well-being of one's mind, and to say that the reason for studying philosophy has not yet come, or is already gone, is like saying that the reason for happiness is not yet come or is no more.

Therefore both old and young must study philosophy. The former so that, with advancing years, they may remain young in blessings through the joyous recollection of things past. The latter so that, while still young, they may at the same time be mature because they have no fear of things to come.

So we must meditate on what brings happiness, since if we have that, we have everything. And if we have it not, all our energies are directed at gaining it.

Whatever I have regularly commended to you, practise and do, for what follows are the first principles of the good life.

THE GODS ARE BLESSED BUT OF NO CONCERN TO US

According to popular opinion, god is immortal and blessed. Accept this for a start. But do not then say of him anything that would be alien to his immortality and blessedness. Simply believe whatever is really consistent with it. For indeed gods exist. Our perception of them is clear. But they are not as

[12] The last in order of the three letters preserved by Diogenes Laertius is comparatively fluent and easily read as a brief account of the way of living that Epicurus recommended. Learn that you have nothing to fear from the inactive blessedness of divine beings, and nothing to feel in death. Learn that tranquillity of mind and a pain-free body constitute happiness. You are then able to find happiness in simple things easily attained, and to choose the most fulfilling happiness because you have thought about all the consequences of your choice. Many of the ideas in this 'Letter' are repeated or extended in the various sayings in the 'Principal Doctrines', 'Epicurus' Exhortation' and the collected fragments. Menoeceus was a pupil of Epicurus.

ordinary people imagine, for they do not retain consistently their first impressions. Indeed he is not impious who destroys the gods of popular belief, but rather he who accepts the popular view. For the utterances of the multitude about gods are not true perceptions derived from sensation, but false assumptions: [For example] that the gods send the greatest rewards [to the good] and ultimate misery to the wicked (because the gods are always favourable to their own virtues and regard whatever is different as alien).[13]

THERE IS NOTHING TO FEAR IN DEATH

Get used to believing that death is nothing to us. For all good and evil lies in sensation and death is the end of all sensation. Therefore, a right understanding that death is nothing to us makes the mortality of life enjoyable, not by adding to it a limitless duration, but by taking away the yearning for immortality. For the man who has truly comprehended that there is nothing terrible in ceasing to live, has nothing terrible to fear in life. Thus a man speaks foolishly when he says he fears death. It will not pain him when it comes. It pains only in prospect. Whatever causes no distress when it is present, gives pain to no purpose when it is anticipated. Death therefore, the most dreaded of ills, is nothing to us. While we are, death is not; when death is come, we are not. Death is thus of no concern either to the living or to the dead. For it is not with the living, and the dead do not exist.

But generally, at one time a man will shun death as the greatest evil and at another long for it as a rest from the miseries of life. But the wise man neither looks for escape from life, nor for its cessation. Life does not offend him, nor does its absence look like any sort of evil. And just as men do not seek simply and only the largest portion of good but the pleasantest, so the wise seek to enjoy the time which is most pleasant and not merely that which is longest.

[13] The Greek here is very difficult to translate and possibly deliberately ambiguous. Another reading for the words in parenthesis is 'for they, always favourable to their own virtues, approve those who are like themselves, and regard whatever is different as alien.' 'They' may be gods who are favourable towards men like themselves, or the common people who look for a repetition of their own prejudices in gods.

And he who advises the young to live well and the old to die well is foolish, not merely because life is desirable, but because the same training teaches us to live well and die well. Worse still is the man who says it were better never to have been born, and 'once born, make haste to pass the gates of Hades'. If he really believes this, why not act upon it? It is easy enough to do so if one is firmly convinced. But if he speaks insincerely, his words are folly among men who reject them.

Remember that the future is neither entirely ours nor entirely lost to us: we may not take its coming for certain, nor must we despair of it as quite certain not to come.

BLESSEDNESS IS A PAIN-FREE BODY AND A TRANQUIL MIND

We must consider some of our desires as natural and others as vain. Of those that are natural, some are necessary, others merely natural. Of necessary desires, some are necessary for happiness, others for the comfort of the body, others for life itself. A clear and positive understanding of these facts will enable each of us to direct every choice and avoidance in accordance with health for the body and tranquillity for the mind. For these are the objectives of a life of blessedness. For the end of all we do is to be free from pain and fear, and when once we have attained this, all turmoil of mind is dispersed and the living creature does not have to wonder as if in search of something missing, nor look for anything to complete the good of mind and body.

PLEASURE IS THE GUIDE IN ALL WE CHOOSE

When we suffer pain from the absence of pleasure, only then do we feel the need for pleasure. [But when we no longer feel the pain] we no longer need the pleasure. In this way, regard pleasure as the beginning and end of a blessed life. For we recognize pleasure as the primary and natural desire, and we return to it in all our judgements of the good, taking the feeling of pleasure as our guide.

But given that pleasure is the primary and natural good, we do not choose every and any pleasure, but often pass by many if they are outweighed by the discomforts they bring. And similarly we consider pain superior to pleasures when submission to the pains for a significant time brings a greater pleasure as a consequence. Thus every pleasure, because it is naturally akin to us, is good, but not every pleasure is fit to be chosen – just as all pain is an evil and yet not all is to be avoided. It is by comparison and by looking at the advantages and disadvantages, that all these things must be judged. For under certain circumstances we treat the good as an evil, and conversely evil as a good.

LIVE SIMPLY

And again, we regard independence of external things as a great good, not so that in all cases we may enjoy only a few things, but in order to be contented with little if we have little, being honestly persuaded that they have the sweetest pleasure in luxury who least need it, and that all that is natural is easy to get, while that which is superfluous is hard. Once the pain due to want is removed, plain flavours give us as much pleasure as an extravagant diet, while bread and water bring the greatest possible pleasure to the life of one in need of them. To become accustomed, therefore, to simple and inexpensive food gives us all we need for health, alerts a man to the necessary tasks of life, and when at intervals we approach luxuries we are in a better condition to enjoy them. Moreover [simple things] fit us to be unafraid of fortune.

When we say that pleasure is the objective, we do not mean the pleasures of the profligate or the pleasures of sensuality, as we are understood to do by some through ignorance, prejudice, or wilful misinterpretation. By 'pleasure' we mean the absence of pain in the body and of turmoil in the mind. The pleasurable life is not continuous drinking, dancing and sex; nor the enjoyment of fish or other delicacies of an extravagant table. It is sober reasoning which searches out the motives for all choice and avoidance, and rejects those beliefs which lay open the mind to the greatest disturbance.

LIVE WITH AN EYE TO CONSEQUENCES

Of all this, the beginning and chief good is care in avoiding undesired consequences. Such prudence is more precious than philosophy itself, for all the other virtues spring from it. It teaches that it is impossible to live pleasurably without also living prudently, honestly and justly; [nor is it possible to lead a life of prudence, honour and justice] and not live pleasantly. For the virtues are closely associated with the pleasant life, and the pleasant life cannot be separated from them.

THE HAPPY MORTAL

Who then is better than the man who holds right opinions concerning gods, who is entirely without fear of death, and who understands the highest good of nature? He understands how easily good things can be attained and kept, and how pain is either short in duration or low in intensity. He laughs at [destiny] which some have set up as the ruler of all things. [He thinks that with us lies the chief power in determining events, some of which happen] according to natural law, others by chance, others through our own agency. He sees that natural law cannot be called to account for itself, that chance is inconstant, but that our own actions are free. It is to them that praise and blame naturally attach. It were better, indeed, to accept the myths about gods than to become a slave to the determinism of the physicists. At least the former holds out some faint hope if we placate the gods, while the latter is inescapable.

He does not regard chance as a god as most men do (for in the acts of a god disorder has no place) nor as an unstable cause. For he believes that good and evil are not dispensed to men by chance in order to make life blessed, although chance supplies the starting point of great good and great evil. He believes it is better to be unfortunate while acting reasonably than to prosper acting foolishly. It is better, in short, that what is well thought out in action [should fail, rather than what is ill thought out] should succeed by chance.

Meditate on these feelings, [Menoeceus], and on things like them, by night and day, alone or with a like-minded friend. You will then never be troubled in waking or in sleep, and will live like a god among men. For a man who lives among immortal blessings is unlike a mortal man.

5 Epicurus' Exhortation
Vatican Sayings[14]

IV. All bodily suffering is negligible: for that which causes acute pain has short duration, and that which endures long in the flesh causes but mild pain.

VII. It is hard for an evil-doer to escape detection, but to obtain security for escaping is impossible.

IX. Necessity is an evil, but there is no necessity to live under the control of necessity.

X. [Remember that you are of mortal nature and have a limited time to live and have devoted yourself to discussions on nature for all time and eternity and have seen 'things that are now and are to come and have been'.]

XI. For most men rest is stagnation and activity madness.

XIV. We are born once and cannot be born twice, but for all time must be no more. But you, who are not [master] of to-morrow, postpone your happiness: life is wasted in procrastination and each one of us dies without allowing himself leisure.

[14] These eighty-one aphorisms were discovered in a manuscript in the Vatican in 1888. The manuscript dates from the fourteenth century and at a first glance contained only a number of longer works such as the *Meditations* of Marcus Aurelius and Epictetus' Stoic *Manual*.

Most of the sayings appear to have been culled from private letters or lost works by Epicurus and are concerned with the happy life. Where the saying is omitted in the present text, it is identical with another saying already present in the 'Principal Doctrines'. Thus 'Vatican Saying' I is 'Principal Doctrine' 1, II is 2, III is 4, V is 5, VI is 35, VIII is 15, XII is 17, XIII is 27, XX is 29, XXII is 19, XLIX is 12, L is 8 and LXXII is 13. Sayings set in square brackets appear to be by Metrodorus or from other Epicureans, and not by Epicurus himself.

Almost all the sayings are immediately accessible to us and need little or no learned annotation. But they do need to be contemplated slowly and individually: thought about, rather than skimmed over as if they constituted a newspaper article.

xv. We value our character as something peculiar to ourselves, whether they are good and we are esteemed by men, or not; so ought we to value the characters of others, if they are well-disposed to us.

xvi. No one when he sees evil deliberately chooses it, but is enticed by it as being good in comparison with a greater evil and so pursues it.

xvii. It is not the young man who should be thought happy, but an old man who has lived a good life. For the young man at the height of his powers is unstable and is carried this way and that by fortune, like a headlong stream. But the old man has come to anchor in old age as though in port, and the good things for which before he hardly hoped he has brought into safe harbourage in his grateful recollections.

xviii. Remove sight, association and contact, and the passion of love is at an end.

xix. Forgetting the good that has been he has become old this very day.

xxi. We must not violate nature, but obey her; and we shall obey her if we fulfil the necessary desires and also the physical, if they bring no harm to us, but sternly reject the harmful.

xxiii. All friendship is desirable in itself, though it starts from the need of help.

xxiv. Dreams have no divine character nor any prophetic force, but they originate from the influx of images.

xxv. Poverty, when measured by the natural purpose of life, is great wealth, but unlimited wealth is great poverty.

xxvi. You must understand that whether the discourse be long or short it tends to the same end.

XXVII. In all other occupations the fruit comes painfully after completion, but in philosophy pleasure goes hand in hand with knowledge; for enjoyment does not follow comprehension, but comprehension and enjoyment are simultaneous.

XXVIII. We must not approve either those who are always ready for friendship, or those who hang back, but for friendship's sake we must even run risks.

XXIX. In investigating nature I would prefer to speak openly and like an oracle to give answers serviceable to all mankind, even though no one should understand me, rather than to conform to popular opinions and so win the praise freely scattered by the mob.

XXX. [Some men throughout their lives gather together the means of life, for they do not see that the draught swallowed by all of us at birth is a draught of death.]

XXXI. Against all else it is possible to provide security, but as against death all of us mortals alike dwell in an unfortified city.

XXXII. The veneration of the wise man is a great blessing to those who venerate him.

XXXIII. The flesh cries out to be saved from hunger, thirst and cold. For if a man possess this safety and hopes to possess it, he might rival even Zeus in happiness.

XXXIV. It is not so much our friends' help that helps us as the confidence of their help.

XXXV. We should not spoil what we have by desiring what we have not, but remember that what we have too was the gift of fortune.

XXXVI. [Epicurus' life when compared to other men's in respect of gentleness and self-sufficiency might be thought a mere legend.]

xxxvii. Nature is weak towards evil, not towards good: because it is saved by pleasures, but destroyed by pains.

xxxviii. He is a little man in all respects who has many good reasons for quitting life.

xxxix. He is no friend who is continually asking for help, nor he who never associates help with friendship. For the former barters kindly feeling for a practical return and the latter destroys the hope of good in the future.

xl. The man who says that all things come to pass by necessity cannot criticize one who denies that all things come to pass by necessity: for he admits that this too happens of necessity.

xli. We must laugh and philosophize at the same time and do our household duties and employ our other faculties, and never cease proclaiming the sayings of the true philosophy.

xlii. The greatest blessing is created and enjoyed at the same moment.

xliii. The love of money, if unjustly gained, is impious, and, if justly, shameful; for it is unseemly to be merely parsimonious even with justice on one's side.

xliv. The wise man when he has accommodated himself to straits knows better how to give than to receive: so great is the treasure of self-sufficiency which he has discovered.

xlv. The study of nature does not make men productive of boasting or bragging nor apt to display that culture which is the object of rivalry with the many, but high-spirited and self-sufficient, taking pride in the good things of their own minds and not of their circumstances.

xlvi. Our bad habits, like evil men who have long done us great harm, let us utterly drive from us.

XLVII. [I have anticipated thee, Fortune, and entrenched myself against all thy secret attacks. And we will not give ourselves up as captives to thee or to any other circumstance; but when it is time for us to go, spitting contempt on life and on those who here vainly cling to it, we will leave life crying aloud in a glorious triumph-song that we have lived well.]

XLVIII. We must try to make the end of the journey better than the beginning, as long as we are journeying; but when we come to the end, we must be happy and content.

LI. You tell me that the stimulus of the flesh makes you too prone to the pleasures of love. Provided that you do not break the laws or good customs and do not distress any of your neighbours or do harm to your body or squander your pittance, you may indulge your inclination as you please. Yet it is impossible not to come up against one or other of these barriers: for the pleasures of love never profited a man and he is lucky if they do him no harm.

LII. Friendship goes dancing round the world proclaiming to us all to awake to the praises of a happy life.

LIII. We must envy no one: for the good do not deserve envy and the bad, the more they prosper, the more they injure themselves.

LIV. We must not pretend to study philosophy, but study it in reality: for it is not the appearance of health that we need, but real health.

LV. We must heal our misfortunes by the grateful recollection of what has been and by the recognition that it is impossible to make undone what has been done.

LVI–LVII. The wise man is not more pained when being tortured [himself, than when seeing] his friend [tortured]: [but if his friend does him wrong], his whole life will be confounded by distrust and completely upset.

LVIII. We must release ourselves from the prison of affairs and politics.

LIX. It is not the stomach that is insatiable, as is generally said, but the false opinion that the stomach needs an unlimited amount to fill it.

LX. Every man passes out of life as though he had just been born.

LXI. Most beautiful too is the sight of those near and dear to us, when our original kinship makes us of one mind; for such sight is a great incitement to this end.

LXII. Now if parents are justly angry with their children, it is certainly useless to fight against it and not to ask for pardon; but if their anger is unjust and irrational, it is quite ridiculous to add fuel to their irrational passion by nursing one's own indignation, and not to attempt to turn aside their wrath in other ways by gentleness.

LXIII. Frugality too has a limit, and the man who disregards it is in like case with him who errs through excess.

LXIV. Praise from others must come unasked: we must concern ourselves with the healing of our own lives.

LXV. It is vain to ask of the gods what a man is capable of supplying for himself.

LXVI. Let us show our feeling for our lost friends not by lamentation but by meditation.

LXVII. A free life cannot acquire many possessions, because this is not easy to do without servility to mobs or monarchs, yet it possesses all things in unfailing abundance; and if by chance it obtains many possessions, it is easy to distribute them so as to win the gratitude of neighbours.

LXVIII. Nothing is sufficient for him to whom what is sufficient seems little.

LXIX. The ungrateful greed of the soul makes the creature everlastingly desire varieties of dainty food.

LXX. Let nothing be done in your life, which will cause you fear if it becomes known to your neighbour.

LXXI. Every desire must be confronted with this question: what will happen to me, if the object of my desire is accomplished and what if it is not?

LXXIII. The occurrence of certain bodily pains assists us in guarding against others like them.

LXXIV. In a philosophical discussion he who is worsted gains more in proportion as he learns more.

LXXV. Ungrateful towards the blessings of the past is the saying, 'Wait till the end of a long life'.

LXXVI. You are in your old age just such as I urge you to be, and you have seen the difference between studying philosophy for oneself and proclaiming it to Greece at large: I rejoice with you.

LXXVII. The greatest fruit of self-sufficiency is freedom.

LXXVIII. The noble soul occupies itself with wisdom and friendship: of these the one is a mortal good, the other immortal.

LXXIX. The man who is serene causes no disturbance to himself or to another.

LXXX. The first measure of security is to watch over one's youth and to guard against what makes havoc of all by means of pestering desires.

LXXXI. The disturbance of the soul cannot be ended nor true joy created either by the possession of the greatest wealth or by honour and respect in the eyes of the mob or by anything else that is associated with causes of unlimited desire.

6 Fragments from Epicurus
Quoted in Greek Literature[15]

(a) FRAGMENTS ASSIGNABLE TO SPECIFIC BOOKS OF EPICURUS

Concerning Choice and Avoidance

1. Freedom from trouble in the mind and from pain in the body are static pleasures, but joy and exultation are considered as active pleasures involving motion.

Problems

2. Will the wise man do things that the laws forbid, knowing that he will not be found out? A simple answer is not easy to find.

The Shorter Summary

3. Prophecy does not exist, and even if it did exist, things that come to pass must be counted nothing to us.

Against Theophrastus

4. But even apart from this argument I do not know how one should say that things in the dark have colour.

Symposium

5. Polyaenus: Do you, Epicurus, deny the existence of the warmth produced by wine? (Some one interrupted:) It does not appear that wine is unconditionally productive of heat.

---

[15] This collection of fragments is gathered from Greek writings of antiquity in which it is reasonably clear that Epicurus is being quoted directly or reported in close paraphrase. Fragments (a) can be assigned to known titles of lost books by Epicurus (a catalogue of his works is given in Diogenes Laertius' *Lives of Eminent Philosophers*, Book X); fragments (b) come from letters; while (c), some of the most interesting, cannot be assigned to any particular place in Epicurus' writings. A fully annotated account of each fragment can be found in C. Bailey, *Epicurus, the Extant Remains* (Oxford, 1926), pp. 388–400. Most are very interesting, particularly where they give us an enhanced picture of Epicurus' own character. A few, e.g. 18, 20 and 27, have little intrinsic value and are merely included for the sake of completeness.

(And a little later:) It seems that wine is not unconditionally productive of heat, but wine of a certain quantity might be said to produce heat in a certain body.

6. Therefore we must not speak of wine as unconditionally productive of heat, but rather say that a certain quantity of wine will produce heat in a certain body which is in a certain disposition, or that a different quantity will produce cold in a different body. For in the compound body of wine there are certain particles out of which cold might be produced, if, as need arises, united with different particles they could form a structure which would cause cold. So that those are deceived who say that wine is unconditionally heating or cooling.

7. Wine often enters the body without exerting any power either of heating or of cooling, but when the structure is disturbed and a particle re-arrangement takes place, the particles which create heat at one time come together and by their number give heat and inflammation to the body, at another they retire and so cool it.

8. Sexual intercourse has never done a man good, and he is lucky if it has not harmed him.

9. It is strange indeed that you were not at all impeded by your youth, as you would say yourself, from attaining, young as you were, a distinction in the art of rhetoric far above all your contemporaries, even the experienced and famous. It is strange indeed, I say, that you were not at all impeded by your youth from winning distinction in the art of rhetoric, which seems to require much practice and habituation, whereas youth can be an impediment to the understanding of the true nature of the world, towards which knowledge might seem to contribute more than practice and habituation.

On the End of Life

10. I know not how I can conceive the good, if I withdraw the pleasures of taste, and withdraw the pleasures of love, and withdraw the pleasures of hearing, and withdraw the pleasurable emotions caused to sight by beautiful form.

11. The stable condition of well-being in the body and the sure hope of its continuance holds the fullest and surest joy for those who can rightly calculate it.

12. Beauty and virtue and the like are to be honoured, if they give pleasure; but if they do not give pleasure, we must bid them farewell.

On Nature

Book i

13. The nature of the universe consists of bodies and void.

14. The nature of all existing things is bodies and space.

Book xi

15. For if it (sc. the sun) had lost its size through the distance, much more would it have lost its colour: for there is no other distance better adapted for such loss than that of the sun.

From Uncertain Works

16. The atom is a hard body free from any admixture of void; the void is intangible existence.

17. Away with them all: for he (Nausiphanes), like many another slave, was in travail with that wordy braggart, sophistic.

(b) FRAGMENTS FROM LETTERS

18. If they have this in mind, they are victorious over the evils of want and poverty.

19. Even if war comes, he would not count it terrible, if the gods are propitious. He has led and will lead a pure life in Matro's company, by favour of the gods.

20. Tell me, Polyaenus, do you know what has been a great joy to us?

To the Philosophers in Mytilene

21. This drove him to such a state of fury that he abused me and ironically called me master.

22. I suppose that those grumblers will believe me to be a disciple of The Mollusc and to have listened to his teaching in company with a few bibulous youths. For indeed the fellow was a bad man and his habits such as could never lead to wisdom.

To Anaxarchus

23. But I summon you to continuous pleasures and not to vain and empty virtues which have but disturbing hopes of results.

To Apelles

24. I congratulate you, Apelles, in that you have approached philosophy free from all contamination.

To Themista

25. If you two don't come to me, I am capable of arriving with a hop, skip, and jump, wherever you and Themista summon me.

To Idomeneus

26. Send us therefore offerings for the sustenance of our holy body on behalf of yourself and your children: this is how it occurs to me to put it.

27. O thou who hast from thy youth regarded all my promptings as sweet.

28. If you wish to make Pythocles rich, do not give him more money, but diminish his desire.

29. We think highly of frugality not that we may always keep to a cheap and simple diet, but that we may be free from desire regarding it.

30.[16] On this truly happy day of my life, as I am at the point of death, I write this to you. The disease in my bladder and stomach are pursuing their course, lacking nothing of their natural severity: but against all this is the joy in my heart at the recollection of my conversations with you. Do you, as I might expect from your devotion from boyhood to me and to philosophy, take good care of the children of Metrodorus.

To Colotes

31. In your feeling of reverence for what I was then saying you were seized with an unaccountable desire to embrace me and clasp my knees and show me all the signs of homage paid by men in prayers and supplications to others; so you made me return all these proofs of veneration and respect to you.

Go on thy way as an immortal and think of us too as immortal.

To Leontion

32. Lord and Saviour, my dearest Leontion, what a cheering you drew from us, when we read aloud your dear letter.

To Pythocles

33. Blest youth, set sail in your bark and flee from every form of culture.

34. I will sit down and wait for your lovely and godlike appearance.

To a Boy or Girl

35. We have arrived at Lampsacus safe and sound, Pythocles and Hermarchus and Ctesippus and I, and there we found Themista and our other friends all well. I hope you too are well and your mamma, and that you are always obedient to pappa and Matro, as you used to be. Let me tell you that the reason

---

[16] This extract from a letter to his friend and follower Idomeneus is quoted by Diogenes Laertius in the 'Life' of Epicurus with which he introduces the 'Letters' and 'Principal Doctrines'. A closely similar letter to Hermarchus is quoted by Cicero (in a Latin translation) in *De Finibus*, Book II, 96 (see below, p. 65). Epicurus was dying painfully of a blockage in the urethra. See Fragment 36.

that I and all the rest of us love you is that you are always obedient to them.

Letter Written in his Last Days

36. Seven days before writing this the stoppage became complete and I suffered pains such as bring men to their last day. If anything happens to me, do you look after the children of Metrodorus for four or five years, but do not spend any more on them than you now spend each year on me.

Letters to Unknown Recipients

37. I am thrilled with pleasure in the body, when I live on bread and water, and I spit upon luxurious pleasures not for their own sake, but because of the inconveniences that follow them.

38. As I said to you when you were going away, take care also of his brother Apollodorus. He is not a bad boy, but causes me anxiety, when he does what he does not mean to do.

39. Send me some preserved cheese, that when I like I may have a feast.

40. You have looked after me wonderfully generously in sending me food, and have given proofs heaven-high of your good will to me.

41. The only contribution I require is that which ... ordered the disciples to send me, even if they are among the Hyperboreans. I wish to receive from each of you two a hundred and twenty drachmae a year and no more.

Ctesippus has brought me the annual contribution which you sent for your father and yourself.

42. He will have a valuable return in the instruction which I have given him.

43. I was never anxious to please the mob. For what pleased them, I did not know, and what I did know, was far removed from their comprehension.

44. Think it not unnatural that when the flesh cries aloud, the mind cries too. The flesh cries out to be saved from hunger, thirst, and cold. It is hard for the mind to repress these cries, and dangerous for it to disregard nature's appeal to her because of her own wonted independence day by day.

45. The man who follows nature and not vain opinions is independent in all things. For in reference to what is enough for nature every possession is riches, but in reference to unlimited desires even the greatest wealth is not riches but poverty.

46. In so far as you are in difficulties, it is because you forget nature; for you create for yourself unlimited fears and desires.

48. It is better for you to be free of fear lying upon a pallet, than to have a golden couch and a rich table and be full of trouble.

49. . . . remembering your letter and your discussion about the men who are not able to see the analogy between phenomena and the unseen nor the harmony which exists between sensations and the unseen and again the contradiction . . .

50. Sweet is the memory of a dead friend.

51. Do not avoid conferring small favours: for then you will seem to be of like character towards great things.

52. If your enemy makes a request to you, do not turn from his petition: but be on your guard; for he is like a dog.

(C) UNASSIGNABLE FRAGMENTS CONCERNING
PHILOSOPHY, PHYSICS AND LIFE

On Philosophy

54. Vain is the word of a philosopher which does not heal any suffering of man. For just as there is no profit in medicine if it does not expel the diseases of the body, so there is no profit in philosophy either, if it does not expel the suffering of the mind.

Physics

55. Nothing new happens in the universe, if you consider the infinite time past.

56. We shall not be considering them any happier or less destructible, if we think of them as not speaking nor conversing with one another, but resembling dumb men.

57. Let us at least sacrifice piously and rightly where it is customary, and let us do all things rightly according to the laws not troubling ourselves with common beliefs in what concerns the noblest and holiest of beings. Further let us be free of any charge in regard to their opinion. For thus can one live in conformity with nature . . .

58. If God listened to the prayers of men, all men would quickly have perished: for they are for ever praying for evil against one another.

On the Happy Life

59. The beginning and the root of all good is the pleasure of the stomach; even wisdom and culture must be referred to this.

60. We have need of pleasure when we are in pain from its absence: but when we are not feeling such pain, though we are in a condition of sensation, we have no need of pleasure. For the pleasure which arises from nature does not produce wickedness, but rather the longing connected with vain fancies.

61. That which creates joy insuperable is the complete removal of a great evil. And this is the nature of good, if one can once grasp it rightly, and then hold by it, and not walk about babbling idly about the good.

62. It is better to endure these particular pains so that we may enjoy greater joys. It is well to abstain from these particular pleasures in order that we may not suffer more severe pains.

63. Let us not blame the flesh as the cause of great evils, nor blame circumstances for our distresses.

64. Great pains quickly put an end to life; long-enduring pains are not severe.

65. Excessive pain will bring you to death.

66. Through love of true philosophy every disturbing and troublesome desire is ended.

67. Thanks be to blessed Nature because she has made what is necessary easy to supply, and what is not easy unnecessary.

68. It is common to find a man who is (poor) in respect of the natural end of life and rich in empty fancies. For of the fools none is satisfied with what he has, but is grieved for what he has not. Just as men with fever through the malignance of their (disease) are always thirsty and desire the most injurious things, so too those whose mind is in an evil state are always poor in everything and in their greed are plunged into ever-changing desires.

69. Nothing satisfies the man who is not satisfied with a little.

70. Self-sufficiency is the greatest of all riches.

71. Most men fear frugality and through their fear are led to actions most likely to produce fear.

72. Many men when they have acquired riches have not found the escape from their ills but only a change to greater ills.

73. By means of occupations worthy of a beast abundance of riches is heaped up, but a miserable life results.

74. Unhappiness comes either through fear or through vain and unbridled desire: but if a man curbs these, he can win for himself the blessedness of understanding.

75. It is not deprivation of these things which is pain, but rather the bearing of the useless pain that arises from vain fancies.

76. The mean-spirited person is puffed up by prosperity and cast down by misfortune.

77. Nature teaches us to pay little heed to what fortune brings, and when we are prosperous to understand that we are unfortunate, and when we are unfortunate not to regard prosperity highly, and to receive unmoved the good things which come from fortune and to range ourselves boldly against the seeming evils which it brings: for all that the many regard as good or evil is fleeting, and wisdom has nothing in common with fortune.

78. He who least needs to-morrow, will most gladly go to meet to-morrow.

79. I spit upon the beautiful and those who vainly admire it, when it does not produce any pleasure.

80. The greatest fruit of justice is serenity.

81. The laws exist for the sake of the wise, not that they may not do wrong, but that they may not suffer it.

82. Even if they are able to escape punishment, it is impossible to win security for escaping: and so the fear of the future which always presses upon them does not suffer them to be happy or to be free from anxiety in the present.

83. The man who has attained the natural end of the human race will be equally good, even though no one is present.

84. A man who causes fear cannot be free from fear.

85. The happy and blessed state belongs not to abundance of riches or dignity of position or any office or power, but to freedom from pain and moderation in feelings and an attitude of mind which imposes the limits ordained by nature.

86. Live unknown.

87. We must say how best a man will maintain the natural end of life, and how no one will willingly at first aim at public office.

7 Quotations from Epicurus in Cicero's Philosophical Works[17]

DE FINIBUS

I, 63. The wise man is little inconvenienced by fortune: things that matter are under the control of his own judgement and reason.
No greater pleasure could be derived from an eternal life than is actually derived from an existence we can see to be finite.

I, 68. The same way of thinking that reinforces our outlook so that we fear neither eternal nor long-term evil hereafter, has perceived that friendship is the strongest safeguard in this life.

II, 21. If the things in which voluptuaries find pleasure could free them from fear of gods and death and pain, and if it could teach them to set bounds to their desires, we would have nothing to blame since on all sides they would be replete with pleasures, and on no side would they be vulnerable to pain or grief, which is the sole evil.[18]

II, 96. Epicurus to Hermarchus, greeting. I am writing in the course of the last and most blessed day of my life. I am suffering

---

[17] Among Cicero's expositions of Greek philosophy for Roman readers, *De Finibus Bonorum et Malorum* (a treatise on theories of ethics) and *De Natura Deorum* (a treatise on what we would now call the philosophy of religion), both written in 45 BC, contain important accounts of Epicurean arguments, but relatively few direct quotations from Epicurus and even fewer that supplement Greek sources. In the present collection only direct quotations are included, together with one or two where the indirect speech suggests that the words are, or are very close to, Epicurus' own. But a proper study of Epicurus would require attention to the whole of Book I of *De Finibus* (an exposition by Torquatus of the Epicurean thesis that the chief good is pleasure and the absence of pain) and the Stoic reply in Book II, together with Book I of *De Natura Deorum* which contains (paragraphs 18–56) Velleius' account of Epicurean gods and (paragraphs 57 to 124) a sceptical Academic reply.

[18] In his comments Cicero implies that this quotation is almost a self-evident invitation to vice, and Torquatus' plea 'You don't perceive [Epicurus'] meaning' is quickly brushed aside. But Epicurus himself clearly does mean that the conditions that would make voluptuaries blameless are never in practice satisfied.

from diseases of the intestines and bladder which could not be more severe ... However, all these sufferings are compensated by the joy of remembering our principles and discoveries. But, as is appropriate in terms of the devotion you have displayed to me and to philosophy since your youth, please look after the children of Metrodorus ... My joy compensates the totality of pain.

II, 100. Death touches us in no way; for what has suffered dissolution, is without sensation; and what is without sensation touches us in no way whatsoever.

II, 101. [from Epicurus' last will. See below, p. 72] ... that his heirs Amynochus and Timocrates, in accordance with Hermarchus' wishes, shall give enough for an annual celebration of his birthday in the month of Gamelion [namely January] and shall also assign a sum for a dinner for his fellow students in philosophy on the twentieth of each month, in order to keep alive the memory of himself and Metrodorus.[19]

TUSCULAN DISPUTATIONS

III, 41–2. Nor yet for my part can I find anything that I can understand as good if I take away from it the pleasures afforded by taste, those that come from listening to music, those that come from the eyes by the sight of figures in motion, or other pleasures produced by any of the senses in the complete man. Nor indeed can it be said that joy of the mind all by itself is to be reckoned among [what is] good. For I recognize that a mind is in a state of rejoicing precisely when it has hope of all the pleasures I have spoken about. That is to say, the hope that nature will be free to enjoy them without any admixture of pain ... I have often asked those who are called wise what would remain in any good if they deducted from it the [pleasures] named (unless it were merely their wish to utter speech void of meaning). I have been able to learn nothing from these men. If they wish to continue prattling about virtues and wisdoms, they

---

[19] Metrodorus was a close colleague of Epicurus' who died about 277 BC.

can mean nothing but the way in which the pleasures I have spoken about above can be effected.

III, 49. Epicurus denies that a pleasurable life is possible unless lived with virtue. He denies that fortune has power over the wise. He prefers plain food to a rich excess. He denies that there can be any time when the wise man is not blessed.

DE NATURA DEORUM

I, 45. That which is blessed and eternal may neither experience trouble itself nor extend trouble to others, and thus can feel neither anger nor favour, since anything like that is a weakness.

DE DIVINATIONE

II, 103. That which is finite has an end.

That which has an end can be perceived from [a point] external to itself.

But that which is everything [i.e., the universe] cannot be perceived from [a point] external to itself.

Therefore, since that which is everything has no end, [the universe] must necessarily be infinite.

8 Sayings of Epicurus in Seneca's Works[20]

IN THE MORAL EPISTLES

ii, 5. Joyful poverty is an honourable thing.

iv, 10. Poverty conducted in accordance with the law of nature is great wealth.

vii, 12. This I wrote not for the money, but for you; for we are enough of an audience for each other.

viii, 7. You must be the slave of philosophy if you would enjoy true freedom.

ix, 20. Whoever does not regard what he has as the amplest wealth, though he be lord of the whole earth, yet is he wretched.

xi, 8. We ought to cherish some man of good character and have him always before our eyes, thus living as if he were watching us, and fashioning all our activities as if he could see them.

xii, 10. To live under constraint is an evil, but no one is constrained to *live* under constraint.

xiii, 16. Among the rest of his faults the fool hath also this: that he is always *beginning* to live.

[20] Seneca (c. 4 BC–AD 65): Stoic, tutor to Nero, chief administrator of the Roman Empire with Burrus AD 54–62 and author of 124 *Moral Epistles* (short essays on life and conduct), ten *Moral Essays* (longer works on anger, bereavement, etc.), a satire on the emperor Claudius, nine tragedies and a work on natural philosophy. Seneca was not an Epicurean, but he is much less averse to the school than Cicero. In particular in the *Moral Epistles* Seneca seems to relish quoting pithy, single-line sayings of Epicurus – much as we might look for a 'thought for today' in the sayings of Jesus even if we are not Christians.

xv, 9. The fool's life is ungracious and fearful: it is directed totally at the future.

xvi, 9. If you live according to nature, you will never be poor; if you live according to opinions, you will never be rich.

xvii, 11. For many, the acquisition of riches has not made an end of troubles, but an alteration.

xviii, 14. Ungoverned anger begets madness.

xix, 10. Before you eat and drink anything, consider carefully who you eat and drink it with: for feeding without a friend is the life of a lion or a wolf.

xx, 9. Believe me, your discourse will seem more striking on a stretcher and in rags; for then it will not be a matter of lip-service but of actual experience.

xxi, 3. [To Idomeneus, a once famous man] If you would be touched by fame, my letters will make you more renowned than all the things which you cherish and for the sake of which you are cherished.

xxi, 7. If you wish to make Pythocles rich, be not adding to his money but subtracting from his desires.

xxii, 14-15. No one departs from life in a state any different from that in which he entered it ... No one departs from life any different from how he was born.

xxiii, 9. It is irritating to be always starting to live ... They live badly who are always beginning to live.

xxiv, 22-3. It is ridiculous to run towards death because you are tired of living, when by your manner of living you have forced yourself to run towards death ... What is more ridiculous than to seek death when you have made your life unquiet by fearing it?

xxv, 5. Do everything as if Epicurus were watching you.

xxvi, 8. Meditate upon death [Seneca offers the gloss 'It is a splendid thing to know well how to die'].

xxv, 6. The time when you should most of all withdraw into yourself is when you are forced to be in a crowd.

xxvii, 9. Wealth is poverty adjusted to the law of nature. [cf. iv, 10]

xxviii, 9. Awareness of wrongdoings is the beginning of salvation.

xxix, 10. I have never wished to please the crowd: for what I know, they do not approve; what they approve, I do not know.

xxx, 14. First he hopes that there is no pain at the last breath; if however there is, he derives some comfort from its very brevity. For no pain which is severe lasts long. And in any event one will find relief at the moment of separation of body and life – even if it is terrible – in knowing that after this pain, no pain is possible. Nor does he doubt that life's breath in an old man is on his very lips, nor that but a little force is needed to disengage it from the body. 'A fire which has seized upon some flammable material needs water to quench it; but that which lacks sustaining fuel goes out of its own accord.'

lii, 3. Some people reach the truth without anybody's assistance and find their own way ... some people need the help of others and won't go at all unless somebody goes ahead to them: but they are good at following.

lxvi, 45. [In Epicurus, there are two benefits which together constitute supreme blessings:] a body free from pain and a mind free from disturbance.

xcvii, 13. For the guilty to remain hidden is possible; to be confident in such concealment is impossible. [Seneca's gloss, xcvii, 16, is 'Good fortune frees many men from punishment, but none from the fear of it.']

IN THE MORAL ESSAYS

'On the Firmness of the Wise man', xv, 4: Fortune rarely obstructs the wise.

'On Leisure', iii, 2: The wise man will not be involved in public affairs unless something prevents him [Seneca points out that Zeno the Stoic takes a very different view to that of Epicurus' injunction to 'Live quietly' – 'Zeno says: He *will* be involved in public affairs unless something prevents him.']

9 Epicurus' Last Will and Testament[21]

On this wise I give and bequeath all my property to Amynomachus, son of Philocrates of Bate and Timocrates, son of Demetrius of Potamus, to each severally according to the items of the deed of gift laid up in the Metroön, on condition that they shall place the garden and all that pertains to it at the disposal of Hermarchus, son of Agemortus, of Mytilene, and the members of his society, and those whom Hermarchus may leave as his successors, to live and study in. And I entrust to my School in perpetuity the task of aiding Amynomachus and Timocrates and their heirs to preserve to the best of their power the common life in the garden in whatever way is best, and that these also (the heirs of the trustees) may help to maintain the garden in the same way as those to whom our successors in the School may bequeath it. And let Amynomachus and Timocrates permit Hermarchus and his fellow-members to live in the house in Melite for the lifetime of Hermarchus.

And from the revenues made over by me to Amynomachus and Timocrates let them to the best of their power in consultation with Hermarchus make separate provision (1) for the funeral offerings to my father, mother, and brothers, and (2) for the customary celebration of my birthday on the tenth day of Gamelion in each year, and for the meeting of all my School held every month on the twentieth day to commemorate Metrodorus and myself according to the rules now in force. Let them also join in celebrating the day in Poseideon which commemorates my brothers, and likewise the day in Metageitnion which commemorates Polyaenus, as I have done hitherto.

And let Amynomachus and Timocrates take care of Epicurus, the son of Metrodorus, and of the son of Polyaenus, so long as they study and live with Hermarchus. Let them likewise provide for the maintenance of Metrodorus' daughter, so long as she is well-ordered and obedient to Hermarchus; and, when she comes of age, give her in marriage to a husband selected by Hermarchus from among the members of the School; and out of the

[21] The text is preserved by Diogenes Laertius.

revenues accruing to me let Amynomachus and Timocrates in consultation with Hermarchus give to them as much as they think proper for their maintenance year by year.

Let them make Hermarchus trustee of the funds along with themselves, in order that everything may be done in concert with him, who has grown old with me in philosophy and is left at the head of the School. And when the girl comes of age, let Amynomachus and Timocrates pay her dowry, taking from the property as much as circumstances allow, subject to the approval of Hermarchus. Let them provide for Nicanor as I have hitherto done, so that none of those members of the school who have rendered service to me in private life and have shown me kindness in every way and have chosen to grow old with me in the School should, so far as my means go, lack the necessaries of life.

All my books to be given to Hermarchus.

And if anything should happen to Hermarchus before the children of Metrodorus grow up, Amynomachus and Timocrates shall give from the funds bequeathed by me, so far as possible, enough for their several needs, as long as they are well ordered. And let them provide for the rest according to my arrangements; that everything may be carried out, so far as it lies in their power. Of my slaves I manumit Mys, Nicias, Lycon, and I also give Phaedrium her liberty.

PHILODEMUS

The Fourfold Remedy[22]

Alpha
Nothing to fear in God.
Nothing to feel in Death.
Good can be attained.
Evil can be endured.

Beta
God is not worth fearing.
Death is not worth a worry.
But good can be attained,
And evil can be endured.

[22] Philodemus of Gadara in Syria (*c.* 110–30s BC) came to Rome about 75 BC and became a major influence in the dissemination of Greek philosophy (seen from an Epicurean viewpoint) among the Roman intelligentsia. Some twenty-five erotic verse epigrams survive, and parts of his prose works from charred papyrus rolls recovered from Piso's villa in Herculaneum where Philodemus lived and taught. No collection of his extant works is available in English, but 'The Remedy', preserved in one of the Herculaneum rolls, is so famous as a compressed account of Epicureanism that it deserves to stand by itself. Alpha is Gilbert Murray's translation of a Greek original which differs slightly from the Herculaneum wording. Beta is an attempt to render the Herculaneum Greek. The four lines correspond with, and each is a masterful epitome of, the first four of Epicurus' own 'Principal Doctrines'. See p. 5.

LUCRETIUS

ON THE NATURE OF THE UNIVERSE
De Rerum Natura

Each of the six books is preceded by a synopsis of its subject matter, indicated by reference to the standard line number in the Latin verse. The text itself has the main headings from each synopsis interpolated, and each sub-item in the synopsis is indicated in the text by an additional space. Every paragraph is given its initial line number.

Square brackets in the text indicate conjectural additions or emendations where the manuscript lines are missing or erroneous. A brief footnote explanation is usually given in such cases. Square brackets are also used sparingly to give a synonym or other very brief explanation, thus avoiding trivial footnotes.

The main Epicurean 'Principles' identified in the synopses to Books I, II and IV are marked in the text by italics in the sentence or sentences which most nearly express them. They are also gathered together for discussion in the Introduction, p. xxivf, above.

BOOK I

Physical And Metaphysical Principles

Synopsis

1–53   Address to Venus as the power of nature [verse translation by Charles Foxley, 1933].

54–61   To Memmius, concerning the subject in hand.

62–79   The Triumph of Epicurus over superstition and religion.

80–101   Religion as the cause of evil deeds.

102–35   The fear of death to be overcome by understanding the nature of life and mind.

136–45   Difficult words are best sweetened by poetry.

The Main Principles, 146–634

146–58   *Principle I. No thing is ever created out of nothing by divine will: everything happens according to natural laws without the aid of gods.*

159–214   Arguments for I.

215–16   *Principle II. No thing is ever put out of existence: natural laws resolve each thing again into its primary parts.*

217–64   Arguments for II.

265–70   *Principle III. Primary particles or 'first beginnings' cannot be discerned with the eye but exist.*

271–328   Arguments for III and *Principle IV: Nothing can touch or be touched unless it is body* (304).

329–35   *Principle V: Void – mere space, untouchable and empty – exists.*

336–417   Arguments for V.

418–29   Existence of *body* proved by sensation.
Existence of *void* proved by location of bodies.

430–48   *Principles VI. Nothing other than body and void is real.*

449–82   Everything else, including time and historical events, is a property or accident of body or void.

483–502   *Principle VII. Bodies are primary particles ('primordia'), or the union of these: primary particles are solid (contain no void) and everlasting.*

503–634   Arguments for VII.

Rejection of Alternatives to VII, 635–920

635–704   Heraclitus: that fire is the material of all things.

705–15   Rejection of other minor Presocratic physicalists.

716–829   Empedocles: that things are composed of the four elements.

830–920   Anaxagoras: that things are clusters of little versions ('homoeomeria') of themselves.

The Infinity of the Universe, 921–1117

921–50   Understanding these difficult matters frees men from the bondage of religion.

951–57   Summary.

958–67   *Principle VIII: The universe has no limit.*

968–1007   Arguments for VIII.

1008–20   *Principle IX. The quantity of matter* (i.e. primordia
           viewed collectively) *is* fixed (see I and II) *but
           infinite.*

1021–51   Our world is not the product of intentions but of
           chance.

1052–1113 There is no 'middle' of the universe.

Conclusion

1114–17

Book 1

O joy of gods and men, kind Pow'r of Love,
Who fill'st the fruitful lands, the sailèd sea,
While starry signs glide round in heav'n above,
True Mother of Rome's Trojan race! Through thee
All living creatures are conceived, and see
The light of day. Thou, goddess,[23] dost beguile
The clouds of heav'n, and storms thy coming flee;
Earth fashions thee sweet flowers, the smooth waves smile,
The sunbeams spread abroad, and heav'n is calm awhile.

When first the sunny days of opening Spring,
With Zephyrs breathing new creation, dawn,
The birds of air first feel thy pow'r and sing;
Then bound the beasts along the merry lawn,
And swim swift rivers. Thus by beauty drawn,
All living Nature follows at thy lead;
O'er flood and fell, where greedy torrents yawn,
In leafy hall of birds and grassy mead,
Thou smit'st their hearts with love, that each renews his breed.

So, since thou rulest Nature all alone,
And none without thee gains the shores of light,
Nor anything is glad or lovely grown,
My nature-poem help me to indite,
The verses which to Memmius mine I write,
Great by thy grace in all things evermore.
Then grant my words unperishing delight.
Meanwhile, I pray, to every sea and shore
Give peace, and hush to sleep the sad, wild works of war.

[23] The invocation is addressed to Venus (the Greek Aphrodite) goddess of love and mother of Aeneas (the Trojan whose flight from that city and foundation of Rome is the subject of Virgil's *Aeneid*). The whole invocation is superficially at variance with the Epicurean view that gods are inactive, uncaring and remote from human affairs (see, for example, II, 646–51 and V, 146–55). In part it is undoubtedly merely following a poetic convention. But it can also be read as an expression of Lucretius' reverence for the power of nature, and his wonder and joy at the life we have, and the world we inhabit.

Thou only canst; for oft the god of wars
Sinks on thy breast and leaves his wild design.
Vanquished by love's eternal wound, great Mars
With smooth neck looking upward doth recline
Rapt in thy beauty, yea his breath is thine.
Thou with his head upon thy sacred breast,
Down bending o'er him, from thy lips divine
Pour forth in winning words this dear request,
'Peace for the race of Rome', great goddess, 'peace and rest.'

For in our own dear country's evil days
I cannot write at all in peace of mind,
Nor can a Memmius fail, undimmed in praise,
To stand by Rome when times are so unkind.
Yet, Memmius,[24] let thine ear be now inclined
And thy keen wits alive to Truth's demand.
Oh, leave thine ever-vexing cares behind,
Slight not mine off'ring ere thou understand,
Nor laugh to scorn what I in faithful earnest planned.

54 For of the most high law of the heaven and the gods I will set out to tell you, and I will reveal the primordia[25] of things, from which nature creates all things, and increases and fosters them, and into which nature too dissolves them again at their perishing: these in rendering our account, it is our habit to call 'matter' or 'the creative bodies' of things, and to name them the 'seeds' of things, and again to term them the 'first-bodies', since from them first all things have their being.

[24] Gaius Memmius, to whom Lucretius addresses the whole poem, was an aristocratic Roman with minor political achievements to his credit. He appears to have been a literary patron and an actual or potential Epicurean.

[25] Primordia (translated 'primary particles' or more literally 'first-beginnings') is the word Lucretius normally uses for the technical Greek word atomoi (atoms). I normally retain the word primordia (singular primordium) in the present translation. See above, p. xxviii. In lines 54–61 Lucretius introduces a set of terms whose meaning is crucial for what he has to say. For a summary see p. 100, note 33. But the word semen ('seed', and a cluster of related meanings), although initially introduced as a synonym for primordium, will have a special function when Lucretius is talking about the capacity of different types of primordia to cluster in ways determined by their shape. Limitations on combination mean it is not the case that anything can come out of anything in a completely random way. Seeds are seeds of a limited or even precise range of things.

62 When the life of man lay foul to see and grovelling upon the earth, crushed by the weight of religion, which showed her face from the realms of heaven, lowering upon mortals with dreadful mien, it was a man of Greece [Epicurus] who dared first to raise his mortal eyes to meet her, and first to stand forth to meet her. Him neither the stories of the gods nor thunderbolts checked, nor the sky with its revengeful roar, but all the more spurred the eager daring of his mind to yearn to be the first to burst through the close-set bolts upon the doors of nature. And so it was that the lively force of his mind won its way, and he passed on far beyond the fiery walls of the world,[26] and in mind and spirit traversed the boundless whole; whence in victory he brings us tidings what can come to be and what cannot, yea and in what way each thing has its power limited, and its deepset boundary-stone. And so in revenge religion is cast beneath men's feet and trampled, and victory raises us to heaven.

80 Herein I have one fear, lest perchance you think that you are starting on the principle of some unholy reasoning, and setting foot upon the path of sin. Nay, but on the other hand, again and again our foe, religion, has given birth to deeds sinful and unholy. Even as at Aulis the chosen chieftains of the Greeks, the first of all the host, foully stained with the blood of Iphigenia the altar of the Virgin of the Cross-Roads.[27] For as soon as the band braided about her virgin locks streamed from her either cheek in equal lengths, as soon as she saw her sorrowing father stand at the altar's side, and near him the attendants hiding their knives, and her countrymen shedding tears at the sight of her, tongue-tied with terror, sinking on her knees she fell to earth. Nor could it avail the luckless girl at such a time that she first had given the name of father to the king. For seized by men's hands, all trembling was she led to the altars, not that, when the

---

[26] The expression is intended literally. Lucretius conceived the world – roughly the earth and heavenly bodies visible from it – as a sphere surrounded by fiery air (see V, 457–70).

[27] The story refers to the sacrifice of Iphigenia at Aulis by her father Agamemnon in order to produce favourable winds to take the Greek fleet to Troy. The Virgin of the Cross-Roads is Artemis, the Roman Diana. The reader will note that Lucretius, writing without the advantage of almost two thousand years of the Christian era at his command, had to supply an example of the evil deeds occasioned by religion from remote mythology.

ancient rite of sacrifice was fulfilled, she might be escorted by
the clear cry of 'Hymen',[28] but, in the very moment of marriage,
a pure victim, she might foully fall, sorrowing beneath a father's
slaughtering stroke, that a happy and hallowed starting might
be granted to the fleet. Such evil deeds could religion prompt.

102 You yourself sometime vanquished by the fearsome threats
of the seer's sayings, will seek to desert from us. Nay indeed,
how many a dream may they even now conjure up before you,
which might avail to overthrow your schemes of life, and
confound in fear all your fortunes. And justly so: for if men
would see that there is a fixed limit to their sorrows, then with
some reason they might have the strength to stand against the
scruples of religion, and the threats of seers. As it is there is no
means, no power to withstand, since everlasting is the punishment they must fear in death. For they know not what is the
nature of the soul [*anima*],[29] whether it is born or else finds its
way into them at their birth, and again whether it is torn apart
by death and perishes with us, or goes to see the shades of Orcus
and his waste pools, or by the gods' will implants itself in other
breasts, as our own Ennius[30] sang (who first bore down from
pleasant Helicon the wreath of deathless leaves, to win bright
fame among the tribes of Italian peoples). And yet despite this,
Ennius sets forth in the discourse of his immortal verse that
there is besides a realm of Acheron, where neither our souls
(*animae*) nor our bodies endure, but as it were images pale in
wondrous wise; and thence he tells that the form of Homer, ever
green and fresh, rose to him, and began to shed salt tears, and
in converse to reveal the nature of things.

127 Therefore we must both give good account of the things
on high, in what way the courses of sun and moon come to be,
and by what force all things are governed on earth, and also
before all else we must see by keen reasoning, whence comes the

---

[28] 'Hymen' – a traditional call at a Greek wedding, possibly the name of a
beautiful young man.

[29] The Latin is *anima* (plural *animae*) conventionally, but in an Epicurean context misleadingly translated 'soul'. I have retained the word '*anima*' in the present
translation. See above, p. xxxvf, and note 7.

[30] Ennius (239–169 BC): highly distinguished and much revered Latin playwright
and epic poet, of whose splendid works only fragments now survive.

anima and the nature of the mind, and what thing it is that meets us and affrights our minds in waking life, when we are touched with disease, or again when buried in sleep, so that we seem to see and hear near by us those who have met death, and whose bones are held in the embrace of earth.

136 Nor does it pass unnoticed of my mind that it is a hard task in Latin verses to set clearly in the light the dark discoveries of the Greeks, above all when many things must be treated in new words, because of the poverty of our tongue and the newness of the themes. Yet your merit and the pleasure of your sweet friendship, for which I hope, urge me to bear the burden of any toil, and lead me on to watch through the calm nights, searching by what words, yes and in what measures, I may avail to spread before your mind a bright light, whereby you may see to the heart of hidden things.

THE MAIN PRINCIPLES, 146–634

146 This terror then, this darkness of the mind, must needs be scattered not by the rays of the sun and the gleaming shafts of day, but by the outer view and the inner law of nature; whose first rule shall take its start for us from this, that *nothing is ever created out of nothing by divine will*. Fear indeed so constrains all mortal men, because they behold many things come to pass on earth and in the sky, the cause of whose working they can by no means see, and think that a divine power brings them about. Therefore, when we have seen that nothing can be created out of nothing, then more rightly after that shall we discern that for which we search, both whence each thing can be created, and in what way all things come to be without the aid of gods.

159 For if things came to being from nothing, every kind might be born from all things, no thing would need a seed. First men might arise from the sea, and from the land the race of scaly creatures, and birds burst forth from the sky; cattle and other herds, and all the tribe of wild beasts, with no fixed law of birth, would haunt tilth and desert. Nor would the same fruits stay constant to the trees, but all would change: all trees might avail to bear all fruits. Why, were there not bodies to bring each thing to birth, how could things have a fixed unchanging mother? But as it is, since all things are produced from fixed seeds, each thing is born and comes forth into the coasts of light, out of that which has in it the substance and first-bodies of each; and it is for this cause that all things cannot be begotten of all, because in fixed things there dwells a power set apart.

174 Or again, why do we see the roses in spring, and the corn in summer's heat, and the vines bursting out when autumn summons them, if it be not that when, in their own time, the fixed seeds of things have flowed together, then is disclosed each thing that comes to birth, while the season is at hand, and the lively earth in safety brings forth the fragile things into the coasts of light? But if they sprang from nothing, suddenly would they arise at uncertain intervals and in hostile times of year, since indeed there would be no first-beginnings which might be kept apart from creative union at an ill-starred season.

184 Nay more, there would be no need for lapse of time for the increase of things upon the meeting of the seed, if they could grow from nothing. For little children would grow suddenly to youths, and at once trees would come forth, leaping from the earth. But of this it is well seen that nothing comes to pass, since all things grow slowly, as is natural, from a fixed seed, and as they grow preserve their kind: so that you can know that each thing grows great, and is fostered out of its own substance.

192 There is this too, that without fixed rain-showers in the year the earth could not put forth its gladdening produce, nor again held apart from food could the nature of living things renew its kind or preserve its life; so that rather you may think that many bodies are common to many things, as we see letters are to words, than that without primary particles anything can come to being.

199 Once more, why could not nature produce men so large that on their feet they might wade through the waters of ocean or rend asunder mighty mountains with their hands, or live to overpass many generations of living men, if it be not because fixed substance has been appointed for the begetting of things, from which it is ordained what can arise? Therefore, we must confess that nothing can be brought to being out of nothing, inasmuch as it needs a seed for things, from which each may be produced and brought forth into the gentle breezes of the air.

208 Lastly, inasmuch as we see that tilled grounds are better than the untilled, and when worked by hands yield better produce, we must know that there are in the earth primordia of things, which we call forth to birth by turning the teeming sods with the ploughshare and drilling the soil of the earth. But if there were none such, you would see all things without toil of ours of their own will come to be far better.

215 Then follows this, that *nature breaks up each thing again into its own first-bodies, nor does she destroy any thing into nothing.*

217 For if anything were mortal in all its parts, each thing would on a sudden be snatched from our eyes, and pass away. For there would be no need of any force, such as might cause disunion in its parts and unloose its fastenings. But as it is, because all things are put together of everlasting seeds, until some force has met them to batter things asunder with its blow, or to make its way inward through the empty voids and break things up, nature suffers not the destruction of anything to be seen.

225 Moreover, if time utterly destroys whatsoever through age it takes from sight, and devours all its substance, how is it that Venus brings back the race of living things after their kind into the light of life, or when she has, how does earth, the quaint artificer, nurse and increase them, furnishing food for them after their kind? How is it that its native springs and the rivers from without, coming from afar, keep the sea full? How is it that the sky feeds the stars? For infinite time and the days that are gone by must needs have devoured all things that are of mortal body. But if in all that while, in the ages that are gone by, those things have existed, of which this sum of things consists and is replenished, assuredly they are blessed with an immortal nature. All things cannot then be turned to nothing.

238 And again, the same force and cause would destroy all things alike, unless an eternal substance held them together, part with part interwoven closely or loosely by its fastenings. For in truth a touch would be cause enough of death, seeing that none

of these things would be of everlasting body, whose texture any kind of force would be bound to break asunder. But as it is, because the fastenings of the first-elements are variously put together, and their substance is everlasting, things endure with body unharmed, until there meets them a force proved strong enough to overcome the texture of each. No single thing then passes back to nothing, but all by dissolution pass back into the first-bodies of matter.

250 Lastly, the rains pass away, when the sky, our father, has cast them headlong into the lap of earth, our mother; but the bright crops spring up, and the branches grow green upon the trees, the trees too grow and are laden with fruit; by them next our race and the race of beasts is nourished, through them we see glad towns alive with children, and leafy woods on every side ring with the young birds' cry; through them the cattle wearied with fatness lay their limbs to rest over the glad pastures, and the white milky stream trickles from their swollen udders; through them a new brood with tottering legs sports wanton among the soft grass, their baby hearts thrilling with the pure milk.

262 Not utterly then perish all things that are seen, since nature renews one thing from out another, nor suffers anything to be begotten, unless she be requited by another's death.

265 Come now, since I have taught you that things cannot be created of nothing nor likewise when begotten be called back to nothing, lest by any chance you should begin nevertheless to distrust my words, because *the primordia of things cannot be perceived with the eyes*, let me tell you besides of other bodies, which you must needs confess yourself are among things and yet cannot be seen.

271 First of all the might of the awakened wind lashes the ocean and overwhelms vast ships and scatters the clouds, and anon scouring the plains with tearing hurricane it strews them with great trees, and harries the mountain-tops with blasts that rend the woods: with such fierce whistling the wind rages and ravens with angry roar. There are therefore, we may be sure, unseen bodies of wind, which sweep sea and land, yes, and the clouds of heaven, and tear and harry them with sudden hurri-

cane. They stream on and spread havoc in no other way than when the soft nature of water is borne on in a flood overflowing in a moment, swollen by a great rush of water dashing down from the high mountains after bounteous rains and hurling together broken branches from the woods, and whole trees too; nor can the strong bridges bear up against the sudden force of the advancing flood. In such a way, turbid with much rain, the river rushes with might and main against the piles: roaring aloud it spreads ruin, and rolls and dashes beneath its waves huge rocks and all that bars its flood. Thus then the blasts of wind too must needs be borne on; and when like some strong stream they have swooped towards any side, they push things and dash them on with constant assault; sometimes in eddying whirl they seize them up and bear them away in swiftly swirling hurricane. Wherefore again and again there are unseen bodies of wind, inasmuch as in their deeds and ways they are found to rival mighty streams, whose body all may see.

298 Then again we smell the manifold scents of things, and yet we do not ever descry them coming to the nostrils, nor do we behold warm heat, nor can we grasp cold with the eyes, nor is it ours to descry voices; yet all these things must needs consist of bodily nature, inasmuch as they can make impact on our senses. For, *if it be not body, nothing can touch and be touched.*

305 Once more, garments hung up upon the shore, where the waves break, grow damp, and again spread in the sun they dry. Yet never has it been seen in what way the moisture of the water has sunk into them, nor again in what way it has fled before the heat. Therefore the moisture is dispersed into tiny particles, which the eyes can in no way see.

311 Nay more, as the sun's year rolls round again and again, the ring on the finger becomes thin beneath by wearing, the fall of dripping water hollows the stone, the bent iron ploughshare secretly grows smaller in the fields, and we see the paved stone streets worn away by the feet of the multitude; again, by the city-gates the brazen statues reveal that their right hands are wearing thin through the touch of those who greet them ever and again as they pass upon their way. All these things then we see grow less, as they are rubbed away: yet what particles leave them at each moment, the envious nature of our sight has shut us out from seeing.

322 Lastly, whatever time and nature adds little by little to things, impelling them to grow in due proportion, the straining sight of the eye can never behold, nor again wherever things grow old through time and decay. Nor where rocks overhang the sea, devoured by the thin salt spray, could you see what they lose at each moment. It is then by bodies unseen that nature works her will.

329 And yet all things are not held close pressed on every side by the nature of body; for there is void in things. To have learnt this will be of profit to you in dealing with many things; it will save you from wandering in doubt and always questioning about the sum of things, and distrusting my words. *There is then a void, mere space untouchable and empty.*

336 For if there were not, by no means could things move; for that which is the office of body, to offend and hinder, would at every moment be present to all things; nothing, therefore, could advance, since nothing could give the example of yielding place. But as it is, through seas and lands and the high tracts of heaven, we descry many things by many means moving in diverse ways before our eyes, which, if there were not void, would not so much be robbed and baulked of restless motion, but rather could in no way have been born at all, since matter would on every side be in close-packed stillness.

346 Again, however solid things may be thought to be, yet from this you can discern that they are of porous body. In rocky caverns the liquid moisture of water trickles through, and all weeps with copious dripping: food spreads itself this way and that into the body of every living thing: trees grow and thrust forth their fruit in due season, because the food is dispersed into every part of them from the lowest roots through the stems and all the branches. Noises creep through walls and fly through the shut places in the house, stiffening cold works its way to the bones: but were there no empty spaces, along which each of these bodies might pass, you would not see this come to pass by any means.

358 Again, why do we see one thing surpass another in weight, when its size is no whit bigger? For if there is as much body in a bale of wool as in lead, it is natural it should weigh as

much since it is the office of body to press all things downwards, but on the other hand the nature of void remains without weight. So because it is just as big, yet seems lighter, it tells us, we may be sure, that it has more void; but on the other hand the heavier thing avows that there is more body in it, and that it contains far less empty space within. Therefore, we may be sure, that which we are seeking with keen reasoning, does exist mingled in things – that which we call void.

370 Herein lest that which some[31] vainly imagine should lead you astray from the truth, I am constrained to forestall it. They say that the waters give place to the scaly creatures as they press forward and open up a liquid path, because the fishes leave places behind, to which the waters may flow together as they yield: and that even so other things too can move among themselves and change place, albeit the whole is solid. In very truth, this is all believed on false reasoning. For whither, I ask, will the scaly creatures be able to move forward, unless the waters have left an empty space? again, whither will the waters be able to give place, when the fishes cannot go forward? either then we must deny motion to every body, or we must say that void is mixed with things, from which each thing can receive the first start of movement. Lastly, if two broad bodies leap asunder quickly from a meeting, surely it must needs be that air seizes upon all the void, which comes to be between the bodies. Still, however rapid the rush with which it streams together as its currents hasten round, yet in one instant the whole empty space cannot be filled: for it must needs be that it fills each place as it comes, and then at last all the room is taken up. But if by chance any one thinks that when bodies have leapt apart, then this comes to be because the air condenses, he goes astray. For in that case that becomes empty which was not so before, and again that is filled which was empty before, nor can air condense in such a way, nor, if indeed it could, could it, I maintain, without void draw into itself and gather into one all its parts.

398 Wherefore, however long you hang back with much

---

[31] As is usual with Epicurean writers, vaguely indicated opponents are Stoic philosophers. The Stoics argued in part that motion was the result of an interchange of place between things. But the Stoic account is very complex. See S. Sambursky, *Physics of the Stoics* (London, 1987).

objection, you must needs confess at last that there is void in things. And besides by telling you many an instance, I can heap up proof for my words. But these light footprints are enough for a keen mind. By them you may detect the rest for yourself. For as dogs ranging over mountains often find by scent the lairs of wild beasts shrouded under leafage, when once they are set on sure traces of their tracks, so for yourself you will be able in such themes as this to see one thing after another, to win your way to all the secret places and draw out the truth thence. But if you are slack or shrink a little from my theme, this I can promise you, Memmius, on my own word: so surely will my sweet tongue pour forth to you bounteous draughts from the deep well-springs out of the treasures of my heart, that I fear lest sluggish age creep over our limbs and loosen within us the fastenings of life, before the whole store of proofs on one single theme be launched in my verses into your ears.

418 But now, to weave again at the web, which is the task of my discourse, all nature then, as it is of itself, is built of these two things: for *there are bodies and the void*, in which they are placed and where they move hither and thither. For that body exists is declared by the feeling which all share alike; and unless faith in this feeling be firmly grounded at once and prevail, there will be naught to which we can make appeal about things hidden, so as to prove aught by the reasoning of the mind. And next, were there not room and empty space, which we call void, nowhere could bodies be placed, nor could they wander at all hither and thither in any direction; and this I have above shown to you but a little while before.

430 Besides these *there is nothing which you could say is parted from all body and sundered from void, which could be discovered, as it were a third nature in the list.*[32] For whatever shall exist, must needs be something in itself; and if it suffer touch, however small and light, it will increase the count of body by a bulk great or maybe small, if it exists at all, and be added to its

---

[32] This principle is the crucial claim of Epicurean one-world realism discussed above, p. xxvf, namely that all and everything that can exist is, or is a property or accident of, body and void, *and there is nothing else.*

sum. But if it is not to be touched, inasmuch as it cannot on any side check anything from wandering through it and passing on its way, in truth it will be that which we call empty void. Or again, whatsoever exists by itself, will either do something or suffer itself while other things act upon it, or it will be such that things may exist and go on in it. But nothing can do or suffer without body, nor afford room again, unless it be void and empty space. And so besides void and bodies no third nature by itself can be left in the list of things, which might either at any time fall within the purview of our senses, or be grasped by any one through reasoning of the mind.

449 For all things that have a name, you will find either properties linked to these two things or you will see them to be their accidents. That is a property which in no case can be sundered or separated without the fatal disunion of the thing, as is weight to rocks, heat to fire, moisture to water, touch to all bodies, intangibility to the void. On the other hand, slavery, poverty, riches, liberty, war, concord, and other things by whose coming and going the nature of things abides untouched, these we are used, as is natural, to call accidents.

459 Even so time exists not by itself, but from actual things comes a feeling, what was brought to a close in time past, then what is present now, and further what is going to be hereafter. And it must be avowed that no man feels time by itself apart from the motion or quiet rest of things.

465 Then again, when men say that 'the rape of Tyndarus' daughter', or 'the vanquishing of the Trojan tribes in war' exist, beware that they do not perchance constrain us to acknowledge that these things exist in themselves, just because the past ages have carried off beyond recall those races of men, of whom, in truth, these were accidents.

469 For firstly, we might well say whatsoever has happened is an accident in one case of the countries, in another even of the regions of space. Or again, if there had been no substance of things nor place and space, in which all things are carried on, never would the flame of love have been fired by the beauty of Tyndaris, nor swelling deep in the Phrygian heart of Alexander have kindled the burning battles of savage war, nor unknown of the Trojans would the timber horse have set Pergama aflame at

dead of night, when the sons of the Greeks issued from its womb.

478 So that you may see clearly that all events from first to last do not exist, and are not by themselves like body, nor can they be spoken of in the same way as the being of the void. Rather you might justly call them the accidents of body and place, in which they are carried on, one and all.

483 *Bodies,* moreover, *are in part the primordia of things, in part those which are created for the union of primordia. Now the true primordia of things, no force can quench; for they by their solid body prevail in the end.* Albeit it seems hard to believe that there can be found among things anything of solid body. For the thunderbolt of heaven passes through walled houses, as do shouts and cries; iron grows white hot in the flame, and stones seethe in fierce fire and leap asunder; then too the hardness of gold is relaxed and softened by heat, and the ice of brass yields beneath the flame and melts; warmth and piercing cold ooze through silver, since when we have held cups duly in our hands we have felt both alike, when the dewy moisture of water was poured in from above. So true is it that in things there is seen to be nothing solid. But yet because true reasoning and the nature of things constrains us, give heed, until in a few verses we set forth that there are things which exist with solid and everlasting body, which we show to be the seeds of things and their primordia, out of which the whole sum of things now stands created.

503 First, since we have found existing a twofold nature of things far differing, the nature of body and of space, in which all things take place, it must needs be that each exists alone by itself and unmixed. For wherever space lies empty, which we call the void, body is not there; moreover, wherever body has its station, there is by no means empty void. Therefore primary particles are solid and free from void.

511 Moreover, since there is a void in things created, solid matter must needs stand all round, nor can anything by true reasoning be shown to hide void in its body and hold it within, except you grant that what keeps it in is solid. Now it can be nothing but a union of matter, which could keep in the void in

things. Matter[33] then, which exists with solid body, can be everl. ing, when all else is dissolved.

520 Next, if there were nothing which was empty and void, the whole would be solid. On the other hand, unless there were bodies determined, to fill all the places that they held, the whole universe would be but empty void space. Body, then, we may be sure, is marked off from void turn and turn about, since there is neither a world utterly full nor yet quite empty. There are therefore bodies determined such as can mark off void space from what is full. These cannot be broken up when hit by blows from without, nor again can they be pierced to the heart and undone, nor by any other way can they be assailed and made to totter; all of which I have above shown to you but a little while before. For it is clear that nothing could be crushed in without void, or broken or cleft in twain by cutting, nor admit moisture nor likewise spreading cold or piercing flame, whereby all things are brought to their end. And the more each thing keeps void within it, the more is it assailed to the heart by these things and begins to totter. Therefore, if the first bodies are solid and free from void, as I have shown, they must be everlasting.

540 Moreover, if matter had not been everlasting, ere this all things had wholly passed away to nothing, and all that we see had been born again from nothing. But since I have shown above that nothing can be created from nothing, nor can what has been begotten be summoned back to nothing, the primordia must needs be of immortal body, into which at their last day all things can be dissolved, that there may be matter enough for renewing things. Therefore primordia are of solid singleness, nor in any other way can they be preserved through the ages from infinite time now gone and renew things.

551 Again, if nature had ordained no limit to the breaking of things, by now the bodies of matter would have been so far

---

[33] Note that Lucretius has five words in use to refer to that part of the universe which is not the void. *Primordia* are the imperceptibly small particles – Epicurus' *atomoi* – which contain no void within themselves and are permanent. *Corpus* is body, and bodies are both primordia themselves and sensible clusters of primordia. Sensible clusters of primordia are things (*res*). *Materia* is matter in a collective sense, the clusters of primordia which in holding together make up things. *Semen*, is seed – sometimes merely a synonym for primordium, more often an indication of primordia of a particular type.

brought low by the breaking of ages past, that nothing could be conceived out of them within a fixed time, and pass on to the full measure of its life, or we see that anything you cite is more easily broken up than put together again. Therefore what the long limitless age of days, the age of all time that is gone by, had broken before now, disordering and dissolving, could never be renewed in all time that remains. But as it is, a set limit to breaking has, we may be sure, been appointed, since we see each thing put together again, and at the same time fixed seasons ordained for all things after their kind in which they may be able to reach the flower of life.

565 There is this too that, though the primordia of matter are quite solid, yet we can give account of all the soft things that come to be, air, water, earth, fires, by what means they come to being, and by what force each goes on its way, when once void has been mingled in things. But on the other hand, if the primordia of things were to be soft, it will not be possible to give account whence hard flints and iron can be created; for from the first all nature will lack a first-beginning of foundation. There are then bodies that prevail in their solid singleness, by whose more close-packed union all things can be riveted and reveal their stalwart strength.

577 Moreover, if no limit has been appointed to the breaking of things, still it must needs be that all the bodies of things survive even now from time everlasting, such that they cannot yet have been assailed by any danger. But since they exist endowed with a frail nature, it is not in harmony with this that they have been able to abide for everlasting time harried through all the ages by countless blows.

584 Once again, since there has been appointed for all things after their kind a limit of growing and of maintaining life, and inasmuch as it stands ordained what all things severally can do by the laws of nature, and what too they cannot, nor is anything so changed, but that all things stand so fast that the diverse birds all in their due order show that the marks of their kind are on their body, they must also, we may be sure, have a body of unchanging material. For if the primordia of things could be vanquished in any way and changed, then, too, it would be doubtful what might come to being, what might not, and in what way each thing has its power limited and its deepest

boundary-stone. Nor could the tribes each after their kind so often recall the nature, habits, manner of life and movements of the parents.

599 Then, further, since there are ultimate points, one after another [on bodies, which are the least thing we can see, likewise, too, there must be a least point][34] on that body, which our senses can no longer descry. That point, we may be sure, exists without parts and is endowed with the least nature. Nor was it ever sundered apart by itself, nor can it be hereafter, since it is itself but a part of another thing and the primary single part. Then other like parts, and again others in order in close array, make up the nature of the first body, and since they cannot exist by themselves, it must needs be that they stay fast there whence they cannot by any means be torn away. Primordia are then of solid singleness. For they are a close dense mass of least parts, never put together out of a union of those parts, but rather prevailing in everlasting singleness. From them nature, keeping safe the seeds of things, suffers not anything to be torn away, nor ever to be removed.

615 Moreover, if there be not a least thing, all the tiniest bodies will be composed of infinite parts, since indeed the half of a half will always have a half, nor will anything set a limit. What difference then will there be between the sum of things and the least of things? There will be no difference. For however completely the whole sum be infinite, yet things that are tiniest will be composed of infinite parts just the same. And since true reasoning cries out against this, and denies that the mind can believe it, you must be vanquished and confess that there are those things which consist of no parts at all, and are of the least nature. And since these exist, those primordia too you must needs own are solid and everlasting.

628 And again, if nature, the creatress, had been used to constrain all things to be dissolved into their least parts, then she could not again renew aught of them, for the reason that things which are not enlarged by any parts, have not those powers which must belong to creative matter, the diverse

---

[34] The words in brackets are the conjectural filling of a probable lacuna of two lines in the text.

fastenings, weights, blows, meetings, movements, by which all things are carried on.

REJECTION OF ALTERNATIVE ACCOUNTS OF MATTER, 635–920

635 Wherefore those who have thought that fire is the substance of things, and that the whole sum is composed of fire alone, are seen to fall very far from true reasoning. Heraclitus[35] is their leader who first enters the fray, of bright fame for his dark sayings, yet rather among the empty-headed than among the Greeks of weight, who seek after the truth. For fools laud and love all things more which they can descry hidden beneath twisted sayings, and they set up for true what can tickle the ear with a pretty sound and is tricked out with a smart ring. For I am eager to know how things could be so diverse, if they are created of fire alone and unmixed. For it would be of no avail that hot fire should condense or grow rare, if the parts of fire had the same nature which the whole sum of fire has as well. For fiercer would be the flame, if the parts were drawn together, and weaker again were they sundered and scattered.

652 But further than this, there is nothing which you can think might come to pass from such a cause, far less might the great diversity of things come from fires condensed or rare. This too there is: if they were to hold that void is mingled in things, the fires will be able to condense or be left rare. But because they see many things to thwart them, they hold their peace and shrink from allowing void unmixed among things; while they fear the heights, they lose the true track, nor again do they perceive that, if void be removed from things, all things must condense and be made one body out of many, such as could not send out anything from it in hot haste; even as fire that brings warmth casts abroad light and heat, so that you may see that it has not parts close-packed. But if perchance they believe that in some other way fires may be quenched in union

[35] Heraclitus of Ephesus flourished about 500 BC. His theories included the contention that the primary stuff of the world was fire and that the agency of change was strife. Lucretius takes him as typical of a number of early Greek 'physicalists' who tried to account for things in terms of one basic kind of stuff, e.g. fire, water or air.

and alter their substance, in very truth if they do not spare to do this at any point, then, we may be sure, all heat will perish utterly to nothing, and all things created will come to be out of nothing. For whenever a thing changes and passes out of its own limits, straightway this is the death of that which was before. Indeed something must needs be left untouched to those fires, lest you find all things returning utterly to nothing, and the store of things born again and growing strong out of nothing.

675 As it is then, since there are certain definite bodies which keep nature safe ever the same, through whose coming and going and shifting order things change their nature and bodies are altered, you can be sure that these primary bodies of things are not of fire. For it would be no matter that some should give place and pass away, and others be added, and some changed in order, if despite this all retained the nature of heat; for whatever they might create would be in every way fire. But, I maintain, the truth is this. There are certain bodies, whose meetings, movements, orders, position, and shapes make fires, and when their order changes, they change their nature, and they are not made like to fire nor to any other thing either, which is able to send off bodies to our senses and touch by collision our sense of touch.

690 Moreover, to say that fire is all things, and that there is no other real thing in the whole count of things, but only fire, as this same Heraclitus does, seems to be raving frenzy. For on behalf of the senses he fights himself against the senses, and undermines those on which all that he believes must hang, whereby he himself has come to know that which he names fire. For he believes that the senses can know fire aright, but not all other things, which are no whit less bright to see. And this seems to me alike idle and frenzied. For to what shall we appeal? What can be surer for us than the senses themselves, whereby we may mark off things true and false? Besides, why should any one rather annul all things, and wish to leave only the nature of heat, than deny that fire exists, and grant in its stead that another nature exists? For it seems equal madness to say the one or the other.

705 Wherefore those who have thought that fire is the substance of things, and that the whole sum may be built of fire, and those who have set up air as the first-beginning for the

begetting of things, or again all who have thought that moisture fashions things alone by itself, or that earth creates all and passes into all the natures of things, seem to have strayed very far away from the truth. Add to them too those who make the first-beginnings of things twofold, linking air to fire or earth to water, and those who think that all can grow up out of four things, fire, earth, wind, and rain.

716 Of these, in the forefront, comes Empedocles[36] of Acragas. He was born in that island, within the three-cornered coasts of its lands, around which flows the Ionian ocean, with many a winding inlet, splashing salt foam from its green waves, while with narrow strait a tearing sea sunders with its waves the coasts of Italy's lands from the island-borders. Here is devastating Charybdis, and here the rumblings of Aetna threaten to gather once more the flames of its wrath, that again in its might it may belch forth the fires bursting from its throat, and once more dash to the sky its flashing flames. And though this mighty country seems in many ways marvellous to the tribes of men, and is said to deserve seeing, rich in goodly things, and strengthened with a mighty wealth of men, yet it is seen to have held nothing in it more glorious than this man, nothing more holy, more marvellous and loved. Nay, the songs of his godlike heart lift up their voice and set forth his glorious discoveries, so that he seems scarce born of human stock.

734 Yet he and those whom I named before, weaker than he by exceeding many degrees, and far beneath him, though they discovered much in good, nay godlike fashion, and gave answers as from the shrine of their hearts in more holy wise and with reasoning far more sure than the Pythian priestess who speaks out from the tripod and laurel of Phoebus, yet in the first-beginnings of things they came to grief: great were they, and great and heavy their fall therein. First because they take away the void from things, but suppose movement, and leave things soft and rare, air, sunlight, fire, earth, beasts, and crops, and yet mingle no void in their body. Then because they hold that there

---

[36] Empedocles of Acragas in Sicily (c. 493-c. 433 BC) held that the world is composed of four basic 'elements' (earth, air, fire and water) and two basic agents of change (love, or a creative force; and strife, or a separating force).

is no limit at all to the cutting of bodies, that no halting-place is set to their breaking, nor again is there any least among things. And that when we see that there is that extreme point in each thing, which is seen to be the least to our senses, so that you can infer from this that the extreme point in things which you cannot see is the least in them. Then follows this. That, since they suppose the first-beginnings of things to be soft, things which we see come to birth and endowed throughout with a mortal body, the whole sum of things must then return to naught, and the store of things be born again, and grow strong out of nothing. And how far both this and that are from the truth, you will know by now. Then again, these things are in many ways hostile, nay poison, the one to the other. Herefore either when they meet they will pass away, or they will so fly apart, as when a storm gathers we see the thunderbolts and rain and wind fly asunder.

763 Again, if from four things all are created and all again are dissolved into those things, how can they be called the first-beginnings of things any more than things the first-beginnings of them, with our thought reversed? For they are begotten turn by turn, and change their colour and all their nature one with the other from all time onward. But if perchance you think that the body of fire and the body of earth and the breezes of air and the dewy moisture so unite, that in union no one of them changes its nature, you will see that nothing can be created out of them, no, not a living thing, nor one with lifeless body, like a tree. Indeed in the mingling of this diverse mass each thing will reveal its own nature, and air will be seen to be mixed together with earth, and heat to cleave to moisture. But first-beginnings ought in the begetting of things to bring to bear a secret and unseen nature, that nothing may stand out which might bar and thwart whatever is created from existing with its own true being.

782 But indeed they trace it back to heaven and heaven's fires, and hold that fire first turns itself into the breezes of the sky, that thence is begotten rain, and of rain is created earth, and then all things pass back again from earth, first moisture, next air, then heat, and that these things never cease their mutual changes, in their path from heaven to earth, from earth to the stars of the firmament. But the first-beginnings ought in no wise to do this.

790 For it must needs be that something abides unchangeable, that all things be not altogether brought to naught. For whenever a thing changes and passes out of its own limits, straightway this is the death of that which was before. Wherefore since the things we have named a little before pass into a state of interchange, they must needs be made of other things, which cannot in any case be altered, lest you find all things returning altogether to naught. Why not rather suppose that there are certain bodies endowed with such a nature, and that, if by chance they have created fire, they can too, when a few are removed and a few added, and their order and movement is changed, make the breezes of the sky, and that thus all things are changed one into another?

803 'But,' you say, 'the facts show clearly that all things are nourished and grow from the earth up into the breezes of the sky; and unless the season at a propitious time fosters them with rain, so that the trees rock beneath the outpouring of the storm-clouds, and the sun for its part cherishes them, and bestows its heat on them, crops, trees, living creatures, none could grow.'

809 Yes, in very truth, unless we too were nurtured by dry food and soft moisture, we should lose our flesh, and all the life too would be loosened from all our sinews and bones. For beyond all doubt we are nurtured and nourished upon things determined, and other things again, each in their turn, on things determined. Yes, we may be sure, it is because many primordia common in many ways to many things are mingled among things, that so diverse things are nourished on diverse food. And often it is of great matter with what others those primordia are bound up, and in what position, and what movements they mutually give and receive; for the same build up sky, sea, earth, rivers, sun, the same too crops, trees, living creatures, but only when mingled with different things and moving in different ways. Indeed scattered abroad in my verses you see many letters common to many words, and yet you must needs grant that verses and words are unlike both in sense and in the ring of their sound. So great is the power of letters by a mere change of order. But the primordia of things can bring more means to bear, by which all diverse things may be created.

830 Now let us also search into the homoeomeria of Anaxagoras,[37] as the Greeks term it, though the poverty of our country's speech does not suffer us to name it in our own tongue. Nevertheless the thing itself is easy to set forth in words. First — what he calls the homoeomeria of things — you must know that he thinks that bones are made of very small and tiny bones, and flesh of small and tiny pieces of flesh, and blood is created of many drops of blood coming together in union, and that gold again can be built up of grains of gold, and the earth grow together out of little earths, that fire is made of fires, and water of water-drops, and all the rest he pictures and imagines in the same way. And yet he does not allow that there is void in things on any side, nor that there is a limit to the cutting up of bodies. Therefore in this point and that he seems to me to go astray just as they did, of whom I told above.

847 Add too to this that he pictures his first-beginnings too weak: if indeed those are primordia, which exist endowed with a nature like things themselves, which suffer none the less, and pass away, nor does anything rein them back from their destruction. For which of them all will hold out beneath strong pressure, so as to escape death in the very jaws of destruction? fire or moisture or breeze? which of these? blood or bones? Not one, I think, when everything alike will be altogether as mortal as the things we see clearly before our eyes vanquished by some violence and passing away. But that things cannot fall away into nothing, nor again grow from nothing, I call to witness what I have before now proved.

857 Moreover, since it is food that increases and nourishes the body, you may know that our veins and blood and bones [and sinews are created of parts alien in kind]; or if they saw that all foods are of mingled substance, and have in them little bodies of sinews, and bones and indeed veins and portions of gore, then it will be that all food, both dry, yes and liquid too, must be thought to consist of things alien in kind, of bones and sinews and matter and blood mingled together. Moreover, if all

---

[37] Anaxagoras flourished about 440 BC. What Lucretius has to say is something of a caricature of Anaxagoras' account of the composition of things. He held that things were composed of imperceptible particles, in any given thing mainly like in substance to the thing they composed. The theory had the potential to develop into an account of different elements combined in various ways, and it is moving in the same direction as the atomic theory of Democritus.

bodies that grow from out the earth are in the earth, the earth must be composed of things alien in kind, which rise up out of the earth. Shift this to another field, you may use the same words again. If in logs flame lurks hidden, and smoke and ash, it must needs be that the logs are composed of things alien in kind. Moreover, all the bodies which the earth nourishes, it increases [from things alien in kind, which rise up out of the earth. So too the bodies which logs emit, are nourished][38] upon things alien in kind which rise up out of the logs.

875 Herein there is left a slight chance of hiding from justice, which Anaxagoras grasps for himself, to hold that all things are mingled, though in hiding, in all things, but that that one thing comes out clear, whereof there are most parts mingled in, stationed more ready to view and in the forefront. But this is very far banished from true reasoning. For it were right then that corn also, when crushed by the threatening strength of rock, should often give out some sign of blood, or one of those things which are nourished in our body, and that when we rub it with stone on stone, gore should ooze forth. In the same way it were fitting that blades of grass too and pools of water should often give out sweet drops with a savour like the richness of the milk of fleecy beasts, and that often when sods of earth are crumbled, kinds of grasses and corn and leaves should be seen, hiding in tiny form, scattered about among the earth, lastly that ash and smoke should be seen in logs, when they were broken off, and tiny flames in hiding. But since facts clearly show that none of these things come to pass, you may be sure that things are not so mingled in other things, but that seeds common to many things lie mingled and hidden in things in many ways.

897 'But often on mighty mountains it comes to pass,' you say, 'that the neighbouring tops of tall trees rub together, when the strong south winds constrain them to it, until at last a flowery flame gathers, and they blaze with fire.'

901 And yet you must know that fire is not implanted in their wood, but there are many seeds of heat, which when they have flowed together through the rubbing, create fires in the forests. But if the flame had been hidden away ready-made in the forests,

---

[38] The text of the manuscripts in lines 873–4 does not make easy sense even with H. Munro's conjectural addition given in square brackets.

the fires could not have been concealed for any time, they would consume the forests one and all, and burn the trees to ashes.

907 Do you not then see now, what I said but a little while ago, that it is often of very great importance with what others those same primordia are bound up, and in what position, and what movements they mutually give and receive, and that the same a little changed with one another can create beams or flames? Even as the words themselves have their letters but little changed, when with sound distinct we signify *beams* or *flames*.

915 Once again, if you think that all that you can clearly discern as perceptible cannot come to being unless you suppose the primary particles of matter to be endowed with a nature like the whole, by this reasoning you see the primary particles of things destroyed. Nay, it will come to be that they will be shaken with quivering mirth and laugh aloud, and wet their face and cheeks with salt tears!

THE INFINITY OF THE UNIVERSE, 921—1117

921 Come now, learn what remains, and listen to clearer words. Nor do I fail to see in mind how dark are the ways; but a great hope has smitten my heart with the sharp spur of fame, and at once has struck into my breast the sweet love of the muses, whereby now inspired with strong mind I traverse the distant haunts of the Pierides, never trodden before by the foot of man. It is my joy to approach those untasted springs and drink my fill. It is my joy to pluck new flowers and gather a glorious coronal for my head from spots whence before the muses have never wreathed the forehead of any man. First because I teach about great things, and hasten to free the mind from the close bondage of religion, then because on a dark theme I trace verses so full of light, touching all with the muses' charm. For that too is seen to be not without good reason. For even as healers, when they essay to give loathsome wormwood to children, first touch the rim all round the cup with the sweet golden moisture of honey, so that the unwitting age of children may be beguiled as far as the lips, and meanwhile may drink the bitter draught of wormwood, and though charmed may not be harmed, but rather by such means may be restored and come to health; so now, since this philosophy full often seems too bitter to those

who have not tasted it, and the multitude shrinks back away from it, I have desired to set forth to you my reasoning in the sweet-tongued song of the muses, and as if to touch it with the pleasant honey of poetry (if perchance I might avail by such means to keep your mind set upon my verses) while you come to see the whole nature of the universe, what is its shape and figure.

951 But since I have taught that the most solid bodies of matter fly about for ever unvanquished through the ages, come now, let us unfold, whether there be a certain limit to their full sum or not; and likewise the void that we have discovered, or room or space, in which all things are carried on, let us see clearly whether it is all altogether bounded or spreads out limitless and immeasurably deep.

958 *The whole universe then is bounded in no direction of its ways*; for then it would be bound to have an extreme point. Now it is seen that nothing can have an extreme point, unless there be something beyond to bound it, so that there is seen to be a spot further than which the nature of our sense cannot follow it. As it is, since we must admit that there is nothing outside the whole sum, it has not an extreme point, it lacks therefore bound and limit. Nor does it matter in which quarter of it you take your stand;[39] so true is it that, whatever place every man takes up, he leaves the whole boundless just as much on every side.

968 Moreover, suppose now that all space were created finite. If one were to run on to the end, to its furthest coasts, and throw a flying dart, would you have it that that dart, hurled with might and main, goes on whither it is sped and flies afar, or do you think that something can check and bar its way? For one or the other you must needs admit and choose. Yet both shut off your escape and constrain you to grant that the universe spreads out free from limit. For whether there is something to check it, and bring it about that it arrives not whither it was

[39] Compare this argument with the one quoted (or paraphrased) by Cicero in *De Divinatione*, p. 67 above.

sped nor plants itself in the goal, or whether it fares forward, it did not start from the end. In this way I will press on, and wherever you shall set the furthest coasts, I shall ask what then becomes of the dart. It will come to pass that nowhere can a bound be set and room for flight ever prolongs the chance of flight.

984 Moreover, if all the space in the whole universe were shut in on all sides, and were created with borders determined, and had been bounded, then the store of matter would have flowed together with solid weight from all sides to the bottom,[40] nor could anything be carried on beneath the canopy of the sky, nor would there be sky at all, nor the light of the sun, since in truth all matter would lie idle piled together by sinking down from limitless time. But as it is, no rest, we may be sure, has been granted to the bodies of the primordia, because there is no bottom at all, whither they may, as it were, flow together, and make their resting-place. All things are for ever carried on in ceaseless movement from all sides, and bodies of matter are even stirred up and supplied from beneath out of limitless space.

998 Lastly, before our eyes one thing is seen to bound another; air is as a wall between the hills, and mountains between tracts of air, land bounds the sea, and again sea bounds all lands; yet the universe in truth there is nothing to limit outside.

1002 Thus the nature of room and the space of the deep is such that neither could the bright thunderbolts course through it in their career, gliding on through the everlasting tract of time, nor bring it about that there remain a whit less to traverse as they travel; so far on every side spread out huge room for things, free from limit in all directions everywhere.

1008 Nay more, nature ordains that *the sum of things does not have power to set a limit to itself,* since she constrains body to

---

[40] The Epicureans took it that all matter was moving 'down'. But in an infinite universe such movement would not be relative to anything and therefore, apart from giving a certain dynamic to matter, would never achieve any goal or 'bottom'. Nevertheless, when coupled with the theory that each primary particle was liable to a random 'swerve' or change of direction (see II, 184–250), the downward fall, amounting in effect to an assertion of the universal motion of primordia, results in a chaos of impacting primary particles, See I, 1021–42. See also p. xxixf above.

be bounded by void, and all that is void to be bounded by body, so that thus she makes the universe infinite by their interchange. Or else at least one of the two, if the other of them bound it not, spreads out immeasurable with nature unmixed. [But space, as I have taught above, spreads out without limit. If then the sum of matter is bounded,] neither sea nor earth nor the gleaming quarters of heaven nor the race of mortal men, nor the hallowed bodies of the gods could exist for the short space of an hour. For driven apart from its unions the store of matter would be carried all dissolved through the great void, or rather in truth it could never have grown together and given birth to anything, since scattered abroad it could not have been brought to meet.

1021 For in very truth, not by design did the primordia of things place themselves each in their order with foreseeing mind, nor indeed did they make compact what movements each should start. But because many of them, shifting in many ways throughout the world, are harried and buffeted by blows from limitless time, by trying movements and unions of every kind, at last they fall into such dispositions as those, whereby our world of things is created and holds together.

1029 And it too, preserved from harm through many a mighty cycle of years, when once it has been cast into the movements suited to its being, brings it about that the rivers replenish the greedy sea with the bounteous waters of their streams, and the earth, fostered by the sun's heat, renews its increase, and the race of living things flourishes, sent up from her womb, and the gliding fires of heaven are alive.

1035 All this they would in no wise do, unless a store of matter might rise up from limitless space, out of which they are used to renew all their losses in due season. For even as the nature of living things, robbed of food, loses its flesh and pines away, so all things must needs be dissolved, when once matter has ceased to come for their supply, turned aside in any way from its due course.

1042 Nor can blows from without on all sides keep together the whole of each world which has come together in union. For they can smite on it once and again, and keep a part in place, until others come, and the sum may be supplied. Yet sometimes they are constrained to rebound and at once afford space and time for flight to the primordia of things, so that they can pass away freed from union. Therefore, again and again, it must be that many things rise up, yes, and in order that even the blows too may not fail, there must needs be a limitless mass of matter on all sides.

1052 Herein shrink far from believing, Memmius, what some[41] say: that all things press towards the centre of a totality, and that it is for this cause that the nature of the world stands fast without any blows from outside, and that top and bottom cannot part asunder in any direction, because all things are pressing upon the centre (if indeed you can believe that anything can stand upon itself): and that all heavy things which are beneath the earth press upwards, and rest placed upside down upon the earth, like the images of things which we see, as it is, through water. And in the same way they maintain that living things walk head downwards, and cannot fall off the earth into the spaces of heaven beneath them any more than our bodies can of their free will fly up into the quarters of heaven: that when they see the sun, we are descrying the stars of night, and that they share with us turn by turn the seasons of the sky, and pass nights equal to our days.

1067 But empty error has commended these false ideas to fools, because they embrace and hold a theory with twisted reasoning. For there can be no centre, since the universe is created infinite. Nor, if indeed there were a centre, could anything at all rest there any more for that, rather than be driven away for some far different reason: for all room and space, which we call void, must through centre or not-centre give place alike to heavy bodies, wherever their motions tend. Nor is there any place, to which when bodies have come, they can lose the force of their weight and stand still in the void; nor must aught that is void support anything, but rather hasten to give place, as its own nature desires. It cannot be then that

---

[41] The theory, again one held by the Stoics, that all things tend to the centre of the world, came, as will be seen, very near the truth, and was an approach to the modern idea of gravitation. Lucretius could not, of course, adopt it, as it was a direct contradiction of the fundamental Epicurean theory that the natural motion of things was always downwards (adapted from Bailey's note).

things can be held together in union in such a way, constrained by a yearning for the centre.

1083 Moreover, since they do not pretend that all bodies press towards the centre, but only those of earth and liquid, the moisture of the sea and mighty waters from the mountains, and those things which are, as it were, enclosed in an earthy frame; but on the other hand, they teach that the thin breezes of air and hot fires at the same time are carried away from the centre, and that for this cause all the sky around is twinkling with stars, and the flame of the sun is fed through the blue tracts of heaven, because all the heat fleeing from the centre gathers itself together there; nor again can the topmost branches grow leafy upon trees, unless from the earth little by little each has food [supplied by nature, their thoughts are not at harmony with themselves.

1102 There must then be an infinite store of matter], lest after the winged way of flames the walls of the world suddenly fly apart, dissolved through the great void, and lest all else follow them in like manner, or the thundering quarters of the sky fall down from above, and the earth in hot haste withdraw itself from beneath our feet, and amid all the mingled ruin of things on earth and of the sky, whereby the frames of bodies are loosed, it pass away through the deep void, so that in an instant of time not a wrack be left behind, except emptied space and unseen first-beginnings. For on whatever side you maintain that the bodies fail first, this side will be the gate of death for things, by this path will all the throng of matter cast itself abroad.

CONCLUSION

1114 These things you will learn thus, led on with little trouble; for one thing after another shall grow clear, nor will blind night snatch away your path from you, but you shall see all the utmost truths of nature: so shall things kindle a light for others.

BOOK II

The Atomic Theory

Synopsis

1–36   The simple ease of happiness [verse paraphrase by W. H. Mallock, 1900].

37–61   Fear of death and religious fears are groundless.

Motion of Primary Particles or 'Primordia', 62–332

62–79   Change and replenishment will be explained: lives perish, life goes on.

80–111   *Principle X. Primary particles move of themselves.*

112–41   Understanding of X gained from motes in a sunbeam.

142–66   The speed of movement of primordia.

167–83   Primordia a better explanatory hypothesis than gods and religion [see Book V, 195–234].

184–250   *Principle XI. Primordia move 'down', and uniformly, irrespective of weight, except for random swerves which set up multiple collisions, groupings and rebounds.*

251–93   The 'swerve' is related to the volitions of living things.

294–307   *Principle XII. The totality of matter and the totality of movements are both constant.*

308–32   Primordia are in constant imperceptible motion: motion is only perceptible in the things primordia compose.

The Shapes of Primary Particles and their Combinations, 333–729

333–41   *Principle XIII. Primordia vary in shape and size.*

342–477   Evidence for and applications of this with respect to the senses.

478–80   *Principle XIII (completed). But the different shapes are finite in number.*

481–521   Evidence for this and consequences of it.

522–31   The number of primordia of a given shape is infinite.

532–80   Evidence for this.

581–88   Things are always a combination of primordia of more than one shape.

589–660   Worship of the Earth as productive God-Mother is poor reasoning. Gods are not thus. The earth is prolific because it contains many kinds of primordia.

661–99   More evidence that kinds of primordia are mixed in any given material thing.

700–29   Not all combinations of kinds of primordia are possible.

The Qualities of Primordial Particles, 730–990

730–841   Primordia have no colour.

842–64   And no heat, sound, taste or smell.

865–930   Nor possibility of having sensation; although sensation is caused by their movements: *Principle XIV (A). Things with sensation are composed of primordia which have no sensation.*

931–43   *Principle XIV (B). Living things with sensations just are primordia grouped in an appropriate way.*

944–62   Examples to show this.

963–90   Primordia in motion cause passions in living things but, of course, do not themselves experience the passions.

991–1022 Summary: we are seeded from sky and earth; death disperses the combinations of primordia that have resulted in sensation. It does not destroy the primordia.

The Formation and Dissolution of Worlds, 1023–174

1023–47   Dare to ask about the nature of worlds beyond ours.

1048–143 There are other worlds than ours produced by natural causes. Ours grew by additions of primordia without control by gods.

1144–63   This world has now begun to decay as all things do.

1164–74   All times when old seem good to those that grow old.

Book II

When storms blow loud, 'tis sweet to watch at ease
From shore, the sailor labouring with the seas:
    Because the sense, not that such pains are his,
But that they are not ours, must always please.

Sweet for the cragsman, from some high retreat
Watching the plains below where legions meet,
    To await the moment when the walls of war
Thunder and clash together. But more sweet,

Sweeter by far on Wisdom's rampired height
To pace serene the porches of the light,
    And thence look down – down on the purblind herd
Seeking and never finding in the night

The road to peace – the peace that all might hold,
But yet is missed by young men and by old,
    Lost in the strife for palaces and powers,
The axes, and the lictors, and the gold.

Oh sightless eyes! Oh hands that toil in vain!
Not such your needs. Your nature's needs are twain,
    And only twain: and these are to be free –
Your minds from terror, and your bones from pain.

Unailing limbs, a calm unanxious breast –
Grant Nature these, and she will do the rest.
    Nature will bring you, be you rich or poor,
Perhaps not much – at all events her best.

What though no statued youths from wall and wall
Strew light along your midnight festival,
    With golden hands, nor beams from Lebanon
Keep the lyre's languor lingering through the hall.

Yours is the table 'neath the high- nispering trees;
Yours is the lyre of .eai and stre .m and breeze,
    The golden flagon, and the echoing dome –
Lapped in the Spring, what care you then for these?

Sleep is no sweeter on the ivory bed
Than yours on moss; and fever's shafts are sped
    As clean through silks damasked for dreaming kings,
As through the hood that wraps the poor man's head.

37 Wherefore since in our body riches are of no profit, nor high birth, nor the glories of kingship, for the rest, we must believe that they avail nothing for the mind as well. Unless perchance, when you see your legions swarming over the spaces of the Campus, and provoking a mimic war, strengthened with hosts in reserve and forces of cavalry, when you draw them up equipped with arms, all alike eager for the fray, when you see the army wandering far and wide in busy haste, then alarmed by all this the scruples of religion fly in panic from your mind, or that the dread of death leaves your heart empty and free from care.

47 But if we see that these thoughts are mere mirth and mockery, and in very truth the fears of men, and the cares that dog them fear not the clash of arms nor the weapons of war, but pass boldly among kings and lords of the world, nor dread the glitter that comes from gold nor the bright sheen of the purple robe, can you doubt that all such power belongs to reason alone, above all when the whole of life is but a struggle in darkness? For even as children tremble and fear everything in blinding darkness, so we sometimes dread in the light things that are no whit more to be feared than what children shudder at in the dark, and imagine will come to pass.

59 This terror then, this darkness of the mind, must needs be scattered not by the rays of the sun and the gleaming shafts of day, but by the outer view and the inner law of nature.[42]

[42] I.e. we should dispel religious and other fears by observing the phenomena and understanding the fundamental principles according to which they occur. Lines 59–61 are repeated from I, 146–8, and occur again, almost as a refrain, in III, 91–3 and VI, 39–41.

MOTION OF PRIMARY PARTICLES OR 'PRIMORDIA',
62–332

62 Come now, I will unfold by what movement the creative
bodies of matter beget diverse things, and break up those that
are begotten, by what force they are constrained to do this, and
what velocity is appointed them for moving through the mighty
void: do you remember to give your mind to my words. For in
very truth matter does not cleave close-packed to itself, since we
see each thing grow less, and we perceive all things flow away,
as it were, in the long lapse of time, as age withdraws them from
our sight: and yet the universe is seen to remain undiminished,
inasmuch as all bodies that depart from anything, lessen that
from which they pass away, and bless with increase that to
which they have come; they constrain the former to grow old
and the latter again to flourish, and yet they abide not with it.

77 Thus the sum of things is ever being replenished, and
mortals live one and all by give and take. Some races wax and
others wane, and in a short space the tribes of living things are
changed, and like runners hand on the torch of life.

80 If you think that the primordia of things can stay still, and
by staying still beget new movements in things, you stray very
far away from true reasoning. For since they wander through
the void, it must needs be that *all the primordia of things move
on either by their own weight or sometimes by the blow of
another*. For when quickly, again and again, they have met and
clashed together, it comes to pass that they leap asunder at once
this way and that. Indeed this is not strange, since they are most
hard with solid heavy bodies, and nothing bars them from
behind. And the more you perceive all the bodies of matter
tossing about, bring it to mind that there is no lowest point in
the whole universe, nor have the primordia any place where
they may come to rest, since I have shown in many words, and
it has been proved by true reasoning, that space spreads out
without bound or limit, immeasurable towards every quarter
everywhere.

95 And since that is certain, we may be sure that no rest is
allowed to the primary particles moving through the deep void.
But rather, plied with unceasing, diverse motion, some when

they have dashed together leap back at great space apart, others too are thrust but a short way from the blow. And all those which are driven together in more close-packed union and leap back but a little space apart, entangled by their own close-locking shapes, these make the strong roots of rock and the brute bulk of iron and all other things of their kind. Of the rest which wander through the great void, a few leap far apart, and recoil afar with great spaces between; these supply for us thin air and the bright light of the sun. Many, moreoever, wander on through the great void, which have been cast back from the unions of things, nor have they anywhere else availed to be taken into them and link their movements.

112 And of this truth, as I am telling it, a likeness and image is ever passing presently before our eyes. For look closely, whenever rays are let in and pour the sun's light through the dark places in houses, you will see many tiny bodies mingle in many ways all through the empty space right in the light of the rays, and as though in some everlasting strife wage war and battle, struggling troop against troop, nor ever crying a halt, harried with constant meetings and partings; so that you may guess from this what it means that the primordia of things are for ever tossing in the great void. So far as may be, a little thing can give a picture of great things and afford traces of a conception.

124 And for this reason it is the more right for you to give heed to these bodies, which you see jostling in the sun's rays, because such jostlings hint that there are movements of matter too beneath them, secret and unseen. For you will see many particles there stirred by unseen blows change their course and turn back, driven backwards on their path, now this way, now that, in every direction everywhere. You may know that this shifting movement comes to them all from the primordia. For first the primordia of things move of themselves; then those bodies which are formed of a tiny union, and are, as it were, nearest to the powers of the primordia, are smitten and stirred by their unseen blows, and they in their turn, build up bodies a little larger. And so the movement passes upwards from the primordia, and little by little comes forth to our senses, so that

those bodies move too, which we can descry in the sun's light;
yet it is not clearly seen by what blows they do it.

142 Next, what speed of movement is given to the primary
particles of matter, you may learn, Memmius, in a few words
from this. First, when dawn strews the land with new light, and
the diverse birds flitting through the distant woods across the
soft air fill the place with their clear cries, we see that it is plain
and evident for all to behold how suddenly the sun is wont at
such a time to rise and clothe all things, bathing them in his
light. And yet that heat which the sun sends out, and that calm
light of his, is not passing through empty space; therefore, it is
constrained to go more slowly, while it dashes asunder, as it
were, the waves of air. Nor again do the several particles of heat
move on one by one, but entangled one with another, and joined
in a mass. Therefore they are at once dragged back each by the
other, and impeded from without, so that they are constrained
to go more slowly. But the primordia, which are of solid
singleness, when they pass through the empty void, and nothing
checks them without, and they themselves, single wholes with
all their parts, are borne, as they press on, towards the one spot
which they first began to seek, must needs, we may be sure,
surpass in speed of motion, and be carried far more quickly than
the light of the sun, and rush through many times the distance
of space in the same time in which the flashing light of the sun
crowds the sky.

.   .   .43

nor to follow up each of the primordia severally, to see by what
means each single thing is carried on.

167 Yet a certain sect, against all this, ignorant [that the bodies]
of matter [fly of their own accord, unvanquished through the
ages,] believe that nature cannot without the power of the gods,
in ways so nicely tempered to the needs of men, change the
seasons of the year, and create the crops, and all else besides,
which divine pleasure wins men to approach, while pleasure

---

43 A significant number of lines are apparently missing at this point so that lines
165–6 are incomplete in themselves. The missing lines could well have fulfilled the
expectation set up in line 62 to explain how primordia unite and disunite to make
and unmake things.

herself, the leader of life, leads on and entices them by the arts of Venus to renew their races, so that the human race may not perish.

174 But when they suppose that the gods have appointed all things for the sake of men, they are seen in all things to fall exceedingly far away from true reason. For however little I know what the primordia of things are, yet this I would dare to affirm from the very workings of the firmament, and to prove from many other things as well, that the nature of the world is by no means made by divine grace for us: so great are the flaws with which it stands beset. And this, Memmius, I will make clear to you hereafter. Now I will set forth what yet remains about the movements.

184 Now is the place, in my opinion, to prove this also to you: *that no bodily thing can of its own force be carried upwards or move upwards*; lest the bodies of flames give you the lie herein. For upwards indeed the smiling crops and trees are brought to birth, and take their increase, upwards too they grow, albeit all things of weight, as far as in them lies, are borne downwards. Nor when fires leap up to the roofs of houses, and with swift flame lick up beams and rafters, must we think that they do this of their own will, shot up without a driving force. Even as when blood shot out from our body spirts out leaping up on high, and scatters gore. Do you not see too with what force the moisture of water spews up beams and rafters? For the more we have pushed them straight down deep in the water, and with might and main have pressed them, striving with pain many together, the more eagerly does it spew them up and send them back, so that they rise more than half out of the water and leap up. And yet we do not doubt, I hold, but that all these things, as far as in them lies, are borne downwards through the empty void. Just so, therefore, flames too must be able when squeezed out to press on upwards through the breezes of air, albeit their weights are fighting, as far as in them lies, to drag them downwards.

206 And again, the nightly torches of the sky which fly on high, do you not see that they trail long tracts of flames behind towards whatever side nature has given them to travel? do you not see stars and constellations falling to earth? The sun too from the height of heaven scatters its heat on every side, and

sows the fields with his light; it is towards the earth then that the sun's heat also tends. And you see, too, thunderbolts flying crosswise through the rain; now from this side, now from that the fires burst from the clouds and rush together; the force of flame everywhere falls towards the earth.

216 Herein I would fain that you should learn this too, that when primordia are being carried downwards straight through the void by their own weight, *at times quite undetermined and at undetermined spots they push a little from their path*: yet only just so much as you could call a change of trend. But if they were not used to swerve, all things would fall downwards through the deep void like drops of rain, nor could collision come to be, nor a blow brought to pass for the primordia: so nature would never have brought anything into existence.

225 But if perchance any one believes that heavier bodies, because they are carried more quickly straight through the void, can fall from above on the lighter, and so bring about the blows which can give creative motions, he wanders far away from true reason.

230 For all things that fall through the water and thin air, these things must needs quicken their fall in proportion to their weights, just because the body of water and the thin nature of air cannot check each thing equally, but give place more quickly when overcome by heavier bodies. But, on the other hand, the empty void cannot on any side, at any time, support anything, but rather, as its own nature desires, it continues to give place. Therefore all things must needs be borne on through the calm void, moving at equal rate with unequal weights. The heavier will not then ever be able to fall on the lighter from above, nor of themselves bring about the blows, which make diverse the movements, by which nature carries things on.

243 Wherefore, again and again, it must needs be that the primordia swerve a little; yet not more than the very least, lest we seem to be imagining a sideways movement, and the truth refute it. For this we see plain and evident, that bodies, as far as in them lies, cannot travel sideways, since they fall headlong from above, as far as we can discern. But that nothing at all swerves from the straight direction of its path, what sense is there which can discern this?

251 Once again, if every motion is always linked onto another, and the new always arises from the old in order determined,[44] and if by swerving the primordia do not initiate a certain start of movement to break through the decrees of fate, so that cause may not follow cause from infinite time; whence comes this free will for living things all over the earth? Whence, I ask, is it wrested from fate, this will whereby we move forward, where pleasure leads each one of us, and swerve likewise in our motions neither at determined times nor in a determined direction of place, but just where our mind has carried us? For without doubt it is his own will which gives to each one a start for this movement, and from the will the motions pass flooding through the limbs.

263 Do you not see too how, when the barriers are flung open, yet for an instant of time the eager might of the horses cannot burst out so suddenly as their mind itself desires? For the whole store of matter throughout the whole body must be roused to movement, that when aroused through every limb it may strain and follow the eager longing of the mind; so that you see a start of movement is brought to pass from the heart, and comes forth first of all from the will of the mind, and then afterwards is spread through all the body and limbs.

274 Nor is it the same as when we move forward impelled by a blow from the strong might and strong constraint of another. For then it is clear to see that all the matter of the body moves and is hurried on against our will, until the will has reined it back throughout the limbs.

----

[44] Once again, a Stoic doctrine is the object of Lucretius' criticisms. It is best represented by Cicero in *On Divination*, I, 125–7: '... nothing has happened which was not going to be, and similarly nothing is going to be concerning which nature does not already contain causes working to bring about precisely that thing ... if there were some human being who could understand the connexion of all causes, he would certainly never be deceived. For whoever grasps the causes of future events, must necessarily grasp all that will be ... For the passage of time is like the unwinding of a rope, bringing about nothing new.' The doctrine gave the Stoics difficulty in accounting for personal moral responsibility: a difficulty Lucretius, following Epicurus, superficially evades by reference to the swerve of particles. There is evidence in Cicero's *On Fate*, sects 22f., confirmed by fragment 54 of Diogenes of Oenoanda (M. F. Smith's numeration; see note 98), that Epicurus took it that the random swerve would in the final analysis break the causal necessity he associated with Democritus and give us 'free will'. But the philosophical question ultimately depends upon what can be understood by free will.

277 Do you not therefore see that, albeit a force outside pushes many men and constrains them often to go forward against their will and to be hurried away headlong, yet there is something in our breast, which can fight against it and withstand it? And at its bidding too the store of matter is constrained now and then to turn throughout the limbs and members, and, when pushed forward, is reined back and comes to rest again.

284 Wherefore in primordia you must also allow that there is another cause of motion besides blows and weights, whence comes this power born in us, since we see that nothing can come to pass from nothing. For weight prevents all things coming to pass by blows, as by some force without. But that the very mind feels not some necessity within in doing all things, and is not constrained like a conquered thing to bear and suffer, this is brought about by the tiny swerve of the primordia in no determined direction of place and at no determined time.

294 Nor was the store of matter ever more closely packed nor again set at larger distances apart. For neither does anything come to increase it nor pass away from it. Therefore *the bodies of the primordia in the ages past moved with the same [sum of] motion as now*, and hereafter will be borne on for ever in the same way. Such things as have been wont to come to being will be brought to birth under the same law, will exist and grow and be strong and lusty, inasmuch as is granted to each by the ordinances of nature. *Nor can any force change the sum of things*; for neither is there anything outside, into which any kind of matter may escape from the universe, nor whence new forces can arise and burst into the universe and change the whole nature of things and alter its motions.

308 Herein we need not wonder why it is that, when all the primordia of things are in motion, yet the whole seems to stand wholly at rest, except when anything starts moving with its entire body. For the entire nature of primordia lies far away from our senses, below their purview. Therefore, since you cannot reach to examine them, they conceal their motions from you too; above all, because such things as we can look upon often hide their motions when withdrawn from us on some distant spot.

317 For often the fleecy flocks cropping the glad pasture on a hill creep on whither each is called and tempted by the grass bejewelled with fresh dew, and the well fed lambs gambol and butt playfully; yet all this seems blurred to us from afar, and to lie like a white mass on a green hill. Moreover, when mighty legions fill the spaces of the plains with their chargings, awaking a mimic warfare, a sheen rises there to heaven and all the earth around gleams with bronze, and beneath a noise is roused by the mighty mass of men as they march, and the hills smitten by their shouts turn back the cries to the stars of the firmament, and the cavalry wheel round and suddenly shake the middle of the plains with their forceful onset, as they scour across them. And yet there is a certain spot on the high hills, whence all seems to be at rest and to lie like a glimmering mass upon the plains.

THE SHAPES OF PRIMARY PARTICLES AND THEIR COMBINATIONS, 333–729

333 Now come, next in order learn of what kind are the beginnings of all things and how far differing in form, and how they are made diverse with many kinds of shapes; not that but a few are endowed with a like form, but that they are not all alike the same one with another. Nor need we wonder. For since there is so great a store of them, that neither have they any limit, as I have shown, nor any sum, it must needs be, we may be sure, that *they are not all of equal bulk nor possessed of the same shape.*

342 Moreover, the race of men, and the dumb shoals of scaly creatures which swim the seas, and the glad herds and wild beasts, and the diverse birds, which throng the gladdening watering-places all around the riverbanks and springs and pools, and those which flit about and people the distant forests: go and take any one of these from among its kind, and you will find that they are different in shape one from another. Nor in any other way could the offspring know its mother, or the mother her offspring; yet we see that they can, and that they are clearly not less known to one another than men.

352 For often before the sculpted shrines of the gods a calf

has fallen, slaughtered hard by the altars smoking with incense, breathing out from its breast the hot tide of blood. But the mother bereft wanders over the green glades and seeks on the ground for the footprints marked by those cloven hoofs, scanning every spot with her eyes, if only she might anywhere catch sight of her lost young, and stopping fills the leafy grove with her lament. Again and again she comes back to the stall, stabbed to the heart with yearning for her lost calf, nor can the tender willows and the grass refreshed with dew and the loved streams, gliding level with their banks, bring gladness to her mind and turn aside the sudden pang of care, nor yet can the shapes of other calves among the glad pastures turn her mind to new thoughts or ease it of its care: so eagerly does she seek in vain for something she knows as her own.

367 Moreover, the tender kids with their trembling cries know their horned mothers and the butting lambs the flocks of bleating sheep. So surely, as their nature needs, do they run back always each to its own udder of milk. Lastly, take any kind of corn, you will not find that every grain is like its fellows, each in its several kind, but that there runs through all some difference between their forms. And in like manner we see the race of shells painting the lap of earth, where with its gentle waves the sea beats on the thirsty sand of the winding shore.

377 Wherefore again and again in the same way it must needs be, since the primordia of things are made by nature and not fashioned by hand to the fixed form of one pattern, that some of them fly about with shapes unlike one another.

381 It is very easy by reasoning of the mind for us to read the riddle why the fire of lightning is far more piercing than is our fire rising from pine-torches on earth. For you might say that the heavenly fire of lightning is made more subtle and of smaller shapes, and so passes through holes which our fire rising from logs and born of the pine-torch cannot pass. Again light passes through horn-lanterns, but the rain is spewed back. Why? unless it be that those bodies of light are smaller than those of which the quickening liquid of water is made. And we see wine flow through the strainer as swiftly as you will; but, on the other hand, the sluggish olive-oil hangs back, because, we may be sure, it is composed of particles either larger or more hooked and entangled one with the other, and so it comes about that

the primordia cannot so quickly be drawn apart, each single one from the rest, and so ooze through the single holes of each thing.

398 There is this too, that the liquids of honey and milk give a pleasant sensation of the tongue, when rolled in the mouth; but on the other hand, the loathsome nature of wormwood and biting centaury set the mouth awry by their noxious taste; so that you may easily know that those things which can touch the senses pleasantly are made of smooth and round bodies, but that on the other hand all things which seem to be bitter and harsh, these are held bound together with particles more hooked, and for this cause are wont to tear a way into our senses, and at their entering in to break through the body.

408 Lastly, all things good or bad to the senses in their touch fight thus with one another, because they are built up of bodies of different shape; lest by chance you may think that the harsh shuddering sound of the squeaking saw is made of particles as smooth as are the melodies of music which players awake, shaping the notes as their fingers move nimbly over the strings. Nor again, must you think that primordia of like shape pierce into men's nostrils, when noisome carcasses are roasting, and when the stage is freshly sprinkled with Cilician saffron, and the altar hard by is breathing the scent of Arabian incense. Nor must you suppose that the pleasant colours of things, which can feed our eyes, are made of seeds like those which prick the pupil and constrain us to tears.

422 For every shape, which ever charms the senses, has been brought to being with some smoothness in the primordia; but, on the other hand, every shape which is harsh and offensive has been formed with some roughness of substance. Other particles there are, moreover, which cannot rightly be thought to be smooth nor altogether hooked with bent points, but rather with tiny angles standing out a little, insomuch that they can tickle the senses rather than hurt them; and of this kind is lees of wine and the taste of endive. Or again, that hot fires and cold frost have particles fanged in different ways to prick the senses of the body, is proved to us by the touch of each.

434 For touch, yes touch, by the holy powers of the gods, is

the sense of the body, either when something from without finds
its way in, or when a thing which is born in the body hurts us,
or gives pleasure as it passes out, or else when the seeds after
collision jostle within the body itself and, roused one by another,
disturb our sense: as if by chance you should with your hand
strike any part of your own body and so make trial. Therefore
the primordia must needs have forms far different, which can
produce such diverse feelings.

444 Or, again, things which seem to us hard and compact,
must be made of particles more hooked one to another, and are
held together close-fastened at their roots, as it were by branching particles. First of all in this class diamond stones stand in
the forefront of the fight, well used to despise all blows, and
stubborn flints and the strength of hard iron, and brass sockets,
which scream aloud as they struggle against the bolts. Those
things indeed must be made of particles more round and smooth,
which are liquid with a fluid body: for indeed a handful of
poppy-seed moves easily just as a draught of water; for the
several round particles are not checked one by the other, and
when struck, it will roll downhill just like water. Lastly, all
things which you perceive flying asunder, like smoke, clouds
and flames, it must needs be that even if they are not made
entirely of smooth and round particles, yet they are not ham-
pered by particles closely linked, so that they can prick the body,
and pass into rocks, and yet not cling one to another. So that
you can easily learn that, whatever we see [borne asunder by the
tearing winds and] meeting our senses [as poison], are of
elements not closely linked but pointed. But because you see
that some things which are fluid, are also bitter, as is the brine
of the sea, count it no wonder. For because it is fluid, it is of
smooth and round particles, and many rugged bodies mingled
in it give birth to pain; and yet it must needs be that they are
not hooked and held together. You must know that they are
nevertheless spherical, though rugged, so that they can roll on
together and hurt the senses. And that you may the more think
that rough are mingled with smooth primordia, from which is
made the bitter body of the sea-god, there is a way of sundering
them and seeing how, apart from the rest, the fresh water, when
it trickles many a time through the earth, flows into a trench
and loses its harshness; for it leaves behind up above the

primordia of its sickly saltness, since the rough particles can more readily stick in the earth.[45]

478 And since I have taught this much, I will hasten to link on a truth which holds to this and wins belief from it, that the primordia of things are limited in the variety of their shapes.

481 If this were not to be so, then once again certain seeds must needs be of unbounded bulk of body. For, within the same tiny frame of any one single seed, the shapes of the body cannot be very diverse.

485 For suppose the primordia to be of three least parts, or if you will, make them larger by a few more; in truth when you have tried all those parts of one body in every way, shifting top and bottom, changing right with left, to see what outline of form in that whole body each arrangement gives, beyond that, if by chance you wish to make the shapes different, you must needs add other parts. Thence it will follow that in like manner the arrangement will ask for other parts, if by chance you still wish to make the shapes different. And so greater bulk in the body follows on newness of forms. Wherefore it is not possible that you can believe that there are seeds with unbounded difference of forms, lest you constrain certain of them to be of huge vastness, which I have taught above cannot be approved. At once you would see barbaric robes and gleaming Meliboean purple, dyed with the colour of Thessalian shells, and the golden tribes of peacocks, steeped in smiling beauty, lie neglected and surpassed by the new colours in things; and the smell of myrrh and the taste of honey would be despised, and the swan's song and the many-toned melodies on Phoebus' strings would in like manner be smothered and mute. For something more excellent than all else would always be arising. Likewise, all things would sink back on the worse side, just as we have told that they would rise towards the better. For, on the other hand, something would be more loathly too than all else to nostrils and ears and eyes, and the taste of the mouth. And since these things are not

---

[45] It is probable that lines are missing here in which Lucretius showed what he takes to be established in lines 479–81, namely that the size of atoms is limited. If this were not so, some would be visible.

so, but a fixed limit to things marks the extreme on either side, you must confess that the first-matter too has a limited difference in shapes.

515 Again from fire right on to the icy frost of winter is but a limited way, and in like manner is the way measured back again. For all heat and cold and tepid warmths in the middle lie between the two, filling up the sum in due order. And so they are brought to being differing with limited degrees, since they are marked off at either end by the twin points, beset on this side by flames, on that by stiffening frosts.

522 And since I have taught this much, I will hasten to link on a truth which holds to it and wins belief from it, that the primordia of things, which are formed with a shape like to one another, are in number infinite. For since the difference of forms is limited, it must needs be that those which are alike are unlimited, or else that the sum of matter is created limited, which I have proved not to be, showing in my verses that the tiny bodies of matter from everlasting always keep up the sum of things, as the team of blows is harnessed on unbroken on every side.

532 For you see that certain animals are more rare, and perceive that nature is less fruitful in them, yet in another quarter and spot, in some distant lands, there may be many in that kind. And so the tale is made up, even as in the race of four-footed beasts we see that elephants with their snaky hands come first of all, by whose many thousands India is embattled with a bulwark of ivory, so that no way can be found into its inner parts: so great is the multitude of those beasts, whereof we see but a very few samples.

541 But still, let me grant this too. Let there be, if you will, some one thing unique, alone in the body of its birth, to which there is not a fellow in the whole wide world. Yet unless there is an unlimited stock of matter, from which it might be conceived and brought to birth, it will not be able to be created, nor, after that, to grow on and be nourished. Nay, in very truth, if I were to suppose this too, that the bodies creative of one single thing were limited as they tossed about the universe, whence, where,

by what force, in what manner will they meet and come together in that vast ocean, that alien turmoil of matter?

551 They have not, I maintain, a plan for union, but as, when many a great shipwreck has come to pass, the great sea is wont to cast hither and thither benches, ribs, yards, prow, masts and swimming oars, so that along all the coasts of the lands floating stern-pieces are seen, giving warning to mortals, to resolve to shun the snares of the sea and its might and guile, nor trust it at any time, when the wiles of the windless waves smile treacherous. Even so, if you once suppose that primordia of a certain kind are limited, then scattered through all time they must needs be tossed hither and thither by the tides of matter, setting towards every side, so that they never can be driven together in union, nor stay fixed in union, nor take increase and grow. Yet that each of these things openly comes to pass, is proved for all to see: things can be brought to birth, and being born, can grow. It is manifest then that there is an infinite number of primordia in every class, by which all things are supplied.

569 And so, neither can the motions of destruction prevail for ever, and bury life in an eternal tomb, nor yet can the motions of creation and increase for ever bring things to birth and preserve them. So war, waged from time everlasting, is carried on by the balanced strife of the primordia. Now here, now there, the vital forces of things conquer and are conquered alike. With the funeral mingles the wailing which babies raise as they come to look upon the coasts of light. Nor has night ever followed on day, or dawn on night, but it has heard mingled with the baby's sickly wailings, the lament that escorts death and the black funeral.

581 Herein it is right to have this truth also surely sealed and to keep it stored in your remembering mind, that there is not one of all the things, whose nature is seen before our face, which is built of one kind of primordia, nor anything which is not created of well-mingled seed. And whatever possesses within it more forces and powers, it thus shows that there are in it most kinds of primordia and diverse shapes.

589 First of all the earth holds within it the primary bodies, by which the springs welling out coldness ever and anon renew the measureless sea, it holds those whence fires are born. For in many places the surface of the earth is kindled and blazes, but the outburst of Aetna rages with fire from its lowest depths. Then further, it holds those whence it can raise for the races of men the smiling crops and glad trees, whence too it can furnish to the tribe of wild beasts, which ranges the mountains, streams, leaves and glad pastures. Wherefore earth alone has been called the Great Mother of the gods, and the mother of the wild beasts, and the parent of our body.

600 Of her in days of old the learned poets of the Greeks sang that borne on from her sacred shrine in her car she drove a yoke of lions, teaching thereby that the great earth hangs in the space of air nor can earth rest on earth. To the car they yoked wild beasts, because, however wild the brood, it ought to be conquered and softened by the loving care of parents. The top of her head they wreathed with a battlemented crown, because embattled on glorious heights she sustains towns; and dowered with this emblem even now the image of the divine mother is carried in awesome state through lands far and wide. On her the diverse nations in the ancient rite of worship call as 'the Mother of Ida', and they give her Phrygian[46] bands to bear her company, because from those lands first they say corn began to be produced throughout the whole world. The mutilated priests they assign to her, because they wish to show forth that those who have offended the godhead of the Mother, and have been found ungrateful to their parents, must be thought to be unworthy to bring offspring alive into the coasts of light. Taut timbrels thunder in their hands, and hollow cymbals all around, and horns menace with harsh-sounding bray, and the hollow pipe goads their minds in the Phrygian mode, and they carry

---

[46] Phrygia was an ancient country comprising the central plateau and central west of Asia Minor. This whole section down to line 643 is an account of the various ways in which the earth had been thought of as a goddess and worshipped accordingly. Lucretius himself, in common with Classical Paganism, had a profound reverence for all nature, including the earth. But he did not regard the earth as a divine being with the characteristics of a super-person. In the end it took Christianity, not Epicureanism, to depersonalise the physical world into an object of contempt, 'fallen' and 'corrupt', and fit only for exploitation.

weapons before them, the symbols of their dangerous frenzy, that they may be able to fill with fear of the goddess's power the thankless minds and unhallowed hearts of the multitude. And so as soon as she rides on through great cities, and silently blesses mortals with unspoken salutation, with bronze and silver they strew all the path of her journey, enriching her with bounteous alms, and snow rose-blossoms over her, overshadowing the Mother and the troops of her escort. Then comes an armed band, whom the Greeks call by name the Curetes of Phrygia, and because now and again they join in mock conflict of arms and leap in rhythmic movement, gladdened at the sight of blood and shaking as they nod the awesome crests upon their heads, they recall the Curetes of Dicte, who are said once in Crete to have drowned the wailing of the infant Jove, while, a band of boys around the baby boy, in hurrying dance all armed, they beat in measured rhythm brass upon brass, that Saturn might not seize and commit him to his jaws, and plant an everlasting wound deep in the Mother's heart. For this cause in arms they escort the Great Mother, or else because they show forth that the goddess preaches that they should resolve with arms and valour to defend their native land and prepare to be a guard and ornament to their parents.

644 Yet all this, albeit well and nobly set forth and told, is nevertheless far removed from true reasoning. For it must be that the very nature of the gods enjoys life everlasting in perfect peace, sundered and separated far away from our world, free from all grief, free from danger, mighty in its own resources, independent of us. It is not won by virtuous service nor touched by wrath.[47] Truly, the earth is without feeling throughout all time, and it is because it has possession of the primordia of many things, that it brings forth many in many ways into the light of the sun.

655 Herein, if any one is resolved to call the sea Neptune and corn Ceres, and likes rather to misuse the title of Bacchus than to utter the true name of the vine-juice, let us grant that he may proclaim that the world is the Mother of the gods, if only in very truth he forbear to stain his own mind with shameful religious awe.

[47] Lines 646–51 repeat I, 44–9, although this is not obvious from the verse translation.

661 And so often fleecy flocks and the warrior brood of horses and horned herds, cropping the grass from one field beneath the same canopy of heaven, and slaking their thirst from one stream of water, yet live their life with different aspect, and keep the nature of their parents and imitate their ways each after his own kind. So great is the difference of matter in any kind of grass you will, so great in every stream.

669 Moreover, any one living creature of them all is made of bones, blood, veins, heat, moisture, flesh and sinews: and they as well are far different, formed as they are with primordia of unlike shape. Then once again, all things that are set ablaze and burnt up by fire, store in their body, if nothing else, yet at least those particles, from which they may be able to toss fire abroad and shoot out light, and make sparks fly, and scatter cinders far and wide.

677 Traversing all other things with the like reasoning of your mind, you will find then that they hide in their body the seeds of many things and contain diverse shapes.

680 Again, you see many things to which both colour and taste are given together with smell. First of all, most of the offerings [burnt on the altars of the gods] must be made of diverse shapes. For the burning smell pierces, where the hue passes not into the limbs, even so the hue in one way, the taste in another, finds its way into our senses. Thus you may know that they differ in the shapes of their primordia. So different forms come together into one mass, and things are made with mingled seeds. Nay, more, everywhere in these actual verses of mine you see many letters common to many words, and yet you must grant that verses and words are formed of different letters, one from another. Not that but a few letters run through them in common, or that no two of them are made of letters all the same, but that they are not all alike the same one with another. So in other things likewise since there are primordia common to many things, yet they can exist with sums different from one another: so that the human race and corn and glad trees are rightly said to be created of different particles.

700 And yet we must not think that all [particles] can be linked together in all ways, for you would see monsters created everywhere, forms coming to being half man, half beast, and

sometimes tall branches growing out from a living body, and many limbs of land-beasts linked with beasts of the sea, and nature too throughout the lands, that are the parents of all things, feeding Chimaeras breathing flame from their noisome mouths.

707 But it is clear to see that none of these things comes to be, since we see that all things are born of fixed seeds and a fixed parent, and can, as they grow, preserve their kind. You may be sure that that must needs come to pass by a fixed law. For its own proper particles separate from every kind of food and pass within into the limbs of everything, and are there linked on and bring about the suitable movements. But, on the other hand, we see nature cast out alien matter on to the ground, and many things with bodies unseen flee from the body, driven by blows, which could not be linked to any part nor within feel the lively motions in harmony with the body and imitate them.

718 But lest by chance you should think that living things alone are bound by these laws, the same condition sets a limit to all things. For even as all things begotten are in their whole nature unlike one to the other, so it must needs be that each is made of primordia of a different shape; not that but a few are endowed with a like form, but that they are not all alike the same one with another. Moreover, since the seeds are different, there must needs be a difference in their spaces, passages, fastenings, weights, blows, meetings, movements, which not only sunder living things, but part earth and the whole sea, and hold all the sky away from the earth.

THE QUALITIES OF PRIMARY PARTICLES, 730–990

730 Come now, listen to discourse gathered by my joyful labour, lest by chance you should think that these white things, which you perceive shining bright before your eyes are made of white primary particles, or that things which are black are born of black seeds; or should believe that things which are steeped in any other colour you will, bear this colour because the bodies of matter are dyed with a colour like it.

737 For the bodies of matter have no colour at all, neither like things nor again unlike them. And if by chance it seems to

you that the mind cannot project itself into these bodies, you
wander far astray. For since those born blind, who have never
experienced the light of the sun, yet know bodies by touch,
never linked with colour for them from the outset of their life,
you may know that for our mind too, bodies painted with no
tint may be clearly concevied. Again, we ourselves feel that
whatever we touch in blind darkness is not dyed with any
colour. And since I convince you that this may be, I will now
teach you that [primordia] are [without colour in themselves].

748 For any colour, whatever it be, changes into any other;
but the primordia ought in no wise to do this. For it must needs
be that something abides unchangeable, that all things be not
utterly brought to nothing. For whenever a thing changes and
passes out of its own limits, straightway this is the death of that
which was before. Therefore take care not to dye with colour
the seeds of things, lest you see all things altogether pass away
to nothing.

757 Moreover, if the nature of colour has not been granted
to primary particles, and yet they are endowed with diverse
forms, out of which they beget and vary colours of every kind,
forasmuch as it is of great matter with what others all the seeds
are bound up, and in what position, and what movements they
mutually give and receive, you can most easily at once give an
account, why those things which were a little while before of
black colour, are able of a sudden to become of marble
whiteness; as [for example] the sea, when mighty winds have
stirred its level waters, is turned into white waves of shining
marble. For you might say that when the substance of that
which we often see black has been mingled up, and the order of
its primordia changed, and certain things added and taken away,
straightway it comes to pass that it is seen shining and white.
But if the level waters of the ocean were made of sky-blue seeds,
they could in no wise grow white.

776 For in whatever way you were to jostle together seeds
which are sky-blue, they can never become a marble colour.
But if the seeds which make up the single unmixed brightness
of the sea are dyed with this colour and that, even as often
out of different forms and diverse shapes some square thing is
made up with a single shape, then it were natural that, as in the
square we perceive that there are unlike forms, so we should

perceive in the water of the ocean, or in any other single and unmixed brightness, colours far different and diverse one from another.

784 Moreover, the unlike shapes do not a whit thwart and hinder the whole from being square in its outline; but the diverse colours in things do check and prevent the whole thing being of a single brightness. Then, further, the reason which leads us on and entices us sometimes to assign colours to the primordia of things, is gone, since white things are not made of white, nor those which are seen black of black, but of diverse colours. And in very truth much more readily will white things be born and rise up out of no colour than out of black, or any other colour you will which fights with it and thwarts it.

795 Moreover, since colours cannot exist without light, nor do the primordia of things come out into the light, you may know how they are not clothed with any colour. For what colour can there be in blind darkness? Nay even in the light it changes according as it shines brightly, struck with a straight or slanting beam of light: as [for example] the plumage of doves, which is set about their throats and crowns their necks, is seen in the sunshine. For anon it comes to pass that it is red with bright garnet, sometimes in a certain view it comes to pass that it seems to mingle green emeralds among coral. And the tail of the peacock, when it is bathed in bounteous light, in like manner changes it colours as it moves round; and since these colours are begotten by a certain stroke of light, you may know that we must not think that they could come to be without it.

810 And since the pupil of the eye receives in itself a certain kind of blow, when it is said to perceive white colour, and another again, when it perceives black and the rest, nor does it matter with what colour things you touch may choose to be endowed, but rather with what sort of shape they are fitted, thus you may know that the primordia have no need of colours, but by their diverse forms produce diverse kinds of touch.

817 Moreover, since no fixed nature of colour belongs to fixed shapes, and all conformations of primordia may exist in any hue you will, why on like grounds are not those things which are made out of them steeped with every kind of colour in every kind? For it were natural that often flying crows too should throw off white colour from white wings, and that black

swans should be made of black seeds or of any other colour you will, simple or diverse.

826 Nay again, the more each thing is pulled asunder into tiny parts, the more can you perceive colour little by little fading away and being quenched: as comes to pass when purple cloth is plucked apart into small pieces: when it has been unravelled thread by thread, the dark purple or the scarlet, by far the brightest colours, is utterly destroyed. So you can know from this that the tiny shreds dissipate all their colour before they are sundered into the seeds of things.

834 Lastly, since you do not allow that all bodies send out sound or smell, it comes to pass, therefore, that you do not assign sound and smell to them. Even so, since we cannot with the eyes discern all things, you may know that some things are made bereft of colour, just as some are without any smell and far parted from sound, yet the keen mind can come to know them no less than it can mark those devoid of other things.

842 But lest by chance you think that the primordia abide bereft only of colour, they are also sundered altogether from warmth and cold, and fiery heat, and are carried along barren of sound and devoid of taste, nor do they give off any scent of their own from their body. Even as when you set about to make the delicious liquid of marjoram or myrrh, or scent of nard, which breathes nectar to the nostrils, first of all it is right to seek, in so far as you may and can find it, the nature of scentless oil, which may send off no breath of perfume to the nostrils, so that it may as little as possible taint and ruin with its own strong smell the scents mingled in its body and boiled along with it.

854 For the same reason the primordia of things are bound not to bring to the begetting of things their own scent or sound, since they cannot give anything off from themselves, nor in the same way acquire any taste at all, nor cold, nor once more warm and fiery heat[48] . . . and the rest. Yet since they are such as to be created mortal, the pliant of soft body, the brittle of crumbling body, the hollow of loose textured, they must needs all be kept apart from the primordia, if we wish to place

---

[48] Something is missing in the manuscripts at this point.

immortal foundations beneath things, on which the sum of life may rest; lest you see all things pass away utterly into nothing.

865 It must needs be that you should admit that *all things which we see to have sensation are yet made of insensible primary particles.*[49] The clear facts, which are known for all to see, neither refute this nor fight against it, but rather themselves lead us by the hand and constrain us to believe that, as I say, living things are begotten of insensible things. Indeed we may see worms come forth alive from noisome dung, when the soaked earth has become muddy from immeasurable rains. Moreover, we may see all things in like manner change themselves. Streams, leaves, and glad pastures change themselves into cattle. Cattle change their nature into our bodies, and from our bodies the strength of wild beasts often gains increase, and the bodies of birds strong of wing. And so nature changes all foods into living bodies, and out of food brings to birth all the senses of living things, in no far different way than she unfolds dry logs into flames and turns all things into fires. Do you not then see now that it is of great matter in what order all the primordia of things are placed, and with what others mingled they give and receive motions?

886 Next then, what is it, that strikes on the very mind, which stirs it and constrains to utter diverse thoughts, that you may not believe that the sensible is begotten of the insensible? We may be sure it is that stones and wood and earth mixed together yet cannot give out vital sense. Herein it will be right to remember this, that I do not say that sensations are begotten at once from all and every of the things which give birth to

[49] The whole sweep of argument in lines 865–943 is much more important than it might seem. Lucretius maintains that things with sensation (including of course human beings) are composed of primordia grouped in an appropriate way, *and* that no primordium by itself has the sensation which is a feature of the composite living body. This allows him in Book III to reject the suggestion that I, a sensible body, might survive my body's dissolution because the component particles (which indeed survive) have the sensation which is identical with my own. According to Lucretius, and it is difficult to disagree on the basis of the Epicurean principles he advances, the sensation which I can have arises from the whole thing I am, structured in the way it is. Similarly one might argue that a harmony in music exists in the combination of several notes, not each note sundered from the whole. The key conclusion is in 930, 'sensation can be begotten out of that which is not sensation.'

sensible things, but that it is of great matter, first of what size
are these bodies, which create the sensible, and with what form
they are endowed, then what they are in their motions, arrangements and positions. And none of these things can we perceive
in logs and sods. And yet, when they are, as it were, made
muddy through the rains, they give birth to little worms, because
the bodies of matter stirred by the newcomer from their old
arrangements are brought into union in the way in which living
things are bound to be begotten.

902 Next, those [Anaxagoras] who think that the sensible
could be created out of sensible bodies which in turn were used
to owe their sense to others, [make the seeds of their own sense
perishable] when they make them soft. For all sensation is linked
to flesh, sinews and veins, which we see are always soft in nature
built up of mortal body. Nevertheless let us grant for a moment
that these [sensible particles] can abide for ever. Still doubtless
they must either have the sense proper to a part, or be thought
to be of a sense like to that of whole living things. But it must
needs be that the parts cannot have sense by themselves; for all
sensation in the limbs depends on us, nor severed from us can
the hand nor any part of the body at all keep sensation by itself.
The conclusion remains that sensible particles are made like
whole living things. Thus it must needs be that they feel likewise
what we feel, so that they may be able to share with us in every
place in the vital sensations. How then will they be able to be
called the primordia of things, and to shun the paths of death,
since they are living things, and living things are one and the
same with mortal things? Yet grant that they can, yet by their
meeting and union, they will make nothing besides a crowd and
jumble of living things, even as (as you may know!) men, herds
of cattle, and wild beasts could not beget anything by clustering
together with one another. But if by chance they lose their own
sense, when inside a body, and receive another, what good was
it that that should be assigned to them which is taken away?
Then, moreover, as we saw before, inasmuch as we perceive the
eggs of birds turn into living chickens, and worms swarm out
when mud has seized on the earth owing to immoderate rains,
we may know that *sensations can be begotten out of that which
is not sensation.*

931 But if by chance any one shall say that sensation can in any case arise from not-sensation by change of substance or, as it were, by a kind of birth, by which it is thrust out into being, it will be enough to make clear and prove to him that birth cannot come to be, except when a union has been formed before, nor is anything changed except after union. First of all, no body at all can have sensation before the nature of the living thing is itself begotten, because, we may be sure, its matter is scattered abroad and is kept in the air, in streams, in earth and things sprung from earth, nor has it *come together in an appropriate way and combined with one another the vital motions*, whereby the all-seeing senses are kindled, and see to the safety of each living thing.

944 Moreover, a heavier blow than its nature can endure, of a sudden fells any living creature, and hastens to stun all the sensations of its body and mind. For the positions of the primary particles are broken up, and the vital motions are checked deep within, until the matter, shaken throughout all the limbs, loosens the vital clusters of the anima from the body, scatters it abroad, and drives it out through every pore. For what else are we to think that a blow can do when it meets each thing, but shake it to pieces and break it up?

954 It comes to pass too, that when a blow meets us with less force, the vital motions that remain are often wont to win. Yes, to win, and to allay the vast disturbances of the blow and summon each part back again into its proper path, and to shake to pieces the movement of death that now, as it were, holds sway in the body, and to kindle the sensations almost lost. For by what other means could living things gather their wits and turn back to life even from the very threshold of death rather than pass on, whither their race is already almost run, and pass away?

963 Moreover, since there is pain when the bodies of matter, disturbed by some force throughout the living flesh and limbs, tremble each in their abode within; and when they settle back into their place, comforting pleasure comes to pass, you may know that the primordia cannot be assailed by any pain, and can find no pleasure in themselves. For they themselves are not

made of any bodies of primordia through whose newness of movement they may be in pain or find any enjoyment of life-giving delight. They are bound then not to be endowed with any sensation.

973 Again, if, in order that all living things may be able to feel, we must after all assign sensation to their primordia, what of those whereof the race of men has its peculiar increment? You must think that they are shaken with quivering mirth and laugh aloud and sprinkle face and cheeks with the dew of their tears. And they have the wit to say much about the mingling of things, and they go on to ask what are their primordia; inasmuch as, being made like to whole mortal men, they too must be built of other particles in their turn, and those again of others, so that you may never dare to make a stop. I will press hard on you, so that, whatsoever you say speaks and laughs and thinks, shall be composed of other particles which do these same things. But if we perceive this to be but raving madness, and a man can laugh, though he has not the increment of laughing particles, and can think and give reasons with learned lore, though he be not made of seeds thoughtful and eloquent, why should those things, which, as we see, have feeling, any the less be able to exist, mingled of seeds which lack sense in every way?

991 To conclude, we are all sprung from heavenly seed. There is the one father of us all, from whom, when life-giving earth, the mother, has taken within her the watery drops of moisture, teeming she brings forth the goodly crops and the glad trees and the race of men. She brings forth too all the tribes of the wild beasts, when she furnishes the food, on which all feed their bodies and pass a pleasant life and propagate their offspring. Wherefore rightly has she won the name of mother. Even so, what once sprung from earth, sinks back into the earth; and what was sent down from the coasts of the sky, returns again, and the regions of heaven receive it.

1002 Nor does death so destroy things as to put an end to the bodies of matter, but only scatters their union. Then she joins anew one with others, and brings it to pass that all things thus alter their forms, and change their colours, and receive sensations, and in an instant of time yield them up again. Thus you may know that it matters with what others the primordia of things are bound up, and in what positions and what motions they mutually give and receive, and may not think that what we see floating on the surface of things or at times coming to birth, and on a sudden passing away, can abide in the possession of eternal primordia. No indeed, even in my verses it is of moment with what others, and in what order each letter is placed. For the same letters signify sky, sea, earth, rivers, sun, the same too crops, trees, living creatures. If not all, yet by far the greater part, are alike, but it is by position that things sound different. So in things themselves likewise when meetings, motions, order, position, shapes are changed, things too are bound to be changed.

THE FORMATION AND DISSOLUTION OF WORLDS, 1023–174

1023 Now turn your mind, I pray, to a true reasoning. For a truth wondrously new is struggling to fall upon your ears, and a new face of things to reveal itself. Yet neither is anything so easy, but that at first it is more difficult to believe, and likewise nothing is so great or so marvellous but that little by little all decrease their wonder at it.

1030 First of all the bright clear colour of the sky, and all it holds within it, the stars that wander here and there, and the moon and the sheen of the sun with its brilliant light; all these, if now they had come to being for the first time for mortals, if all unforeseen they were in a moment placed before their eyes, what story could be told more marvellous than these things, or what that the nations would less dare to believe beforehand? Nothing, I believe, so worthy of wonder would this sight have been. Yet think how no one now, wearied with satiety of seeing, deigns to gaze up at the shining quarters of the sky!

1040 Wherefore cease to reject a theory from your mind, struck with terror at its mere newness. But rather with eager judgement weigh things, and, if you see them true, lift your hands and yield, or, if it is false, gird yourself to battle. For our mind now seeks to reason, since the sum of space is boundless out beyond the walls of this world, what there is far out there, whither the intellect desires always to look forward, and whither the unfettered projection of our mind flies on unchecked.

1048 First of all, we find that in every direction everywhere, and on either side, above and below, through all the universe, there is no limit, as I have shown, and indeed the truth cries out for itself and the nature of the deep shines clear. Now in no way must we think it likely, since towards every side is infinite empty space, and seeds in unnumbered numbers in the deep universe fly about in many ways driven on in everlasting motion, that this one world and sky was brought to birth, but that beyond it all those bodies of matter do nothing.

1058 Above all, since this world was so made by nature, as the seeds of things themselves of their own accord, jostling from time to time, were driven together in many ways, rashly, idly, and in vain, and at last those united, which, suddenly cast together, might become ever and anon the beginnings of great things, of earth and sea and sky, and the race of living things. Wherefore, again and again, you must needs confess that there are here and there other gatherings of matter, such as is this, which the ether holds in its greedy grip.

1067 Moreover, when there is much matter ready to hand, when space is there, and no thing, no cause delays, things must, we may be sure, be carried on and completed. As it is, if there is so great a store of seeds as the whole life of living things could not number, and if the same force and nature abides which could throw together the seeds of things, each into their place in like manner as they are thrown together here, it must needs be that you confess that there are other worlds in other regions, and diverse races of men and tribes of wild beasts.

1077 This there is too, that in the sum of things there is nothing single, nothing born unique and growing unique and alone, but it is always of some tribe, and there are many things in the same race.

1080 First of all turn your mind to living creatures. You will find that in this wise is begotten the race of wild beasts that haunts the mountains. In this wise the stock of men. In this wise again the dumb herds of scaly fishes, and all the bodies of flying fowls. Wherefore you must confess in the same way that sky and earth and sun, moon, sea and all else that exists, are not unique, but rather of number numberless. Inasmuch as the deep-fixed boundary-stone of life awaits these as surely, and they are just as much of a body that has birth, as every race which is here on earth, abounding in things after its kind.

1090 And if you learn this surely, and cling to it, nature is seen, free at once, and quit of her proud rulers, doing all things of her own accord alone, without control of gods. For – by the holy hearts of the gods, which in their tranquil peace pass placid years, and a life of calm – who is able to rule the whole sum of the boundless? Who can hold in his guiding hand the mighty reins of the deep? Who can turn round all firmaments at once, and warm all fruitful lands with heavenly fires, or be at all times present in all places? Who can make darkness with clouds, and shake the calm tracts of heaven with thunder, and then shoot thunderbolts, and often make havoc of his own temples, or moving away into deserts rage furiously there, plying the bolt, which often passes by the guilty and does to death the innocent and undeserving?

1105 And since the time of the world's birth, and the first birthday of sea and earth, and the rising of the sun, many bodies have been added from without, and seeds added all around, which the great universe in its tossing has brought together; that from them sea and lands might be able to increase, and from them too the mansion of the sky might gain new room and lift its high vault far away from the lands, and the air might rise up.

1112 For from all places all bodies are separated by blows each to its own kind, and they pass on to their own tribes; moisture goes to moisture, with earthy substance earth grows, fires forge fires, and sky sky, until nature, parent of all, with perfecting hand has brought all things on to the last end of growing; as it comes to pass, when there is now no whit more which is sent within the veins of life, than what flows out and passes away.

1120 Here the growth of all things must stop, here nature by her powers curbs increase. For whatsoever things you see waxing large with joyful increase, and little by little climbing the steps to full-grown years, take more into themselves than they send out from their body, so long as food is passed easily into all their veins, and so long as the things are not so widely spread that they throw off much, and cause waste greater than that on which their growth feeds. For of a surety you must throw up your hands and grant that many bodies flow away and pass from things; but more must needs be added to them, until they have reached the topmost point of increase.

1130 Then little by little age breaks their powers and their full-grown strength, and wastes away on the downhill path. For verily the huger a thing is, and the wider it is, when once its bulk begins to go, the more bodies now does it scatter abroad and throw off from itself, nor is its food easily dispersed into all its veins, nor is there store enough, whence matter may arise and be supplied to equal the vast ebb which it gives out. With reason then they perish, when all things have been made rare by the ebb, and yield before the blows from without, inasmuch as at last food fails the aged life, nor do bodies from without cease to thump upon it, and wear it away, and to overcome it with hostile blows.

1144 Thus even the walls of the wide world all round will be stormed and fall into decay and crumbling ruin. For it is food which must needs repair all things and renew them, food must support them, and food sustain all things. Yet all is vain, since neither the veins can bear to receive what is enough, nor does nature furnish all that is needful. Yea, even now its life is broken, and the worn-out earth scarce creates tiny animals, though once it created all the tribes, and brought to birth huge bodies of wild beasts. For it was no golden rope, I maintain, which let down the races of living things from heaven above on to the fields, nor did the sea or the waves, that lash the rocks, create them, but the same earth conceived them, which now nourishes them of her substance.

1157 Moreover, at first by herself of her own accord she created for mortals the smiling crops and glad vine-plants, herself brought forth sweet fruits and glad pastures; which now scarce wax great, though aided by our toil. We wear out our oxen and the strength of our husbandmen. We exhaust the iron ploughshare, though scarce supplied by the fields so much do they grudge their produce and increase our toil.

1164 And now the aged ploughman shaking his head sighs ever and again that the toil of his hands has perished all for nothing, and when he matches present days against days that are past, he often praises the fortunes of his father. So too gloomily the planter of the worn-out, wrinkled vine rails at the trend of the times, and wearies heaven, and grumbles to think how the generations of old, rich in piety, easily supported life on a narrow plot, since aforetime the limit of land was far less to each man. Nor does he grasp that all things waste away little by little and pass to the grave, worn out by age and the passing of life.

BOOK III

Mind, Life And Death

Synopsis

1–30   Address to Epicurus [verse translation by Charles Foxley, 1933].

31–93   Review of subjects past; the new subject is to dispel fear of death.

The Relation between Mind, Body and Anima, 94–416

94–136   Mind is a part of the body along with anima.

137–60   Mind and anima are of the same nature.

161–76   Both are bodily.
177–230   Both are very tiny particles.

231–57   Both are breath, heat, air and something else of extreme minuteness and speed.

258–322   How the parts of the anima mingle in us, and in other animals.

323–58   Life is caused by the union of body and anima.

359–69   Eyes are not doors out of which the mind looks.

370–95   Rebuttal of other theories.

396–416   Mind is the core of life.

Proofs that Mind and Body have a Common Birth and Death, 417–829

417–24   In what follows, mind and anima may sometimes be spoken of as one thing by means of the word 'anima'.

425–44   (i) When a vessel (the body) is shattered, the contents (anima) seep away.

445–58   (ii) Mind and body grow and fail conjointly in life.

459–62   (iii) Both are alike subject to pain.

463–75   (iv) Both are alike subject to disease.

476–86   (v) Both are alike subject to wine.

487–509   (vi) Both are restored together after violent illness.

510–25   (vii) Both are susceptible to alteration by medicine.

526–47   (viii) Anima often retreats piecemeal.

548–57   (ix) Mind, like other organs, has a place in the body and cannot function in separation any more than an eye can.

558–79   (x) Neither mind nor body can live in separation.

580–91   (xi) Departure of anima destroys the body's physical structure.

592–614   (xii) Violent physical shocks or blows all but dislodge the anima.

615–23   (xiii) Mind has a specific location in the body.

624–33   (xiv) Mind in isolation has no possibility of sensation: hence we imagine the dead as if with ears, etc.

634–69   (xv) Signs of animation in severed limbs show the divisibility of the anima, and what is divisible cannot be eternal.

670–78   (xvi) If mind is immortal, why have we no memories of things before our birth?

679–97   (xvii) If mind is implanted at birth, how does it develop with the body?

698–712   (xviii) If implanted, and permeates the living body, how could the mind survive bodily dissolution?

713–40   (xix) Animae do not seek or fashion bodies for themselves. The anima is part of any living body.

741–75   (xx) Mind grows with, and according to, the nature of each animal-type, but it is a new entity in each individual [some commentators identify five separate short arguments in this section].

776–83   (xxi) The absurdity of supposing minds queueing up awaiting bodies.

784–99   (xxii) If the mind is independent of the body, why is it so clearly *not* located in much of the body (e.g. not in an arm or leg)?

800–29   (xxiii) Everlasting things must be absolutely solid [like primary particles]. The anima is not thus, nor is it a privileged entity protected by the force of life.

Therefore Death is Nothing to Us, 830–1094

830–42   Death is no concern of mortal man.

843–69   Our physical replication is not the reconstruction of our identity as persons.

870–93   It is an error of understanding to imagine yourself when you are dead as if you were in any way still yourself as you are when alive.

894–911   Do not pity yourself or others as dead: death is rest.

912–30   Sleep yearns not for wakefulness, nor death for life.

931–77   It is natural and decent for old lives to give way to new. Accept this.

978–1013   It is life, not death, that contains Hell's engines of torture.

1014–23   Fear of punishment *now* is the real Hell for sinners.

1024–52   All those who have been great men sleep in peace; seek not to be an exception to this.

1053–75   Restless man, be at peace in yourself and in understanding the nature of things.

1076–94   And seek not a useless prolonging of life, for a long life in no way shortens the eternity to come which is nothing to you.

Book III

O thou, whose lamp first in so black a night
Illumining the goods of life outshone,
Of Grecian race the glory and delight,
I mark thy footsteps and I follow on.
For love and not for vain comparison
My longing is to copy well thy course.
Shall the light swallow vie with stately swan?
Or can the trembling kid's poor limbs find force
To match in even race the stride of the strong horse?

Thou, father, art our author, and we take
A father's counsel when thy book's unrolled.
As bees will sip each bloom in flow'ry brake,
We likewise feed on all thy words of gold,
Most worthy words unending life to hold.
For where thy godlike thought is quick to trace
The ways of Nature and thy voice is bold,
From mind fears flee, the welkin's walls give place,
And show me all that's done throughout the realms of Space.

The sacred splendor of the gods appears,
Their peaceful homes unshaken by the gale;
No hoary snow-show'rs vex their vernal years,
Nor frosty flakes congealed to piercing hail;
No low'ring skies with stormy drift assail;
But laughing light spreads round them far and wide,
And cloudless heav'ns to fold them cannot fail.
Kind Nature doth for all their needs provide,
Unreached by gnawing care, unchanged by time and tide.

But Hell's dark regions nowhere do we meet,
Though now the Earth doth all transparent shine;
To Science works in Space beneath our feet
Reveal their every action and design.
There settles on my life a joy divine,
A thrill withal of more than human awe,

That, guided by that wondrous pow'r of thine,
Which Nature's every secret movement saw.
I view the clear expanse of universal Law.

31 I have already shown of what kind are the beginnings of all things, with what diverse shapes they differ, and how of their own accord they fly on, impelled by everlasting motion, and in what manner each several thing can be created out of them. Next after this it seems that the nature of the mind and the anima must now be displayed in my verses, and the old fear of Acheron driven headlong away, which utterly confounds the life of men from the very root, clouding all things with the blackness of death, and suffering no pleasure to be pure and unalloyed.

41 For, although men often declare that disease and a life of disgrace are more to be feared than the lower realm of death, and that they know that the nature of the anima is of blood, or else of wind (if by chance their whim so wills it) and thus they have no need at all of our philosophy, you may be sure by this that all is idly vaunted to win praise, and not because the truth is itself accepted.

48 These same men, exiled from their country and banished far from the sight of men, stained with some foul crime, beset with every kind of care, live on all the same, and, spite of all, to whatever place they come in their misery, they make sacrifice to the dead, and slaughter black cattle and despatch offerings to the gods of the dead, and in their bitter plight far more keenly turn their hearts to religion.

55 Wherefore it is more fitting to watch a man in doubt and danger, and to learn of what manner he is in adversity; for then at last a real cry is wrung from the bottom of his heart: the mask is torn off, and the truth remains behind.

59 Moreover, avarice and the blind craving for honours, which constrain wretched men to overlap the boundaries of right, and sometimes as comrades or accomplices in crime to struggle night and day with surpassing toil to rise up to the height of power — these sores in life are fostered in no small degree by the fear of death. For most often scorned disgrace and biting poverty are seen to be far removed from pleasant settled life, and are, as it were, a present dallying before the gates of death; and while men, spurred by a false fear, desire to flee far

from them, and to drive them far away, they amass substance by civil bloodshed and greedily multiply their riches, heaping slaughter on slaughter. Hardening their heart they revel in a brother's bitter death, and hate and fear their kinsmen's board.

74 In like manner, often through the same fear, they waste with envy because someone is powerful, is regarded, or walks clothed with bright renown; while they complain that they themselves are wrapped in darkness and the mire. Some of them come to ruin to win statues and a name; and often through fear of death so deeply does the hatred of life and the sight of the light possess men, that with sorrowing heart they compass their own death, forgetting that it is this fear which is the source of their woes, which assails their honour, which bursts the bonds of friendship, and overturns affection from its lofty throne. For often ere now men have betrayed country and beloved parents, seeking to shun the realms of Acheron.

87 For even as children tremble and fear everything in blinding darkness, so we sometimes dread in the light things that are no whit more to be feared than what children shudder at in the dark, and imagine will come to pass.

91 This terror then, this darkness of the mind, must needs be scattered, not by the rays of the sun and the gleaming shafts of day, but by the outer view and the inner law of nature.

THE RELATION BETWEEN MIND, BODY AND ANIMA, 94-416

94 First I say that the mind,[50] which we often call the understanding, in which is placed the reasoning and guiding power of life, is a part of a man no whit the less than hand and foot and eyes are created parts of the whole living being.

98 [Yet many wise men have thought] that the sensation of the mind is not placed in any part determined, but is a certain

---

[50] Lucretius' distinction between mind (*animus*), which is a concentration of anima particles in one bodily location and is the centre of will and thought, and the vital principle (*anima*), which is made of similar particles but extended throughout a living body and mixed with other body particles, is of the utmost importance. But note that from line 417 onwards he permits *anima* to include *animus* when the distinction may be ignored.

vital habit of the body, which the Greeks call a harmony,[51] in that it makes us live with sensation, although in no part does an understanding exist; as when often good health is said to belong to the body, and yet it is not itself any part of a healthy man. In this wise they do not set the sensation of the mind in any part determined; and in this they seem to me to wander very far astray. Thus often the body (which is clear to see) is sick, when, at the same time we feel pleasure in some other hidden part. And contrariwise it happens that the reverse often comes to be in turn, when one wretched in mind feels pleasure in all his body; in no other wise than if, when a sick man's foot is painful, all the while, may be, his head is in no pain. Moreover, when the limbs are given up to soft sleep, and the heavy body lies slack and senseless, yet there is something else in us, which at that very time is stirred in many ways, and admits within itself all the motions of joy and baseless cares of heart.

117 Now that you may be able to learn that the anima too is in the limbs, and that it is not by a harmony that the body is wont to feel, first of all it comes to pass that when a great part of the body is removed, yet often the life lingers on in our limbs. And then again, when a few bodies of heat are scattered abroad and some air has been driven out through the mouth, that same life of a sudden abandons the veins and leaves the bones. So you may be able to know from this that not all kinds of bodies have an equal part to play, nor do all equally support existence, but that rather those, which are the seeds of wind and burning heat, are the cause that life lingers in the limbs. There is then heat and a life-giving wind in the very body, which abandons our dying frame.

130 Wherefore, since the nature of mind and anima has been revealed as a part of man, give up the name of harmony, which was handed down to musicians from high Helicon: or else they themselves have dragged it forth from some other source, and brought it over to this thing, which then was without a name of its own. Whatever it is, let them keep it: do you listen to the rest of my discourse.

---

[51] Lucretius is referring to a theory of Aristoxenus (a pupil of Aristotle and a famous musical theorist) which treated the soul as a tuning or harmony of the body. The view is reported in Cicero's *Tusculan Disputations*, I, 19.

136 Now I say that mind and anima are held in union one with the other, and form of themselves a single nature, but that the head, as it were, and lord in the whole body is the reason, which we call mind or understanding, and it is firmly seated in the middle region of the breast.[52] For here it is that fear and terror throb, around these parts are soothing joys; here then is the understanding and the mind. The rest of the anima, spread abroad throughout the body, obeys and is moved at the will and inclination of the understanding.

145 The mind alone by itself has understanding for itself and rejoices for itself, when no single thing stirs either anima or body. And just as, when head or eye hurts within us at the attack of pain, we are not tortured at the same time in all our body; so the mind sometimes feels pain by itself or waxes strong with joy, when all the rest of the anima through the limbs and frame is not roused by any fresh feeling. Nevertheless, when the understanding is stirred by some stronger fear, we see that the whole anima feels with it throughout the limbs, and then sweat and pallor break out over all the body, and the tongue is crippled and the voice is choked, the eyes grow misty, the ears ring, the limbs give way beneath us, and indeed we often see men fall down through the terror in their mind. So any one may easily learn from this that the anima is linked in union with the mind; for when it is smitten by the force of the mind, straightway it strikes the body and pushes it on.

161 This same reasoning shows that the nature of mind and anima is bodily. For when it is seen to push on the limbs, to pluck the body from sleep, to change the countenance, and to guide and turn the whole man – none of which things we see can come to pass without touch, nor touch in its turn without body – must we not allow that mind and anima are formed of bodily nature?

168 Moreover, you see that our mind suffers along with the body, and shares its feelings together in the body. If the shuddering shock of a weapon, driven within and laying bare

[52] Lucretius is using an account of human physiology which was old-fashioned by the standards of Alexandrian science even when he wrote. Fortunately the philosophical argument is not disturbed by reading 'brain' (as even Cicero admitted as a possibility) for 'middle region of the breast'.

bones and sinews, does not reach the life, yet faintness follows, and a pleasant swooning to the ground, and a turmoil of mind which comes to pass on the ground, and from time to time, as it were, a hesitating will to rise. Therefore it must needs be that the nature of the mind is bodily, since it is distressed by the blow of bodily weapons.

177 Now of what kind of body this mind is, and of what parts it is formed, I will go on to give account to you in my discourse. First of all I say that it is very fine in texture, and is made and formed of very tiny particles. That this is so, if you give attention, you may be able to learn from what follows.

180 Nothing is seen to come to pass so swiftly as what the mind pictures to itself coming to pass and started to do itself. Therefore the mind bestirs itself more quickly than any of the things whose nature is manifest for all to see. But because it is so very nimble, it is bound to be formed of exceeding round and exceeding tiny seeds, so that its particles may be able to move when smitten by a little impulse. For so water moves and oscillates at the slightest impulse, seeing it is formed of little particles, quick to roll. But, on the other hand, the nature of honey is more stable, its fluid more sluggish, and its movement more hesitating; for the whole mass of its matter clings more together, because, we may be sure, it is not formed of bodies so smooth, nor so fine and round. For a light trembling breath can constrain a high heap of poppy-seed to scatter from top to bottom before your eyes: but, on the other hand, a pile of stones or corn-ears it can by no means separate. Therefore, in proportion as bodies are tinier and smoother, so they are gifted with nimbleness. But, on the other hand, all things that are found to be of greater weight or more spiky, the more firm set they are. Now, therefore, since the nature of the mind has been found nimble beyond the rest, it must needs be formed of bodies exceeding small and smooth and round. And this truth, when known to you, will in many things, good friend, prove useful, and will be reckoned of service.

208 The following fact, too, declares the nature of the mind, of how thin a texture it is formed, and in how small a place it might be contained, could it be gathered in a mass: that as soon as the unruffled peace of death has laid hold on a man, and the

nature of mind and anima has passed away, you could discern nothing there, that sight or weight can test, stolen from the entire body.[53]

216 And so it must needs be that the whole anima is made of very tiny seeds, and is linked on throughout veins, flesh, and sinews; inasmuch as, when it is all already gone from the whole body, yet the outer contour of the limbs is preserved unbroken, nor is a jot of weight wanting. Even so it is, when the flavour of wine has passed away or when the sweet breath of a perfume is scattered to the air, or when its savour is gone from some body; still the thing itself seems not a whit smaller to the eyes on that account, nor does anything seem withdrawn from its weight, because, we may be sure, many tiny seeds go to make flavours and scent in the whole body of things. Wherefore once and again you may know that the nature of the understanding and the anima is formed of exceeding tiny seeds, since when it flees away it carries with it no jot of weight.

231 Nevertheless we must not think that the nature [of the understanding] is simple. For it is a certain thin breath that deserts the dying, mingled with heat, and heat moreover draws air with it; nor indeed is there any heat, that has not air too mixed with it. For because its nature is rare, it must needs be that many primordia of air move about in it. Already then we have found the nature of the anima to be triple; and yet all these things are not enough to create sensation, since the mind does not admit that any of these can create the motions that bring about sensation [or the thoughts of the mind].

[53] Lucretius is arguing in the context of popular beliefs that at death something, anima (the 'soul' or 'vital principle'), *departs* from the body. His thesis, that the anima is composed, like everything else, of primary particles, would thus lead to the expectation that if these *leave* the body at death, there ought to be a loss of bodily weight at that moment. But this is not observed. Therefore, argues Lucretius, the anima particles must be exceedingly tiny: too tiny for their subtraction from the body to be measurable as a weight loss. He might have argued, in accordance with II, 931–43, that at death nothing leaves the body. What happens is that the 'appropriate' grouping of primordia breaks down. To do this would have been more philosophically effective, but it would also have ignored the prevalent conviction that something *departs* at the last breath. (One of the meanings in Latin for *anima* is 'last breath'.)

241 It must needs be then that some fourth nature[54] too be added to these. But it is altogether without name. Nothing exists more nimble than it, nothing more fine, nor made of smaller or smoother particles. It first sends abroad the motions that bring sensation among the limbs: for it is first stirred, being made up of small shapes. Then heat receives the motions and the hidden power of wind, and then air. Then all things are set moving, the blood receives the shock and all the flesh feels the thrill. Last of all it passes to the bones and marrow, be it pleasure or the heat of opposite kind. Yet not for nothing can pain pierce thus far within, nor any biting ill pass through, but that all things are so disordered that there is no more place for life, and the parts of the anima scatter abroad through all the pores of the body. But for the most part a limit is set to these motions, as it were, on the surface of the body: and by this means we avail to keep our life.

258 Now, as I long to give account in what way these parts are mingled one with another, and in what manner bound together so that they can act, against my will the poverty of my country's tongue holds me back. Yet, despite that, I will touch the theme, as best I can in brief. For the primordia course to and fro among themselves with their own motions, so that no single one can be put apart, nor can its powers be set in play divided from others by empty space, but they are, as it were, the many forces of a single body. Even as in the flesh of any living creature anywhere there is smell and a certain heat and savour, and yet of all these is made up the bulk of a single body.

271 Thus heat and air and the hidden power of wind mingled create one nature together with that nimble force, which sends among them from itself the beginning of motion, whence the motion that brings sensation first arises throughout the flesh.

---

[54] This fourth 'nature' in the anima is *not* an admission by the Epicureans that life cannot be accounted for without recourse to some non-material entity. The fourth nature is 'a force without a name, made of tiny bodies'. Its activity is what each living thing has to have in order to remain a sensible entity. Clearly Lucretius could employ no such concept, but had physics progressed further he might have identified the 'fourth nature' as electrical charges attaching to molecules or as some such elusive and tiny entity which is nevertheless part of the universe of primordial matter and void space.

For right deep within, this nimble force lies hid far below, nor is there anything further beneath than this in our bodies, and it is moreover the very anima of the whole anima. Even as in our limbs and our whole body the force of the mind and the power of the anima is secretly immingled, because it is formed of small and rare bodies. So, you see, this force without a name, made of tiny bodies, lies concealed, and is moreover, as it were, the very anima of the whole anima and holds sway in the whole body.

282 In like manner it must needs be that wind and air and heat function mingled together throughout the limbs and, although one is more or less prominent than the rest, yet a unitary thing is seen to be composed of all. Otherwise heat and wind, and the power of air, put an end to sensation, and by their separation break it up.

288 Moreover the mind possesses that heat, which it dons when it boils with rage, and the fire flashes more keenly from the eyes. Much cold breath too it has, which goes along with fear, and starts a shuddering in the limbs and stirs the whole frame. And it has too that condition of air lulled to rest, which comes to pass when the breast is calm and the face unruffled. But those creatures have more of heat, whose fiery heart and passionate mind easily boils up in anger.

296 Foremost in this class is the fierce force of lions, who often as they groan break their hearts with roaring, and cannot contain in their breast the billows of their wrath. But the cold heart of deer is more full of wind, and more quickly it rouses the chilly breath in its flesh, which makes a shuddering motion start in the limbs. But the nature of oxen draws its life rather from calm air, nor ever is the smoking torch of anger set to it to rouse it overmuch, drenching it with the shadow of murky mist, nor is it pierced and frozen by the chill shafts of fear: it has its place midway between the two, the deer and the raging lions.

307 So is it with the race of men. However much training gives some of them an equal culture, yet it leaves those first traces of the nature of the mind of each. Nor must we think that such maladies can be plucked out by the roots, but that one man will more swiftly fall into bitter anger, another be a little sooner assailed by fear, while a third will take some things more gently than is right. And in many other things it must needs be that the diverse natures of men differ, and the habits that follow thereon.

But I cannot now set forth the secret causes of these, nor discover names for all the shapes of the primary particles, whence arises this variety in things. One thing herein I see that I can affirm, that so small are the traces of the characteristics which reason could not dispel for us, that nothing hinders us from living a life worthy of the gods.

323 This nature then of the anima is protected by the whole body, and is itself the guardian of the body, and the cause of its life. For the two cling together by common roots, and it is seen that they cannot be torn asunder without destruction.

327 Even as it is not easy to tear out the scent from lumps of frankincense, but that its nature too passes away. So it is not easy to draw out the nature of mind and anima from the whole body, but all alike is dissolved. With primordia so closely interlaced from their very birth both are begotten, endowed with a life shared in common, nor, as is clear to see, can the power of body or mind feel apart, either for itself without the force of the other. But by the common motions of the two on this side and on that is sensation kindled and fanned throughout our flesh.

337 Moreover, the body is never begotten by itself, nor grows alone, nor is seen to last on after death. For never, as the moisture of water often gives off heat (which has been lent to it, and is not for that reason torn asunder itself, but remains unharmed) never, I say, in this way can the abandoned frame bear the separation of the anima, but it utterly perishes torn asunder and rots away. So from the beginning of existence, body and anima, in mutual union, learn the motions that give life. Yes, even when hidden in the mother's limbs and womb, so that separation cannot come to pass without hurt and ruin. So you can see, since the cause of their life is linked together, that their natures too must be linked in one.

350 For the rest, if any one is for proving that the body does not feel, and believes that it is the anima mingled with the whole body that takes up this motion, which we call sensation, he is fighting even against plain and true facts. For who will ever tell us what the feeling of the body is, if it be not what the clear fact itself has shown and taught us? 'But when the anima has passed away, the body is utterly deprived of sensation.' Yes, for it loses

that which was not its own in life, and many other things besides it loses, when it is driven out of life.

359 To say, moreover, that the eyes can see nothing, but that the mind looks out through them as when doors are opened, is hard, seeing that the feeling in the eyes leads us the other way. For that feeling drags us on and forces us to the very pupils. Indeed we often cannot see bright things, because our sight is thwarted by the light. But that does not happen with doors. For the doors, through which we see, do not suffer any pain when they are opened. Moreover, if our eyes are as doors, then the mind, it is clear, ought to discern things better if the eyes were taken out and removed, door-posts and all.[55]

370 Herein you could by no means accept the teaching, which the judgement of that venerable man Democritus[56] sets before us, that the primordia of anima and body alternate, set each next each, first one and then the other, and so weave the web of our limbs. For, as the particles of anima are far smaller than those of which our body and flesh are composed, so too they are less in number, and only here and there are scattered through our frame. So that you may warrant this: that the primary particles of anima preserve distances apart as great as are the smallest bodies which, when cast upon us, can first start the motions of sensation in the body.

381 For sometimes we do not feel the clinging of dust on the body, nor know that chalk has been shaken on us and settled on our limbs, nor do we feel a mist at night, nor the slender threads of the spider that strike against us, when we are caught in its meshes as we move, nor know that his twisted web has fallen on our head, or the feathers of birds or the flying down from plants, which from its exceeding lightness, for the most part falls

---

[55] The argument in 359–69 is an interesting anticipation of objections to the Cartesian 'ghost in the machine' version of mind/body dualism.

[56] Democritus of Abdera flourished in the 420s BC. He was a voluminous writer, and the main proponent of atomism as an account of the physical universe. None of his works survive. Epicurus, probably because of his comparative historical nearness, and the suggestion that he owed much to Democritus, is not well disposed to the earlier philosopher. Lucretius on the other hand, always speaks of Democritus with great respect.

not lightly. Nor do we feel the passage of every kind of crawling creature nor each single footstep, which gnats and other insects plant upon our body. Indeed, so many things must first be stirred in us, before the seeds of the anima, mingled with our bodies throughout our frame, feel that the primary particles have been shaken, and before they can by jostling in these spaces set between, rush together, unite and leap back in turn.[57]

396 Now the mind is more the keeper of the fastnesses of life, more the monarch of life than is the power of the anima. For without the mind and understanding no part of the anima can hold out in the frame for a tiny moment of time, but follows in its train without demur, and scatters into air, and deserts the chill frame in the frost of death. Yet one, whose mind and understanding have abode firm, abides in life. However much the trunk is mangled with the limbs hewn all around, though the anima be rent from him all around and wrested from his limbs, he lives and draws in the breath of heaven to give him life. Robbed, if not of all, yet of a great part of his vitality, still he lingers on and clings to life. Even as, when the eye is mangled all around, if the pupil has abode unharmed, then the living power of sight stands firm, if only you do not destroy the whole ball of the eye, and cut all round the pupil, and leave it by itself: for that will not be done without the destruction of the eyes too. But if that tiny part in the middle of the eye is eaten away, at once light is gone, and darkness follows on, however much the bright ball is in other places unharmed. In such a compact are anima and mind ever bound together.

PROOFS THAT MIND AND BODY HAVE A COMMON BIRTH AND DEATH, 417–829

417 Come now, so that you may be able to learn that the minds and the light animae of living things have birth and death, I will hasten to set forth verses long sought out and found with glad effort, worthy to guide your life.

421 But you may link both [anima and mind] in a single name, and when, to choose an example, I continue to speak of

---

[57] It is difficult to make good sense of the Latin in lines 394–5.

the anima, proving that it is mortal, you may take it that I speak of mind as well, inasmuch as they are at one each with the other and compose a single thing.

425 First of all, since I have shown that it [anima] is finely made of tiny bodies and of primordia far smaller than the liquid moisture of water or cloud or smoke – (for it far surpasses them in speed of motion, and is more prone to move when smitten by some slender cause; for indeed it is moved by images of smoke and cloud: even as when slumbering in sleep we see altars breathing steam on high, and sending up their smoke; for beyond all doubt these are images that are borne to us) – now therefore, since, when vessels are shattered, you behold the water flowing away on every side, and the liquid parting this way and that, and since cloud and smoke part asunder into air, you must believe that the anima too is scattered and passes away far more swiftly, and is dissolved more quickly into its primordia, when once it is withdrawn from a man's limbs, and has departed. For indeed, since the body, which was, as it were, the vessel of the anima, cannot hold it together, when by some chance it is shattered and made rare, by the blood withdrawn from the veins, how could you believe that the anima could be held together by any air, which is more rare than our body [and can contain it less]?

445 Moreover, we feel that the understanding is begotten along with the body, and grows together with it, and along with it comes to old age. For as children totter with feeble and tender body, so a weak judgement of mind goes with it. Then when their years are ripe and their strength hardened, greater is their sense and increased their force of mind. Afterward, when now the body is shattered by the stern strength of time, and the frame has sunk with its force dulled, then the reason is maimed, the tongue raves, the mind stumbles, all things give way and fail at once. And so it is natural that all the nature of the mind should also be dissolved, even as is smoke, into the high breezes of the air; inasmuch as we see that it is born with the body, grows with it, and, as I have shown, at the same time becomes weary and worn with age.

459 Then follows this that we see that, just as the body itself suffers wasting diseases and poignant pain, so the mind too has its biting cares and grief and fear. Therefore it is natural that it should also share in death.

463 Nay more, during the diseases of the body the mind often wanders astray. For it loses its reason and speaks raving words, and sometimes in a heavy lethargy is carried off into a deep unending sleep, when eyes and head fall nodding, in which it hears not voices, nor can know the faces of those who stand round, summoning it back to life, bedewing faces and cheeks with their tears. Therefore you must needs admit that the mind too is dissolved, inasmuch as the contagion of disease pierces into it. For both pain and disease are alike fashioners of death, as we have been taught ere now by many a man's decease.

476 Again, when the stinging strength of wine has entered into a man, and its heat has spread abroad throughout his veins, why is it that there follows a heaviness in the limbs, his legs are entangled as he staggers, his tongue is sluggish, and his mind heavy, his eyes swim, shouting, sobbing, quarrelling grows apace, and then all the other signs of this sort that go along with them; why does this come to pass, except that the mastering might of the wine is wont to confound the soul even within the body? But whenever things can be so confounded and entangled, they testify that, if a cause a whit stronger shall have made its way within, they must needs perish, robbed of any further life.

487 Nay more, some man, often before our very eyes, seized suddenly by violent disease, falls, as though by a lightning-stroke, and foams at the mouth. He groans and shivers throughout his frame. He loses his wits. His muscles grow taut. He writhes. He breathes in gasps, and tossing to and fro wearies his limbs. Because, you may be sure, his anima rent asunder by the violence of disease throughout his frame, is confounded, and gathers foam, as on the salt sea the waters boil beneath the stern strength of the winds. Further, the groaning is wrung from him, because his limbs are racked with pain, and more than all because the particles of voice are driven out, and are carried crowding forth from his mouth, along the way they are wont, where is their paved path. Loss of wits comes to pass, because the force of mind and anima is confounded, and, as I have shown, is torn apart and tossed to and fro, rent asunder by that same poison. Thereafter, when by now the cause of malady has ebbed, and the biting humours of the distempered body return to their hiding-places, then, as it were staggering, he first rises, and little by little returns to all his senses, and regains his anima. When mind and anima then, even within the body, are tossed by such great maladies, and in wretched plight are rent asunder and distressed, why do you believe that without the body in the open air they can continue life amid the warring winds?

510 And since we perceive that the mind is cured, just like the sick body, and we see that it can be changed by medicine, this too forewarns us that the mind has a mortal life. For whosoever attempts and essays to alter the mind, or seeks to change any other nature, must indeed add parts to it or transfer them from their order, or take away some small whit at least from the whole. But what is immortal does not permit its parts to be transposed, nor that any whit should be added or depart from it. For whenever a thing changes and passes out of its own limits, straightway this is the death of that which was before. And so whether the mind is sick, it gives signs of its mortality, as I have proved, or whether it is changed by medicine. So surely is true fact seen to run counter to false reasoning, and to shut off retreat from him who flees, and with double-edged refutation to prove the falsehood.

526 Again, we often behold a man pass away little by little and limb by limb lose the sensation of life. First of all the toes and nails on his feet grow livid, then the feet and legs die, thereafter through the rest of his frame, step by step, pass the traces of chill death. Since the nature of the anima is split up, nor does it come forth all intact at one moment, it must be counted mortal. But if by chance you think that it could of its own power draw itself inwards through the frame, and contract its parts into one place, and so withdraw sensation from all the limbs, yet nevertheless that place, to which so great abundance of anima is gathered together, must needs be seen to be possessed of greater sensation. But since such a place is nowhere found, you may be

sure, as we said before, [the anima] is rent in pieces and scattered abroad, and so perishes. Nay more, if it were our wish to grant what is false, and allow that the anima could be massed together in the body of those who as they die leave the light of day part by part, still you must confess that the anima is mortal, nor does it matter whether it passes away scattered through the air, or is drawn into one of all its various parts and deadens, since sense more and more in every part fails the whole man, and in every part less and less of life remains.

548 And since the mind is one part of man, which abides rooted in a place determined, just as are ears and eyes and all the other organs of sense which guide the helm of life; and, just as hand and eye or nostrils, sundered apart from us, cannot feel nor be, but in fact are in a short time melted in corruption, so the mind cannot exist by itself without the body and the man himself. For the body seems to be, as it were, the vessel of the mind, or anything else you like to picture more closely bound to it, inasmuch as the body clings to [the mind] with binding ties.

558 Again, the living powers of body and mind prevail by union, one with the other, and so enjoy life. For neither without body can the nature of mind by itself alone produce the motions of life, nor yet bereft of anima can body last on and feel sensation. We must know that just as the eye by itself, if torn out by the roots, cannot discern anything apart from the whole body, so, it is clear, anima and mind by themselves have no power. Doubtless because in close mingling throughout veins and flesh, throughout sinews and bones, their primordia are held close by all the body, nor can they freely leap asunder with great spaces between. And thus enclosed they make those sense-giving motions which outside the body, cast out into the breezes of air after death, they cannot make, because they are not in the same way then held together. For indeed air will be a living body, if the anima can hold itself together, and confine itself to those motions, which it made before in the sinews and within the body itself. Wherefore, again and again, when the whole protection of the body is undone, and the breath of life is driven without, you must needs admit that the sensations of the mind

and the anima are dissolved, since the cause of life in anima and body is closely linked.

580 Again, since the body cannot endure the severing of the anima, but that it decays with a foul stench, why do you doubt that the force of the anima has gathered together from deep down within, and has trickled out, scattering abroad like smoke, and that the body has changed and fallen crumbling in such great ruin, because its foundations have been utterly moved from their seat, as the anima trickles forth through the limbs, and through all the winding ways, which are in the body, and all the pores? So that in many ways you may learn that the nature of the anima issued through the frame sundered in parts, and that even within the body it was rent in pieces in itself, before it slipped forth and swam out into the breezes of the air.

592 Nay more, while it moves still within the limits of life, yet often from some cause the anima seems to be shaken and to move, and to wish to be released from the whole body. The face seems to grow flaccid, as at the hour of death, and all the limbs to fall limp on the bloodless trunk. Even so it is, when, as men say, the heart has had a shock, or the heart has failed; when all is alarm, and one and all struggle to clutch at the last link of life. For then the mind is shaken through and through, and all the power of the anima, and both fall in ruin with the body. So a cause a whit stronger might bring dissolution.

603 Why do you doubt after all this but that the anima, if driven outside the body, frail as it is, without in the open air, robbed of its shelter, would not only be unable to last on through all time, but could not hold together even for a moment? For it is clear that no one, as he dies, feels his anima going forth whole from all his body, nor coming up first to the throat and the gullet up above, but rather failing in its place in a quarter determined; just as he knows that the other senses are dissolved each in their own place. But if our mind were immortal, it would not at its death so much lament that it was dissolved, but rather rejoice that it went forth and left its slough, as does a snake.

615 Again, why is the understanding and judgement of the mind never begotten in head or feet or hands, but is fixed for all men in one abode in a quarter determined? Why, except that places determined are assigned to each thing for its birth and in which each distant thing can abide when it is created, that so it may have its manifold parts arranged so that the order of its limbs can never be seen reversed?[58] So surely does one thing follow on another, nor is flame wont to be born of flowing streams, nor cold to be conceived in fire.

624 Moreover, if the nature of the anima is immortal and can feel when sundered from our body, we must, I hold, suppose it endowed with five senses. Nor in any other way can we picture to ourselves animae wandering in the lower world of Acheron. And so painters and the former generations of writers have brought before us [images] of animae endowed with senses. Yet neither eyes nor nose nor even hand can exist for the anima apart from body, nor again tongue apart or ears. Animae cannot therefore feel by themselves or even exist.

634 And since we feel that the sensation of life is present in the whole body, and we see that the whole is a living thing, if some force suddenly hew it in the middle with swift blow, so that it severs each half apart, beyond all doubt the force of the anima too will be cleft in twain, torn asunder and riven together with the body. But what is cleft and separates into any parts, disclaims, assuredly, that its nature is everlasting.

642 They tell how often scythe-bearing chariots, glowing in the mellay of slaughter, so suddenly lop off limbs, that the part which falls lopped off from the frame is seen to shiver on the ground while, in spite of all this, the mind and spirit of the man cannot feel the pain, through the suddenness of the stroke. At the same time, because his mind is swallowed up in the fervour of the fight; with the body that is left him he makes for the fight and the slaughter, and often knows not that his left arm with its shield is gone, carried away by the wheels among the horses and the ravening scythes; and another sees not that his right arm has dropped, while he climbs up and presses onward. Then another struggles

---

[58] Words may be missing here. The Latin as it stands does not make sense.

to rise when his leg is lost, while at his side on the ground his dying foot twitches its toes. And the head lopped off from the warm living trunk keeps on the ground the look of life and the wide-open eyes, until it has yielded up all the last vestiges of soul.

657 Nay more, if you should choose to chop into many parts with an axe the body of a snake with quivering tongue, angry tail, and long body, you will then perceive all the hewn parts severally writhing under the fresh blow, and scattering the ground with gore, and the fore part making open-mouthed for its own hinder part, in order that, smitten by the burning pain of the wound, it may quench it with its bite. Shall we say then that there is a whole anima in all those little parts? But by that reasoning it will follow that one living creature had many animae in its body. Thus the anima which was one together with the body has been severed; wherefore both body and anima must be thought mortal, since each alike is cleft into many parts.

670 Moreover, if the nature of the anima is immortal,[59] and it enters into the body at our birth, why can we not remember also the part of our life already gone, why do we not preserve traces of things done before? For if the power of the mind is so much changed that all remembrance of things past is lost to it, that state is not, I maintain, a far step from death. Therefore you must needs admit that the anima, which was before, has perished, and that that which now is, has been new created.

679 Moreover, if, when our body is already formed, the living power of the mind is wont to be put in just when we are born, when we are crossing the threshold into life, it would not then be natural that it should be seen to grow with the body, together with the limbs in the very blood. But it is natural that it should

[59] Lucretius is here taking up an account of human immortality which was important in classical philosophy (it is evident for example in the *Phaedo* and other of Plato's writings) and in semi-philosophical religions such as Pythagoreanism. The account is that the essential human person or 'soul' has an immortal existence (*from* everlasting *to* everlasting) or, at the very least, has many successive embodiments in different bodies – not necessarily all human. As Lucretius argues: since we never remember our former or pre-natal selves, this gives reasonable grounds for concluding we had no pre-natal existence. It also provides an analogy by means of which we can grasp that our post-mortem existence will be a similar nothingness.

live all alone by itself as in a den, yet so that the whole body nevertheless is rich in sensation.

686 Wherefore, again and again, we must not think that animae are without a birth, or released from the law of death. For neither can we think that they could be so closely linked to our bodies if they were grafted into them from without — but that all this is so, plain fact on the other hand declares. For the anima is so interlaced through veins, flesh, sinews, and bones that the teeth, too, have their share in sensation; as toothache shows and the twinge of cold water, and the biting on a sharp stone if it be hid in a piece of bread. Nor, when animae are so interwoven, can they, it is clear, issue forth entire, and unravel themselves intact from all the sinews and bones and joints.

698 But if by chance you think that the anima is wont to be grafted in us from without, and then permeate through our limbs, all the more will it perish as it fuses with the body. For that which permeates dissolves, and so passes away. For even as food parcelled out among all the pores of the body, when it is sent about into all the limbs and members, perishes and furnishes a new nature out of itself, so anima and mind, however whole they may pass into the fresh-made body, still are dissolved as they permeate, while through all the pores there are sent abroad into the limbs the particles, whereof this nature of the mind is formed, which now holds sway in our body, born from that which then perished, parcelled out among the limbs. Therefore it is seen that the nature of the anima is neither without a birthday nor exempt from death.

713 Moreover, are seeds of anima left or not in the lifeless body? For if they are left and are still there, it will follow that it cannot rightly be held immortal, since it has left the body maimed by the loss of some parts. But if it has been removed and fled from the limbs while still entire, so that it has left no part of itself in the body, how is it that corpses, when the flesh is now putrid, teem with worms, and how does so great a store of living creatures, boneless and bloodless, swarm over the heaving frame? But if by chance you believe that animae are grafted in the worms from without, and can pass severally into their bodies, and do not consider why many thousands of

animae should gather together, whence one only has departed, yet there is this that seems worth asking and putting to the test, whether all those animae go hunting for all the seeds of the little worms, and themselves build up a home to live in, or whether they are, as it were, grafted in bodies already quite formed. But there is no ready reason why they should make the bodies themselves, why they should be at such pains. For indeed, when they are without a body, they do not flit about harassed by disease and cold and hunger. For the body is more prone to suffer by these maladies, and it is through contact with the body that the mind suffers many ills. But still grant that it be ever so profitable for them to fashion a body wherein to enter; yet there seems to be no way whereby they could.

737 Animae then do not fashion for themselves bodies and frames. Nor yet can it be that they are grafted in bodies already made. For neither will they be able to be closely interwoven, nor will contact be made by a sharing of sensation.

741 Again, why does fiery passion go along with the grim brood of lions, and cunning with foxes? Why is the habit of flight handed on to deer from their sires, so that their father's fear spurs their limbs? And indeed all other habits of this sort: why are they always implanted in the limbs and temper from the first moment of life, if it be not because a power of mind determined by its own seed and breed grows along with the body of each animal?

748 But if the anima were immortal and were wont to change its bodies, then living creatures would have characters intermingled. The dog of Hyrcanian seed would often flee the onset of the horned hart, and the hawk would fly fearful through the breezes of air at the coming of the dove. Men would be witless, and the fierce tribes of wild beasts wise. For it is argued on false reasoning, when men say that an immortal anima is altered, when it changes its body. For what is changed, is dissolved, and so passes away. For the parts are transferred and shift from their order. Therefore they must be able to be dissolved too throughout the limbs, so that at last they may all pass away together with the body.

760 But if they say that the animae of men always pass into human bodies, still I will ask how an anima can become foolish

after being wise, why no child has reason, why the mare's foal is not as well trained as the bold strength of a horse. We may be sure they will be driven to say that in a weak body the mind too is weak. But if that indeed comes to pass, you must admit that the anima is mortal, since it changes so much throughout the frame, and loses its former life and sense.

765 Or in what manner will the force of mind be able along with each several body, to wax strong and attain the coveted bloom of life, unless it be partner too with the body at its earliest birth? Or why does it desire to issue forth abroad from the aged limbs? Does it fear to remain shut up in a decaying body, lest its home, worn out with the long spell of years, fall on it? But an immortal thing knows no dangers.

776 Again, that animae should be present at the wedlock of Venus and the birth of wild beasts, seems to be merely laughable. That immortal animae should stand waiting for mortal limbs in numbers numberless, and should wrangle one with another in hot haste, which first before the others may find an entrance! Unless by chance the animae have a compact sealed, that whichever arrives first on its wings, shall first have entrance, so that they strive not forcibly at all with one another!!

784 Again, a tree cannot exist in the sky, nor clouds in the deep waters, nor can fishes live in the fields, nor blood be present in wood, nor sap in stones. It is determined and ordained where each thing can grow and have its place. So the nature of the mind cannot come to birth alone without body, nor exist far apart from sinews and blood. But if this could be, far sooner might the force of mind itself exist in head or shoulders, or right down in the heels, and be wont to be born in any part you will, but at least remain in the same man or the same vessel. But since even within our body it is determined and seen to be ordained where anima and mind can dwell apart and grow, all the more must we deny that it could continue or be begotten outside the whole body. Therefore, when the body has perished, you must needs confess that the anima too has passed away, rent asunder in the whole body.

800 Nay, indeed, to link the mortal with the everlasting, and to think that they can feel together and act one upon the other, is but foolishness. For what can be pictured more at variance, more estranged within itself and inharmonious, than that which is mortal should be linked in union with the immortal and everlasting to brave raging storms?

806 Moreover, if ever things abide for everlasting, it must needs be *either* that, because they are of solid body, they beat back assaults, nor suffer anything to come within them which might unloose the close-locked parts within, such as are the bodies of matter whose nature we have declared before; *or* that they are able to continue throughout all time, because they are exempt from blows, as is the void, which abides untouched, nor suffers a whit from assault; *or else* because there is no supply of room all around, into which, as it were, things might part asunder and be broken up (even as the sum of sums is eternal) nor is there any room without into which they may scatter. Nor are there bodies which might fall upon them and break them up with stout blow.

819 But if by chance the anima is rather to be held immortal for this reason, because it is fortified and protected from things fatal to life, or because things harmful to its life come not at all, or because such as come in some way depart defeated before we can feel what harm they do us [clear facts show us that this is not so]. For besides that it falls sick along with the diseases of the body, there comes to it that which often torments it about things that are to be, and makes it ill at ease with fear, and wears it out with care; and when its evil deeds are past and gone, yet sin brings remorse. There is too the peculiar frenzy of the mind and forgetfulness of the past, yes, and it is plunged into the dark waters of lethargy.

THEREFORE DEATH IS NOTHING TO US, 830–1094

830 Death, then, is nothing to us,[60] nor does it concern us a whit, inasmuch as the nature of the mind is but a mortal possession.

---

[60] It is almost as if the whole energy of the poem is focused upon the triumphant overcoming of the dread of death declared in line 830. It is certainly the case that no

832 And even as in the time gone by we felt no ill, when the
Carthaginians came from all sides to the shock of battle, when
all the world, shaken by the hurrying turmoil of war, shuddered
and reeled beneath the high coasts of heaven, in doubt to which
people's sway must fall all human power by land and sea. So,
when we shall be no more, when there shall have come the
parting of body and anima, by whose union we are made one,
you may know that nothing at all will be able to happen to us,
who then will be no more, or move our feeling. No, not if earth
shall be mingled with sea, and sea with sky.

843 And even if the nature of mind and the power of anima has
feeling, after it has been rent asunder from our body, yet it is
nothing to us, who are made one by the mating and marriage of
body and anima. Nor, if time should gather together our
substance after our decease and bring it back again as it is now
placed, if once more the light of life should be vouchsafed to us,
yet, even were that done, it would not concern us at all, when
once the remembrance of our former selves were snapped in
twain.

852 And even now we care not at all for the selves that we
once were, not at all are we touched by any torturing pain for
them. For when you look back over all the lapse of immeasurable time that now is gone, and think how manifold are the
motions of matter, you could easily believe this too, that these
same seeds, whereof we now are made, have often been placed

---

other poet or writer has set out such an impassioned acceptance of the fitness and
justice of human mortality as Lucretius sets out in the 264 lines that conclude this
book, his 'hymn to mortality' as it has been called. It is not merely a rational but
emotionally uncompelling conclusion to the arguments which precede it. It is also, at
depth, a rolling back of fear: not only of religious fear about what might happen after
death (nothing will happen), but of the fear of non-existence. The fear which Philip
Larkin expresses to such effect in his 1977 poem 'Aubade':

> . . . the total emptyness for ever,
> The sure extinction that we travel to
> And shall be lost in always . . .

Lucretius constantly invites us to think of ourselves as a real part of a natural
universe in which life is wonderful and capable of being made good, but is not fit to
be a part of things forever, and would become a terrible affliction to us if it were
forever.

in the same order as they are now; and yet we cannot recall that in our mind's memory; for in between lies a break in life, and all the motions have wandered everywhere far astray from sense.

862 For, if by chance there is to be grief and pain for a man, he must needs himself too exist at that time, that ill may befall him. Since death forestalls this, and prevents the being of him on whom these misfortunes might crowd, we may know that we have nothing to fear in death, and that he who is no more cannot be wretched, and that it were no whit different if he had never at any time been born, when once immortal death hath stolen away mortal life.

870 And so, when you see a man chafing at his lot, that after death he will either rot away with his body laid in earth, or be destroyed by flames, or the jaws of wild beasts, you may be sure that his words do not ring true, and that deep in his heart lies some secret apprehension, however much he denies to himself that he believes he will have any feeling in death.

876 For he does not, I maintain, grant what he professes, nor the grounds of his profession, nor does he remove and cast himself root and branch out of life, but all unwitting supposes something of himself to live on.

879 For when in life each man pictures to himself that it will come to pass that birds and wild beasts will mangle his body in death, he pities himself. For neither does he separate himself from the corpse, nor withdraw himself enough from the outcast body, but thinks that it is he, and, as he stands watching, taints it with his own feeling. Hence he chafes that he was born mortal, and sees not that in real death there will be no second self, to live and mourn to himself his own loss, or to stand there and be pained that he lies mangled or burning. For if it is an evil in death to be mauled by the jaws and teeth of wild beasts, I cannot see how it is not sharp pain to be laid upon hot flames and cremated, or to be placed in honey and stifled [i.e., embalmed], and to grow stiff with cold, lying on the surface on the top of an icy rock, or to be crushed and ground by a weight of earth above.

894 'Now no more shall your glad home welcome you, nor your good wife and sweet children run up to snatch the first

kisses, and touch your heart with a silent thrill of joy. No more shall you have power to prosper in your ways, or to be a sure defence to your own. Pitiful you are,' men say, 'and pitifully has one evil day taken from you all the many prizes of life.' Yet to this they add not: 'nor does there abide with you any longer any yearning for these things.'

902 But if they saw this clearly in mind, and followed it out in their words, they would free themselves from great anguish and fear of mind. 'You, indeed, even as you are now fallen asleep in death, shall so be for all time to come, released from every pain and sorrow. It is we who have wept with tears unquenchable for you, as you were turned to ashes close by us on the awesome place of burning, and that unending grief no day shall take from our hearts.'

909 But of him who speaks thus we should ask, what there is so exceeding bitter, if it comes at the last to sleep and rest, that any one should waste away in never-ending lamentation.

912 This too men often do, when they are lying at the board, and hold their cups in their hands, and shade their faces with garlands: they say from the heart, 'Brief is this enjoyment for us puny men: soon it will be past, nor ever thereafter will it be ours to call it back.' As though in death this were to be foremost among their ills, that thirst would burn the poor wretches and parch them with its drought, or that there would abide with them a yearning for any other thing.

919 For never does any man long for himself and life, when mind and body alike rest in slumber. For all we care, sleep may then be never-ending, nor does any yearning for ourselves then beset us. And yet at that time those primary particles stray not at all far through our frame away from the motions that bring sense, when a man springs up from sleep and gathers himself together. Much less then should we think that death is to us, if there can be less than what we see to be nothing; for at our dying there follows a greater turmoil and scattering abroad of matter, nor does any one wake and rise again, whom the chill shears of life has once overtaken.

931 Again, suppose that the nature of things should of a sudden lift up her voice, and thus in these words herself rebuke some

one of us: 'Why is death so great a thing to you, mortal, that
you give way to such sickly lamentation? Why groan and weep
at death? For if the life that is past and gone has been pleasant
to you, and all its blessings, as though heaped in a vessel full of
holes, have not run through and perished unenjoyed, why do
you not retire like a guest sated with the banquet of life, and
with calm mind embrace, you fool, a rest that knows no care?
But if all you have reaped has been wasted and lost, and life is a
stumbling-block, why seek to add more, all to be lost again
foolishly and pass away unenjoyed? Why not rather make an
end of life and trouble? For there is nothing more which I can
devise or discover to please you. All things are ever as they were.
If your body is not yet wasted with years, nor your limbs worn
and decayed, yet all things remain as they were, even if you
should live on to overpass all generations, nay rather, if you
should never die.'

950 What answer can we make, but that nature brings a just
charge against us, and sets out in her pleading a true cause? But
if now some older man, smitten in years, should make lament,
and pitifully bewail his decease more than is just, would she not
rightly raise her voice and chide him in sharp tones?

954 'Away with tears henceforth, you rogue, set a bridle on
your laments. You have enjoyed all the prizes of life and now
waste away. But because you long ever for what is not with you,
and despise the gifts at hand, uncompleted and unenjoyed your
life has slipped from you and, before you could think it, death is
standing by your head, before you have the heart to depart filled
and sated with good things. Yet now give up all these things so
ill-fitted for your years, and with calm mind, come, yield them
to your sons: for so you must.'

963 She would be right, I think, in her plea, right in her
charge and chiding. For the old ever gives place, thrust out by
new things, and one thing must be restored at the expense of
others. But no one is sent down to the pit and to black Tartarus.
There must needs be matter that the generations to come may
grow; yet all of them too will follow you when they have had
their fill of life. Yes, just as you, these generations have passed
away before, and will pass away again.

970 So one thing shall never cease to rise up out of another,
and life is granted to none for freehold, to all on lease. Look

back again to see how the past ages of everlasting time, before
we are born, have been as nothing to us. These then nature
holds up to us as a mirror of the time that is to come, when we
are dead and gone. Is there anything that looks terrible in this?
Anything that seems gloomy? Is it not a calmer rest than any
sleep?

978 Yes, we may be sure, all those things of which stories tell
us in the depths of Acheron, are in our life. Neither does
wretched Tantalus fear the great rock that hangs over him in
the air, as the tale tells, numbed with idle terror; but rather it is
in life that the vain fear of the gods threatens mortals. They fear
the fall of the blow which chance may deal to each.

984 Nor do birds make their way into Tityus,[61] as he lies in
Acheron, nor can they verily in all the length of time find food
to grope for deep in his huge breast. However vast the mass of
his outstretched limbs, though he cover not only nine acres with
his sprawling limbs, but the whole circle of earth, yet he will not
be able to endure everlasting pain, nor for ever to supply food
from his own body. But our own Tityus is one whom the birds
mangle as he lies smitten with love. Yes, aching anguish devours
him, or care cuts him deep through some other passion.

995 The Sisyphus in our life too is clear to see, he who open-
mouthed seeks from the people the rods and cruel axes, and
evermore comes back conquered and dispirited. For to seek for
a power, which is but in name, and is never truly given, and for
that to endure for ever grinding toil, this is to thrust uphill with
great effort a stone, which after all rolls back from the topmost
peak, and headlong makes for the levels of the plain beneath.

1003 Then to feed for ever the ungrateful nature of the mind,
to fill it full with good things, yet never satisfy it, as the seasons
of the year do for us, when they come round again, and bring
their fruits and their diverse delights, though we are never filled

---

[61] Tityus was a son of Earth, a vast being and one of the Titans, who was confined
in Hades while vultures tore at his liver as a punishment for the attempted rape of
Leto. Lines 978–1013 list a series of well-known mythological tortures which
Lucretius relates to the realities of this world: Sisyphus condemned to roll a rock up a
hill from the top of which it always rolls down again; the daughters of Danus who
murdered their husbands who were condemned forever to try to fill leaking buckets.
Cerberus was the monstrous dog that guarded the entrance to Hades.

full with the joys of life, this, I believe, is the story of the maidens in the flower of youth, who pile the water into the vessel full of holes, which yet can in no way be filled full.

1011 Cerberus and the furies, moreover, and the lack of light, Tartarus, belching forth awful vapours from his jaws:[62] things which are not anywhere, nor verily can be.

1014 But it is fear of punishment for misdeeds in life (fear notable as the deeds are notable) and the atonement for crime, the dungeon and the terrible hurling down from the rock,[63] scourgings, executioners, the rack, pitch, the metal plate, torches; for although they are not with us, yet the self-knowing mind, fearing for its misdeeds, sets goads to itself, and sears itself with lashings, nor does it see meanwhile what end there can be to its ills, or what limit at last to punishment. Yes, and it fears that these same things may grow worse after death. Here after all on earth the life of fools becomes a hell.

1024 This too you might say to yourself from time to time: 'Even Ancus the good closed his eyes on the light of day, he who was a thousand times better than you.[64] And since him many other kings and rulers of empires have fallen, who held sway over mighty nations. Even he himself, who once paved a way over the great sea, and made a path for his legions to pass across the deep, and taught them on foot to pass over the salt pools, and made naught of the roarings of ocean, prancing upon it with his horses, even he lost the light of day, and breathed out his soul from his dying body. The son of the Scipios, thunderbolt of war, terror of Carthage, gave his bones to earth, even as though he had been the meanest house-slave. Yes, and the inventors of sciences and delightful arts, yes and the comrades of the sisters of Helicon: among whom Homer, who sat alone,

---

[62] Some lines are probably missing at this point.

[63] The Tarpeian Rock on the Capitol at Rome from which murderers and traitors were thrown to their deaths.

[64] As lines 978–1013 listed the mythical punishments of the condemned, so lines 1024–44 list famous men who simply no longer exist: Ancus Martius, the legendary fourth king of Rome; Xerxes who led the Persian army across the Hellespont on a pontoon bridge in 480 BC; Scipio who defeated Hannibal at Zama in 202 BC thus removing the Carthaginian threat to Rome; Homer; Democritus; and 'Epicurus himself'.

holding his sceptre, has fallen into the same sleep as the rest.
Again, after a ripe old age warned Democritus that the mindful
motions of his memory were waning, of his own will he met
death and offered her up his head. Epicurus himself died, when
he had run his course in the light of life, Epicurus, who surpassed
the race of men in understanding and quenched the light of all,
even as the sun rising in the sky quenches the stars.

1045 Will you then hesitate and chafe to meet your doom?
You, whose life is wellnigh dead while you still live and look on
the light, who waste in sleep the greater part of your years, and
snore when wide awake, nor ever cease to see dream-visions,
who has a mind harassed with empty fear, nor can discover
often what is amiss with you, when like a sot you are beset,
poor wretch, with countless cares on every side, and wander
drifting on the shifting currents of your mind.'

1053 If only men, even as they clearly feel a weight in their
mind, which wears them out with its heaviness, could learn too
from what causes that comes to be, and whence so great a mass,
as it were, of ill lies upon their breast, they would not pass their
lives, as now for the most part we see them; knowing not each
one of them what he wants, and longing ever for change of
place, as though he could thus lay aside the burden. The man
who is tired of staying at home, often goes out abroad from his
great mansion, and of a sudden returns again, for indeed abroad
he feels no better. He races to his country home, furiously
driving his ponies, as though he were hurrying to bring help to
a burning house. He yawns at once, when he has set foot on the
threshold of the villa, or sinks into a heavy sleep and seeks
forgetfulness, or even in hot haste makes for town, eager to be
back. In this way each man struggles to escape himself: yet,
despite his will he clings to the self, which, we may be sure, in
fact he cannot shun, and hates himself, because in his sickness
he knows not the cause of his malady. But if he saw it clearly,
every man would leave all else, and study first to learn the
nature of things, since it is his state for all eternity, and not for
a single hour, that is in question, the state in which mortals
must expect all their being, that is to come after their death.

1076 Again, what evil craving for life is this which constrains us with such force to live so restlessly in doubt and danger? Indeed a fixed end of life is ordained for mortals, nor can we avoid death, but we must meet it.

1080 Moreover, we always move and spend our time amid the same things, nor by length of life is any new pleasure hammered out. But so long as we have not what we crave, it seems to surpass all else. Afterwards, when that is ours, we crave something else, and the same thirst for life besets us ever, open-mouthed. It is uncertain too what fortune time to come may carry to us, or what chance may bring us, or what issue is at hand.

1087 Nor in truth by prolonging life do we take away a jot from the time of death, nor can we subtract anything whereby we may be perchance less long dead.

1090 Therefore live you on to complete as many generations as you will: nevertheless that same everlasting death will await you, nor will he for a less long time be no more, who has made an end of life with to-day's light, than he who perished many months or years ago.

BOOK IV

Sensation And Sexuality

Synopsis

1–25 Lucretius' mission [verse translation by Thomas Creech, 1682, cf. I, 926–50].

26–44 The new subject proposed and connected with Book III.

45–53 And connected with Book II.

Existence and Nature of 'Simulacra' or 'Images', 54–215

54–109 That simulacra exist as emanations from things.

110–28 Their extreme thinness.

129–42 And occasional spontaneous formation.

143–75 And fragility.

176–215 And speed, as of light.

Simulacra Account for Sensation, 216–721

216–38 In general they acount for sensations.

239–68 An account of vision.

269–323 An account of mirrors.

324–78 Four puzzles about vision.

379–86 The mind, not the eyes, is sometimes deceived.

387–468 Examples of this.

469–521   Refutation of scepticism: *Principle XIIIC. Sensation is Reliable Because it Cannot be Gainsaid by Anything More Reliable than Itself.*

522–3   Now to account for senses other than vision:

524–614   Sound and speech.

615–32   Taste.

633–72   Why what is food to one sort of creature, is poison to another.

673–705   Smell.

706–21   Smells and colours, like tastes, do not universally please.

Thought and the Functioning of Mind and Will, 722–1036

722–76   How simulacra enter the mind and are re-associated in imagination and dreams.

777–822   How association between simulacra in the mind functions.

823–57   What we are able to do is the result of our bodily organs, not the purpose for which they were made. Artifacts, not natural things, have purposes.

858–76   Nutrition.

877–906   How the mind moves the rest of the body.

907–61   Sleep.

962–1036 Why men and animals have particular kinds of dreams.

Sex and its Troubles, 1037–287

1037–57   The stimulus to sexual arousal.

1058–72   And the disappointments.

1073–120   The insatiability of sexual desire.

1121–40   And its wealth-consuming sloth.

1141–91   And the ways we delude ourselves about the quali-
           ties of the loved one.

1192–209   The pleasures of genuine sex are mutual.

1209–32   How children variously resemble their parents and
           forefathers.

1233–77   Infertility sometimes results from defects in the
           semen, sometimes from the physical posture of the
           woman.

1278–87   The habit of pleasant living together can engender
           genuine love that abides.

Book IV

I feel, I rising feel, poetic heats;
And, now inspir'd, trace o'er the Muses' seats,
Untrodden yet: 'Tis sweet to visit first
Untouch'd and virgin streams, and quench my thirst:
I joy to crop fresh flow'rs, and get a crown
For new and rare inventions of my own:
So noble, great, and gen'rous the design,
That none of all the mighty tuneful Nine
E'er grac'd a head with laurels, like to mine.
For first, I teach great things in lofty strains,
And loose men from religion's grievous chains:
Next, tho' my subject's dark, my verse is clear,
And sweet; with fancy flowing ev'ry where;
And this design'd: For as physicians use,
In giving children draughts of bitter juice,
To make them take it, tinge the cup with sweet,
To cheat the lip; this first they eager meet,
And then drink on, and take the bitter draught,
And so are harmlessly deceiv'd, not caught:
For, by such cheats, they get their strength, their ease,
Their vigour, health, and baffle the disease.
So since our method of philosophy
Seems harsh to some; since most our maxims fly;
I thought it was the fittest way to dress
These rigid principles in verse might please,
With fancy sweet'ning them, to bribe thy mind
To read my book, and lead it on to find
The nature of the world, the rise of things;
And what vast profit too that knowledge brings.

26 And since I have taught what was the nature of the mind,
and whereof composed it grew in union with the body, and in
what way rent asunder it passed back into its primary particles:
now I will begin to tell you what very closely concerns this

theme. There are what we call simulacra of things;[65] which, like films stripped from the outermost body of things, fly forward and backward through the air, and they too, when they meet us in waking hours, affright our minds; yes, and in sleep too, when we often gaze on wondrous shapes, and the simulacra of those who have lost the light of day, which in awful wise have often roused us, as we lay languid in sleep; lest by chance we should think that ghosts escape from Acheron, or that shades fly abroad among the living, or that something of us can be left after death, when body alike and the nature of mind have perished and parted asunder into their several primordia. That we may learn from this, however dull be our wits. I say then that likenesses of things and their shapes are given off by things from their outermost body.

45 [But since I have taught of what manner are the beginnings of all things, and how, differing in their diverse forms, of their own accord they fly on, spurred by everlasting motion; and in what way each several thing can be created from them, now I will begin to tell you what exceeding nearly concerns this theme, that there are what we call sumulacra of things, which may be named, as it were, films or even rind, because the image bears an appearance and form like to that, whatever it be, from whose body it appears to be shed, ere it wanders abroad.][66]

THE EXISTENCE AND NATURE OF 'SIMULACRA' OR 'IMAGES', 54–215

54 First of all, since among things clear to see many things give off bodies, in part scattered loosely abroad, even as wood gives

[65] The Latin word is *simulacrum* (Plural *simulacra*). It is Lucretius' preferred technical term for the Greek word *eidola* which is usually rendered 'idols' in most English translations. But such a translation sounds very odd in Lucretius' text. Hence the somewhat more intuitively helpful Latin term *simulacra* is retained in the present translation. Lucretius sometimes varies it with the word *imago*, 'image', and other locutions, but the same technical concept explained in his text is regularly intended.

[66] Following the introduction, lines 1–25, Lucretius provides two starts to Book IV: lines 26–44, which connect it with the subject matter of Book III; and lines 45–53, which connect it with Book II. This double start is usually seen as one of the signs that the whole poem was not tidied up or completely finished when Lucretius died, lines 45–53 having been left over from an earlier plan to follow Book II with Book IV.

off smoke and fires heat, and in part more closely knit and packed together, as when now and then the grasshoppers lay aside their smooth coats in summer, and when calves at their births give off a caul from their outermost body, and likewise when the slippery serpent rubs off its vesture on the thorns; for often we see the brambles laden with these wind-blown spoils from snakes. And since these things come to pass, a thin image from things too must needs be given off from the outermost body of things. For why these films should fall and part from things any more than films that are thin, none can breathe a word to prove; above all, since on the surface of things there are many tiny bodies, which could be cast off in the same order wherein they stood, and could preserve the outline of their shape, yea, and be cast the more quickly, inasmuch as they can be less entangled, in that they are few, and placed in the forefront.

72 For indeed we see many things cast off and give out bodies in abundance, not only from deep beneath, as we said before, but often too from the surface, such as their own colour. And commonly this is done by awnings, yellow and red and steely-blue, when stretched over great theatres they flap and flutter, spread everywhere on masts and beams. For there they tinge the assembly in the tiers beneath, and all the bravery of the stage [and the gay-clad company of the elders,] and constrain them to flutter in their colours. And the more closely are the hoardings of the theatre shut in all around, the more does all the scene within laugh, bathed in brightness, as the light of day is straitened. Since then the canvas gives out this hue from its outermost body, each several thing also must needs give out thin likenesses, since in either case they are throwing off from the surface. There are then sure traces of forms, which fly about everywhere, endowed with slender bulk, nor can they be seen apart one by one.

90 Moreover, all smell, smoke, heat, and other like things stream forth from things, scattering loosely, because while they arise and come forth from deep within, they are torn in their winding course, nor are there straight outlets to their paths, whereby they may hasten to issue all in one mass. But, on the other hand, when the thin film of surface-colour is cast off, there

is nothing which can avail to rend it, since it is ready at hand, and placed in the forefront.

98 Lastly, whenever simulacra appear to us in mirrors, in water, and in every shining surface, it must needs be, seeing that they are endowed with an appearance like the things, that they are made of the images of things given off. There are then thin shapes of things and likenesses, which, although no one can see them one by one, yet thrown back with constant and ceaseless repulse, give back a picture from the surface of the mirrors, and it is seen that they cannot by any other means be so preserved that shapes so exceeding like each several thing may be given back.

110 Come now and learn of how thin a nature this image is formed. And to begin with, since primordia are so far beneath the ken of our senses, and so much smaller than the things which our eyes first begin to be unable to descry, yet now that I may assure you of this too, learn in a few words how fine in texture are the beginnings of all things.

116 First of all there are living things sometimes so small that a third part of them could by no means be seen. Of what kind must we think any one of their entrails to be? What of the round ball of their heart or eye? What of their members? What of their limbs? How small are they? Still more, what of the several primordia from which their anima and the nature of their mind must needs be formed? Do you not see how fine and how tiny they are? Moreover, whatever things breathe out a pungent savour from their body, panacea, sickly wormwood, and strongly-smelling abrotanum, and bitter centaury; if by chance [you press] any one of these lightly between two [fingers, the scent will for long cling to your fingers, though never will you see anything at all: so that you may know how fine is the nature of the primary particles, whereof the scent is formed . . .][67]. . . and not rather learn that many simulacra of things wander abroad in many ways with no powers, unable to be perceived?

[67] After line 126 a considerable number of lines are missing: There is evidence that the single (lost) manuscript, from which all the surviving manuscripts ultimately derive, contained twenty-six lines per page. If a whole page has been lost this would mean that fifty-two lines have gone. Their probable subject matter is indicated by the passage in square brackets.

129 But that you may not by chance think that after all only those simulacra of things wander abroad, which come off from things, there are those too which are begotten of their own accord, and are formed of themselves in this sky which is called air; which moulded in many ways are borne along on high, and being fluid continue to change their appearance, and to turn into the outline of forms of every kind; even as from time to time we see clouds lightly gathering together in the deep sky, and staining the calm face of the firmament, caressing the air with their motion. For often the faces of giants are seen to fly along and to trail a shadow far and wide, and sometimes mighty mountains and rocks torn from the mountains are seen to go on ahead and to pass before the sun; and then a huge beast seems to draw on and lead forward the storm clouds.

143 Come now, in what swift and easy ways those simulacra are begotten, and flow unceasingly from things and fall off and part from them, [I will now explain]. For continually the outermost surface is streaming away from things, that so they may cast it off. And when this reaches some things, it passes through them, as above all through glass: but when it reaches rough stones or the substance of wood, there at once it is torn, so that it cannot give back any simulacrum. But when things that are formed bright and dense are set athwart its path, such as above all is the mirror, neither of these things comes to pass. For neither can they pass through, as through glass, nor yet be torn; for the smoothness is careful to ensure their safety. Wherefore it comes to pass that the simulacra stream back from it to us. And however suddenly, at any time you will, you place each several thing against the mirror, the image comes to view; so that you may know that from the outermost body there flow off unceasingly thin webs and thin shapes of things. Therefore many simulacra are begotten in a short moment, so that rightly is the creation of these things said to be swift. And just as the sun must needs shoot out many rays of light in a short moment, so that the whole world may unceasingly be filled, so too in like manner from things it must needs be that many simulacra of things are borne off in an instant of time in many ways in all directions on every side; inasmuch as to whatever side we turn

the mirror to meet the surface of things, things in the mirror
answer back alike in form and colour.

168 Moreover, even when the weather in the sky has but
now been most clear, exceeding suddenly it becomes foully
stormy, so that on all sides you might think that all darkness
has left Acheron, and filled the great vault of the sky; so terribly,
when the noisome night of clouds has gathered together, do the
shapes of black fear hang over us on high; yet how considerable
a part of these is a simulacrum there is no one who could say or
give an account in words.

176 Come now, with what swift motion the simulacra are
carried on, and what speed is given them as they swim through
the air, so that a short hour is spent on a long course, towards
whatever place they each strain on with diverse impulse, I will
proclaim in verses of sweet discourse rather than in many; even
as the brief song of a swan is better than the clamour of cranes,
which spreads abroad among the clouds of the south high in
heaven.

183 First of all very often we may see that light things made
of tiny bodies are swift. In this class there is the light of the sun
and his heat, because they are made of tiny primordia, which,
as it were, are knocked forward, and do not pause in passing on
through the space of air between, smitten by the blow from
those that follow. For in hot haste the place of light is taken by
light, and as though driven in a team, one flash is goaded by
another flash. Wherefore in like manner it must needs be that
simulacra can course through space unthinkable in an instant of
time. First because it is a tiny cause,[68] far away behind, which
drives and carries them forward, and after that, in that they are
borne on with so swift a lightness of bulk; and then because
they are given off endowed with texture so rare that they can
easily pass into anything you will, and as it were ooze through
the intervening air.

[68] The speed of the unimpeded primary particle is much greater than that of any
compound of particles however small (see II, 127). For the same reason the impact
(roughly the momentum deriving from its speed) of the unimpeded particle is greatest,
and it can therefore impart greater speed to any object which it hits. Simulacra are
sent on their way by the impact of single particles from within the compound, and
the 'tiny cause' is thus able to impart great speed to them. (Adapted from Bailey's
note.)

199 Moreover, when particles of things are given out abroad from deep within, like the sun's light and heat, these are seen to fall in a moment of time and spread themselves over the whole expanse of heaven, and to fly over sea and earth and flood the sky. What then of those things which are ready at once in the forefront? When they are cast off and nothing hinders their discharge, do you not see that they must needs move swifter and further, and course through many times the same expanse of space in the same time in which the rays of the sun crowd the sky? This, too, more than all seems to show forth truly in what swift motion simulacra of things are borne on, that as soon as a bright surface of water is placed beneath the open sky, when the heaven is starry, in a moment the calm beaming stars of the firmament appear in answer in the water. Do you not then see now in how short an instant of time the image falls from the coasts of heaven to the coasts of earth?

SIMULACRA ACCOUNT FOR SENSATION, 216–721

216 Wherefore more and more you must needs confess that bodies are sent off such as strike the eyes and awake our vision. And from certain things scents stream off unceasingly: just as cold streams off from rivers, heat from the sun, spray from the waves of the sea, which gnaws away walls all around the shores. Nor do diverse voices cease to fly abroad through the air. Again, often moisture of a salt savour comes into our mouth, when we walk by the sea, and on the other hand, when we watch wormwood being diluted and mixed, a bitter taste touches it. So surely from all things each separate thing is carried off in a stream, and is sent abroad to every quarter on all sides, nor is any delay or respite granted in this flux, since we feel unceasingly, and we are suffered always to descry and smell all things, and to hear them sound.

230 Moreover, since a shape felt by the hands in the darkness is known to be in some way the same as is seen in the light and the clear brightness, it must needs be that touch and sight are stirred by a like cause. If then we handle a square thing, and it stirs our touch in the darkness, what square thing can fall upon our sight in the light, except its image? Wherefore it is clear that

the cause of seeing lies in the images, nor without them can anything be seen.

239 Next those things which I call the simulacra of things are borne everywhere, and are cast off and meted out to every side. But because we can see them only with our eyes, for that cause it comes to pass that, to whatever side we turn our sight, all things there strike against it with their shape and hue. And how far each thing is away from us, the image causes us to see and provides that we distinguish. For when it is given off, straightway it pushes and drives before it all the air that has its place between it and the eyes, and thus it all glides through our eyeballs, and, as it were, brushes through the pupils, and so passes on. Therefore it comes to pass that we see how far away each thing is. And the more air is driven on in front, and the longer the breeze which brushes through our eyes, the further each thing is seen to be removed. But you must know that these things are brought to pass by means exceeding quick, so that we see what it is and at the same time how far it is away. Herein by no means must we deem there is cause to wonder why the simulacra which strike the eyes cannot be seen one by one, but the whole things are descried. For when wind too lashes us little by little, and when piercing cold streams on us, we are not wont to feel each separate particle of that wind and cold, but rather all at once, and then we perceive blows coming to pass on our body, just as if something were lashing us and giving us the feeling of its body without. Moreover, when we strike a stone with our finger, we touch the very outside of the rock and its colour on the surface, yet we do not feel the colour with our touch, but rather we feel the very hardness of the rock deep down beneath.

269 Come now and learn why the image is seen beyond the mirror; for indeed it seems removed far within. It is even as those things which in very truth are seen outside a door, when the door affords an unhindered sight through it, and lets many things out of doors be seen from the house. For that vision too is brought to pass by two twin airs. For first the air on our side of the jambs is seen in such a case, then follow the folding doors themselves on right and left, afterwards the light outside brushes

through the eyes, and a second air, and then those things which in very truth are seen without the doors. So when first the image of the mirror has cast itself adrift, while it is coming to our pupils, it pushes and drives before it all the air which has its place between it and our eyes, and so makes us able to perceive all this air before the mirror. But when we have perceived the mirror itself too, straightway the image which is borne from us passes to the mirror, and being cast back returns to our eyes and drives on and rolls in front of it another air, and makes us see this before itself, and therefore seems to be just so much distant from the mirror. Wherefore, again and again, it is not right at all that we should wonder [that this appearance comes to be both for those things which are really seen out of doors, and also][69] for those things which send back a vision from the level surface of the mirrors; since in either case it is brought about by the two airs. Next it comes to pass that the part of our limbs which is on the right is seen in mirrors on the left, because when the image comes to the plane of the mirror and strikes against it, it is not turned round unchanged, but is dashed back straight; just as if one were to dash a plaster mask, before it is dry, against a pillar or a beam, and it at once were to preserve its shape turned straight to meet us, and were to mould again its own features dashed back towards us. Thus it will come to pass that what was before the right eye, now in turn is the left, and the left in exchange is now the right. It comes to pass too that the image is handed on from mirror to mirror, so that even five or six simulacra are wont to be made. For even when things are hidden far back in an inner part of the room, yet, however far distant from the sight along a twisting path, it may be that they will all be brought out thence by winding passages, and, thanks to the several mirrors, be seen to be in the house. So surely does the image reflect from mirror to mirror, and when a left hand is presented, it comes to pass that it is changed to the right, and then once again it is changed about and returns to where it was before. Moreover, all flank-curved [concave?] mirrors, endowed with a curve like to our flanks, send back to us right-handed simulacra, either because the image if borne across from one part of the mirror to another, and then flies towards us, twice

___

[69] The words in brackets indicate the probable meaning of a missing line.

dashed back, or else because the image is twisted around, when it has arrived, because the curved shape of the mirror teaches it to turn round towards us. Moreover, you would believe that simulacra walk step by step and place their feet as we do, and imitate our gait, just because, from whatever part of the mirror you retire, straightway the images cannot be turned back from it, inasmuch as nature constrains all things to be carried back, and leap back from things, sent back at equal angles.

324 Bright things moreover the eyes avoid, and shun to look upon. The sun, too, blinds, if you try to raise your eyes to meet him, because his own power is great, and the simulacra from him are borne through the clear air, sinking heavily into the deep, and strike upon the eyes, disordering their texture. Moreover, any piercing brightness often burns the eyes for the reason that it contains many seeds of fire, which give birth to pain in the eyes, finding their way in. Moreover, whatever the jaundiced look upon becomes sickly-yellow, because many seeds of yellow stream off from their bodies to meet the simulacra of things, and many also are mixed in their eye, which by their infection tinge all things with their pallor.

337 Now we see things that are in the light out of the darkness, because, when the black air of the gloom, which is nearer, first enters and seized on the open eyes, there follows in hot haste a bright air full of light, which, as it were, cleanses the eyes and scatters abroad the dark shadows of the former air. For the latter is many times more nimble, many times finer and more potent. And as soon as it has filled the passages of the eyes with light, and opened up those which before the black air had beleaguered, straightway follow the simulacra of the things which are lying in the light, and excite our eyes so that we see. But, on the other hand, we cannot do this in the darkness out of the light, because the air of the gloom, which is denser, comes on afterwards, and fills all the channels and beleaguers the passages of the eyes, so that none of the simulacra of things can be cast upon them and stir them.

353 And when we see from afar off the square towers of a town, it comes to pass for this cause that they often look round, because every angle from a distance is seen flattened, or rather it is not seen at all, and the blow from it passes away, nor does its

stroke come home to our eyes, because, while the simulacra are being borne on through much air, the air by its frequent collisions constrains it to become blunted. When for this cause every angle alike has escaped our sense, it comes to pass that the structures of stone are worn away as though turned on the lathe; yet they do not look like things which are really round to a near view, but a little resembling them as though in shadowy shape.

364 Likewise our shadow seems to us to move in the sunshine, and to follow our footsteps and imitate our gait; if indeed you believe that air bereft of light can step forward, following the movements and gait of men. For that which we are wont to name a shadow can be nothing else but air devoid of light. But in very truth it is because in certain spots in due order the ground is bereft of the light of the sum wherever we, as we move on, cut it off, and likewise the part of it which we have left is filled again; for this cause it comes to pass that, what was but now the shadow of our body, seems always to follow unaltered straight along with us. For always new rays of light are pouring out, and the former perish, like wool drawn into a flame.

377 Therefore readily is the ground robbed of light, and is likewise filled again and washes away its own black shadows.

379 And yet we do not grant that in this the eyes are a whit deceived. For it is theirs to see in what several spots there is light and shade: but whether it is the same light or not, whether it is the same shadow which was here, that now passes there, or whether that rather comes to pass which I said a little before, this the reasoning of the mind alone must needs determine, nor can the eyes know the nature of things. Do not then be prone to impute to the eyes this fault in the mind.

387 The ship, in which we journey, is borne along, when it seems to be standing still. Another, which remains at anchor, is thought to be passing by. The hills and plains seem to be flying towards the stern, past which we are driving on our ship with skimming sail. All the stars, fast set in the vault of the firmament, seem to be still, and yet they are all in ceaseless motion, inasmuch as they rise and return again to their distant settings, when they have traversed the heaven with their bright body. And in like manner sun and moon seem to abide in their places,

yet actual fact shows that they are borne on. And mountains rising up afar off from the middle of the waters, between which there is a free wide issue for ships, yet seem united to make a single island. When children have ceased turning round themselves, so sure does it come to appear to them that the halls are turning about, and the pillars racing round, that scarcely now can they believe that the whole roof is not threatening to fall in upon them. And again, when nature begins to raise on high the sunbeam ruddy with twinkling fires, and to lift it above the mountains, those mountains above which the sun seems to you to stand, as he touches them with his own fire, all aglow close at hand, are scarce distant from us two thousand flights of an arrow, may often scarce five hundred casts of a javelin: but between them and the sun lie the vast levels of ocean, strewn beneath the wide coasts of heaven, and many thousands of lands are set between, which diverse races inhabit, and tribes of wild beasts. And yet a pool of water not deeper than a single finger-breadth, which lies between the stones on the paved street, affords us a view beneath the earth to a depth as vast as the high gaping mouth of heaven stretches above the earth; so that you, seem to descry the clouds and the heaven and bodies wise hidden beneath the earth – yet in a magic sky.

420 Again, when our eager horse has stuck fast amid a river, and we look down into the hurrying waters of the stream, the force seems to be carrying on the body of the horse, though he stands still, athwart the current, and to be thrusting it in hot haste up the stream; and wherever we cast our eyes all things seem to be borne on and flowing forward, as we are ourselves. Though a colonnade runs on straight-set lines all the way, and stands resting on equal columns from end to end, yet when its whole length is seen from the top end, little by little it contracts to the pointed head of a narrow cone, joining roof with floor, and all the right hand with the left, until is has brought all together into the point of a cone that passes out of sight.

432 It happens to sailors on the sea that the sun seems to rise from the waves, and again to set in the waves, and hide its light; since verily they behold nothing else but water and sky; so that you must not lightly think that the senses waver at every point.

436 But to those who know not the sea, ships in the harbour

seem to press upon the water maimed, and with broken poop. For all the part of the oars which is raised up above the salt sea spray, is straight, and the rudders are straight above; but all that is sunk beneath the water, seems to be broken back and turned round, yes, and to turn upwards again and twist back so that it almost floats on the water's surface. And when winds in the night season carry scattered clouds across the sky, then the shining signs seem to glide athwart the storm-clouds, and to be moving on high in a direction far different from their true course.

446 Then if by chance a hand be placed beneath one eye and press it, it comes to pass by a new kind of perception that all things which we look at seem to become double as we look, double the lights of the lamps with their flowery flames, double the furniture throughout the whole house in twin sets, and double the faces of men, double their bodies.

453 Again, when sleep has bound our limbs in sweet slumber, and all the body lies in complete rest, yet then we seem to ourselves to be awake and moving our limbs, and in the blind gloom of night we think to see the sun and the light of day, and, though in some walled room, we seem to pass to new sky, new sea, new streams, and mountains, and on foot to cross over plains, and to hear sounds, when the stern silence of night is set all about us, and to give answer, when we do not speak.

462 Wondrously many other things of this sort we see, all of which would fain spoil our trust in the senses; all in vain, since the greatest part of these things deceives us on account of the opinions of the mind, which we add ourselves, so that things not seen by the senses are counted as seem. For nothing is harder than to distinguish things manifest from things uncertain, which the mind straightway adds to itself.

469 Again, if any one thinks that nothing is known, he knows not whether that can be known either, since he admits that he knows nothing. Against him then I will refrain from joining issue, who plants himself with his head in the place of his feet.

473 And yet were I to grant that he knows this too, yet I would ask this question. Since he has never before seen any truth in things, whence does he know what is knowing, and not

knowing each in turn? What thing has proved that the doubtful differs from the certain?

478 You will find that the concept of the true is begotten first from the senses, and that *the senses cannot be gainsaid*.[70] For something must be found with a greater surety, which can of its own authority refute the false by the true. Next then, what must be held to be of greater surety than sense? *Will reason, sprung from false sensation, avail to speak against the senses, when it is wholly sprung from the senses?* For unless they are true, all reason too becomes false. Or will the ears be able to pass judgement on the eyes? Or touch on the ears? Or again will the taste in the mouth refute this touch? Will the nostrils disprove it, or the eyes show it false? It is not so, I think. For each sense has its faculty set apart, each its own power, and so it must needs be that we perceive in one way what is soft or cold or hot, and in another the diverse colours of things, and see all that goes along with colour.

494 Likewise, the taste of the mouth has its power apart; in one way smells arise, in another sounds. And so it must needs be that one sense cannot prove another false. Nor again will they be able to pass judgement on themselves, since equal trust must at all times be placed in them. Therefore, whatever they have perceived on each occasion, is true. And if reason is unable to unravel the cause, why those things which close at hand were square, are seen round from a distance, still it is better through lack of reasoning to be at fault in accounting for the cause of either shape, rather than to let things clear seen slip abroad from your grasp, and to assail the grounds of belief, and to pluck up the whole foundations on which life and existence rest.

507 For not only would all reasoning fall away; life itself too would collapse straightway, unless you chose to trust the senses, and avoid headlong spots and all other things of this kind which must be shunned, and to make for what is opposite to these.

---

[70] The reliability of the senses is a crucial principle for the Epicureans. The thought in these lines is that reason is itself based on the senses, so if sensation is false or unreliable so must reason be. In a famous passage from Democritus quoted by Galen, Democritus has the senses reply to criticism, 'Poor mind, do you take your evidence from us and then try to overthrow us? Our overthrow is your fall.' For Democritus on knowledge and sensation (and as a precursor of Epicurus) see Jonathan Barnes, *Early Greek Philosophy* (Harmondsworth, 1987), pp. 244–88.

Know, then, that all this is but an empty store of words, which has been drawn up and arrayed against the senses.

513 Again, just as in a building, if the first ruler is awry, and if the square is wrong and out of the straight lines, if the level sags a whit in any place, it must needs be that the whole structure will be made faulty and crooked, all awry, bulging, leaning forwards or backwards, and out of harmony, so that some parts seem already to long to fall, or do fall, all betrayed by the first wrong measurements. Even thus your reasoning of things must be awry and false, when it springs from false senses.

522 Now it is left to explain in what manner the other senses perceive each their own object – a path by no means stony to tread.

524 First of all, every kind of sound and voice is heard, when they have found their way into the ears and struck upon the sense with their body. For that voice too and sound are bodily you must grant, since they can strike on the senses. Moreover, the voice often scrapes the throat and shouting makes the windpipe over-rough as it issues forth; since, indeed, the primordia of voices have risen up in greater throng through the narrow passsage, and begun to pass forth: and then, in truth, when the passages are crammed, the door too is scraped. There is no doubt then that voices and words are composed of bodily elements, so that they can hurt. And likewise it does not escape you how much body is taken away and drawn off from men's very sinews and strength by speech continued without pause from the glimmer of rising dawn to the shades of dark night, above all if it is poured out with loud shouting. And so the voice must needs be of bodily form, since one who speaks much loses a part from his body. Now roughness of voice comes from roughness in its primordia, and likewise smoothness is begotten of their smoothness. Nor do the primordia pierce the ears with like form, when the trumpet bellows deep with muffled tones, and when the barbarous Berecyntian pipe shrieks with shrill buzzing sound, and when the swans at night from the cold marches of Helicon lift with mournful voice their clear lament.

549 These voices then, when we force them forth from deep within our body, and shoot them abroad straight through our

mouth, the pliant tongue, artificer of words, severs apart, and the shaping of the lips in its turn gives them form. Therefore, when it is no long distance from which each single utterance starts and reaches to us, it must needs be that the very words too are clearly heard and distinguished sound by sound. For each utterance preserves its shaping and preserves its form. But if the space set between be over great, passing through much air, the words must needs be jostled together, and the utterance disordered, while it flies across the breezes. And so it comes to pass that you can perceive the sound, yet not distinguish what is the meaning of the words: so confounded and entangled does the utterance come to you.

563 Again one single word often awakes the ears of all in an assembly, shot out from the crier's mouth. Therefore one voice flies apart immediately into many voices, since it sunders itself into all the several ears, imprinting on the words a shape and a clear-cut sound. But that part of the voices which falls not straight upon the ears, passes by and perishes scattered in vain through the air.

570 Some beating upon solid spots are cast back, and give back the sound, and at times mock us with the echo of a word. And when you see this clearly, you could give account to yourself and others, in what manner among solitary places rocks give back the counterparts of words each in due order, when we seek our comrades wandering amid the dark hills, and with loud voice summon them scattered here and there.

577 I have seen places give back even six or seven cries, when you sent forth but one: so surely did one hill beat back to another and repeat the words trained to come back again. Such places the dwellers around fancy to be the haunt of goat-footed satyrs and nymphs, and they say that there are fauns, by whose clamour spreading through the night and sportive revels they declare that the dumb silence is often broken; and that sounds of strings are awakened, and sweet sad melodies, which the pipe pours forth, stopped by the fingers of players; and that the race of country folk hears far and wide, when Pan, tossing the piny covering of his half-monstrous head, ofttimes with curling lip runs over the open reeds, so that the pipe ceases not to pour forth woodland music.

590 All other marvels and prodigies of this kind they tell, lest

by chance they be thought to live in lonely places, deserted even of the gods. Therefore they boast such wonders in discourse, or else are led on in some other way, even as the whole race of man is over greedy for an audience.

595 For the rest, we need not wonder by what means voices come and arouse the ears through places, though which the eyes cannot see things clear to view. Often too we see a talk carried on through closed doors, because, we may be sure, voice can pass unharmed through winding pores in things, but simulacra refuse to pass. For they are torn asunder, unless they stream through straight pores, as are those in glass, through which every image can fly.

603 Moreover, a voice is severed in every direction, since voices are begotten one from another, when once one voice has issued forth and sprung apart into many, even as a spark of fire is often wont to scatter itself into its several fires. And so places hidden far from sight are filled with voices; they are in a ferment all around, alive with sound. But all simulacra press on in the direct line, as they have once been started. Therefore no one can see beyond the wall, but can perceive voices outside. And yet even this voice, while it passes through the walls of the house, is dulled, and enters the ear all confounded, and we seem to hear a sound rather than words.

615 Nor do the tongue and palate, whereby we perceive taste, need longer account or give more trouble. First of all we perceive taste in our mouth, when we press it out in chewing our food, just as if one by chance begins to squeeze with the hand and dry a sponge full of water. Then what we press out is all spread abroad through the pores of the palate. and through the winding passages of the loose-meshed tongue. Therefore, when the bodies of the oozing savour are smooth, they touch pleasantly, and pleasantly stroke all around the moist sweating vault above the tongue. But, on the other hand, the more each several thing is filled with roughness, the more does it prick the sense and tear it in its onslaught. Next pleasure comes from the savour within the limit of the palate; but when it has passed headlong down through the jaws, there is no pleasure while it is all being spread abroad into the limbs. Nor does it matter a whit with what diet the body is nourished, provided only you can digest what you

take, and spread it abroad in the limbs, and keep an even moistness in the stomach.

633 Now to explain how for different creatures there is different food and poison, or for what cause, what to some is noisome and bitter, can yet seem to others most sweet to eat. And there is herein a difference and disagreement so great that what is food to one, is to others biting posion; even as there is a certain serpent, which, when touched by a man's spittle, dies and puts an end to itself by gnawing its own body. Moreover, to us hellebore is biting poison, but it makes goats and quails grow fat.

642 That you may be able to learn by what means this comes to be, first of all it is right that you remember what we have said before now, that the seeds contained in things are mingled in many ways. Besides all living creatures which take food, just as they are unlike to outer view and a diverse outward contour of the limbs encloses them each after their kind, so also are they fashioned of seeds of varying shape. And further, since the seeds are unlike, so must the spaces and passages, which we call the openings, be different in all their limbs, and in the mouth and palate too. Some of these then must needs be smaller, some greater, they must be three-cornered for some creatures, square for others, many again round, and some of many angles in many ways. For according as the arrangement of shapes and the motions demand, so the shapes of the openings must needs differ, and the passages vary according to the texture which shuts them in. Therefore, when what is sweet to some becomes bitter to others, for the man to whom it is sweet, the smoothest bodies must needs enter the pores of the palate caressingly, but, on the other hand, for those to whom the same thing is sour within, we can be sure it is the rough and hooked bodies which penetrate the passages.

663 Now from these facts it is easy to learn of each case: thus when fever has attacked a man, and his bile rises high, or the violence of disease is aroused in some other way, then his whole body is disordered, and then all the positions of the primordia are changed about; it comes to pass that the bodies which before suited his taste, suit it no longer, and others are better fitted, which can win their way in and beget a sour taste.

For both kinds are mingled in the savour of honey; as I have often shown you above ere now.

673 Come now, I will tell in what manner the impact of smell touches the nostrils. First there must needs be many things whence the varying stream of scents flows and rolls on, and we must think that it is always streaming off and being cast and scattered everywhere abroad; but one smell is better fitted to some living things, another to others, on account of the unlike shapes of the types of primordium. And so through the breezes bees are drawn on however far by the scent of honey, and vultures by corpses. Then the strength of dogs sent on before leads on the hunters whithersoever the cloven hoof of the wild beasts has turned its steps; and the white goose, saviour of the citadel of Romulus's sons, scents far ahead the smell of man. So diverse scents assigned to diverse creatures lead on each to its own food, and constrain them to recoil from noisome poison, and in that way are preserved the races of wild beasts.

687 This very smell then, whenever it stirs the nostrils, may in one case be thrown further than in another. But yet no smell at all is carried as far as sound, as voice, I forebear to say as the bodies which strike the pupil of the eyes and stir the sight. For it strays abroad and comes but slowly, and dies away too soon, its frail nature scattered little by little among the breezes of air. Firstly, because coming from deep within it is not readily set loose from the thing. Nor that smells stream off and depart from things far beneath the surface is shown because all things seem to smell more when broken, when crushed, when melted in the fire. Again, one may see that it is fashioned of larger primordia than voice, since it does not find a path through stone walls, where voice and sound commonly pass. Wherefore too you will see that it is not so easy to trace in what spot that which smells has its place. For the blow grows cool as it dallies through the air, nor do tidings of things rush hot to the sense. And so dogs often go astray, and have a look for the footprints.

706 Yet this does not happen only among smells and in the class of savours, but likewise the forms and colours of things are not all so well fitted to the senses of all, but that certain of them are too pungent to the sight of some creatures. Nay,

indeed, ravening lions can by no means face and gaze upon the cock, whose wont it is with clapping wings to drive out the night, and with shrill cry to summon dawn; so surely do they at once bethink themselves of flight, because, we may be sure, there are in the body of cocks certain seeds, which, when they are cast into the eyes of lions, stab into the pupils, and cause sharp pain, so that they cannot bear up against them in fierce confidence; and yet these things cannot in any way hurt our eyes, either because they do not pierce them or because, although they do, a free outlet from the eyes is afforded them, so that they cannot by staying there hurt the eyes in any part.

THOUGHT AND THE FUNCTIONING OF MIND AND WILL, 722–1036

722 Come now, let me tell you what things stir the mind, and learn in a few words whence come the things which come into the understanding.

724 First of all I say this, that many simulacra of things wander about in many ways in all directions on every side, fine images, which easily bcome linked with one another in the air, when they come across one another's path, like spider's web and gold leaf. For indeed these simulacra are far finer in their texture than those which fill the eyes and arouse sight, since these pierce through the pores of the body and awake the fine nature of the mind within, and arouse its sensation.

732 And so we see Centaurs and the limbs of Scyllas, and the dog-faces of Cerberus and simulacra of those who have met death, and whose bones are held in the embrace of earth. This is because simulacra of every kind are borne everywhere, some which are created of their own accord even in the air, some which depart in each case from diverse things, and those again which are made and put together from the shapes of these. For in truth the image of the Centaur comes not from a living thing, since there never was the nature of such a living creature, but when by chance the images of man and horse have met, they cling together readily at once, as we have said ere now, because of their subtle nature and fine fabric. All other things of this kind are fashioned in the same way. And when they move nimbly with exceeding lightness, as I have shown ere now, any

one such subtle image stirs their mind; for the mind is fine and of itself wonderfully nimble.

749 That these things come to pass as I tell, you may easily learn from this. Inasmuch as the one is like the other, what we see with the mind, and what we see with the eyes, they must needs be created in like manner.

752 Now, therefore, since I have shown that I see a lion maybe, by means of simulacra, which severally stir the eyes, we may know that the mind is moved in like manner, in that it sees a lion and all else neither more nor less than the eyes, except that it sees finer simulacra.

757 And when sleep has relaxed the limbs, the understanding of the mind is for no other cause awake, but that these same simulacra stir our minds then, as when we are awake, insomuch that we seem surely to behold ever one who has quitted life, and is holden by death and the earth.

762 Nature constrains this to happen just because all the senses of the body are checked and at rest throughout the limbs, nor can they refute the falsehood by true facts. Moreover, the memory lies at rest, and is torpid in slumber, nor does it argue against us that he, whom the understanding believes that it beholds alive, has long ago won to death and doom. For the rest, it is not wonderful that the simulacra should move and toss their arms and their other limbs in rhythmic time. For it happens that the image in sleep seems to do this; inasmuch as when the first image passes away and then another comes to birth in a different posture, the former seems then to have changed its gesture. And indeed we must suppose that this happens in quick process: so great is the speed, so great the store of things, so great, in any one instant that we can perceive, the abundance of the little parts of images, whereby the supply may be continued.

777 And in these matters many questions are asked, and there are many things we must make clear, if we wish to set forth the truth plainly. First of all it is asked why, whatever the whim may come to each of us to think of, straightway his mind thinks of that very thing.

781 Do the simulacra keep watch on our will, and does the image rise up before us, as soon as we desire, whether it pleases

us to think of sea or land or sky? Gatherings of men, a procession, banquets, battles, does nature create all things at a word, and make them ready for us? And that too when in the same place and spot the minds of others thinking of things all far different.

788 What, again, when in sleep we behold simulacra dancing forward in rhythmic measure, and moving their supple limbs, when alternately they shoot out swiftly their supple arms, and repeat to the eyes a gesture made by the feet in harmony? So simulacra are steeped in art, and wander about trained to be able to tread their dance in the nighttime!

794 Or will this be nearer truth? Within a single *time*, which we perceive, that is, when a single word is uttered, many *times* lie unnoted, which reasoning discovers. Therefore it comes to pass that in any time, however small, the several primordia are there ready at hand in all the several spots. So great is the speed, so great the store of things.

800 Therefore when the first image passes away and then another comes to birth in a different posture, the former seems then to have changed its gesture. Again, because they are fine, the mind cannot discern them sharply, save those which it strains to see; therefore all that there are besides these pass away, save those for which it has made itself ready. Moreover, the mind makes itself ready, and hopes it will come to pass that it will see what follows upon each several thing; therefore it comes to be.

807 Do you not see the eyes too, when they begin to perceive things which are fine, strain themselves and make themselves ready, and that without that it cannot come to pass that we see things sharply? And yet even in things plain to see you might notice that, if you do not turn your mind to them, it is just as if the thing were sundered from you all the time, and very far away. How then is it strange, if the mind loses all else, save only the things to which it is itself given up? Then too on small signs we base wide opinions, and involve ourselves in the snare of self-deceit.

818 It happens too that from time to time an image of a different kind rises before us, and what was before a woman, seems now to have become a man before our very eyes, or else

one face or age follows after another. But that we should not think this strange, sleep and its forgetfulness secure.

823 Herein you must eagerly desire to shun this fault, and with foresighted fear to avoid this error. Do not think that the bright light of the eyes was created in order that we may be able to look before us,[71] or that, in order that we may have power to plant long paces, therefore the tops of shanks and thighs, based upon the feet, are able to bend. Or again, that the forearms are jointed to the strong upper arms and hands given us to serve us on either side in order that we might be able to do what was needful for life.

832 All other ideas of this sort, which men proclaim, by distorted reasoning set effect for cause, since nothing at all was born in the body that we might be able to use it, but what is born creates its own use. Nor did sight exist before the light of the eyes was born, nor pleading in words before the tongue was created, but rather the birth of the tongue came long before discourse, and the ears were created much before sound was heard, and in short all the limbs, I maintain, existed before their use came about. They cannot then have grown for the purpose of using them.

842 But, on the other side, to join hands in the strife of battle, to mangle limbs and befoul the body with gore; these things were known long before gleaming darts flew abroad, and nature constrained men to avoid a wounding blow, before the left arm, trained by art, held up the defence of a shield. And of a surety to trust the tired body to rest was a habit far older than the soft-spread bed, and the slaking of the thirst was born before

---

[71] The argument in lines 823–57 that natural things, including the appropriately devised features of living things, *find* uses while artifacts are *given* them by the design of intelligent animals, is important. Not only is it distancing the Epicureans from Stoic versions of the design argument for the existence of God (see Cicero, *De Natura Deorum*, II, 87–115), but it is also, ultimately, opening the way to a natural selection theory of the evolution of life. Such a rejection of purposes in nature was not unique to the Epicureans. It is also characteristic of, for example, Strato of Lampsacus (a successor of Artistotle and contemporary of Epicurus himself). The Epicurean contentions were that the natural universe neither needed nor could be given an external explanation such as being made for our convenience, *and* that its apparently purposeful individual features had merely acquired useful functions, not been made or designed for them.

cups. These things, then, which are invented to suit the needs of life, might well be thought to have been discovered for the purpose of using them. But all those other things lie apart, which were first born themselves, and thereafter revealed the concept of their usefulness. In this class first of all we see the senses and the limbs; wherefore, again and again, it cannot be that you should believe that they could have been created for the purpose of useful service.

858 This, likewise, is no cause for wonder, that the nature of the body of every living thing of itself seeks food. For indeed I have shown that many bodies ebb and pass away from things in many ways, but most are bound to pass from living creatures. For because they are sorely tried by motion and many bodies by sweating are squeezed and pass out from deep beneath, many are breathed out through their mouths, when they pant in weariness; by these means then the body grows less, and all the nature is undermined; and on this follows pain. Therefore food is taken to support the limbs and renew strength when it passes within, and to muzzle the gaping desire for eating through all the limbs and veins. Likewise, moisture spreads into all the spots which demand moisture; and the many gathered bodies of heat, which furnish the fires to our stomach, are scattered by the incoming moisture, and quenched like a flame, that the dry heat may no longer be able to burn our body. Thus then the panting thirst is washed away from our body, thus the hungry yearning is satisfied.

877 Next, I will explain how it comes to pass that we are able to plant our steps forward, when we wish, how it is granted us to move our limbs in diverse ways, and what force is wont to thrust forward this great bulk of our body. Attend to my words.
    880 I say that first of all simulacra of walking fall upon our mind, and strike the mind, as we have said before. Then comes the will; for indeed no one begins to do anything, before the mind has seen beforehand what it will do, and inasmuch as it sees this beforehand, an image of the thing is formed. And so, when the mind stirs itself so that it wishes to start and step forward, it straightway strikes the force of the anima which is spread abroad in the whole body throughout limbs and frame.

And that is easy to do, since it is held in union with it. Then the anima goes on and strikes the body, and so little by little the whole mass is thrust forward and set in movement.

892 Moreover, at such times the body too becomes rarefied, and air (as indeed it needs must do, since it is always quick to move), comes through the opened spaces, and pierces through the passages in abundance, and so it is scattered to all the tiny parts of the body. Here then it is brought about by two causes acting severally, that the body, like a ship, is borne on by sails and wind. Nor yet herein is this cause for wonder; that such tiny bodies can twist about a body so great, and turn round the whole mass of us. For in very truth the wind that is finely wrought of a subtle body drives and pushes on a great ship of great bulk, and a single hand steers it, with whatever speed it be moving, and twists a single helm whithersoever it will; and by means of pulleys and tread-wheels a crane can move many things of great weight, and lift them up with light poise.

907 Now in what ways this sleep floods repose over the limbs, and lets loose the cares of the mind from the breast, I will proclaim in verses of sweet discourse, rather than in many; even as the brief song of the swan is better than the clamour of cranes, which spreads abroad among the cloud of the south high in heaven. Do you lend me a fine ear and an eager mind, lest you should deny that what I say can be, and with a breast that utterly rejects the words of truth part company with me, when you are yourself in error and cannot discern.

916 First of all sleep comes to pass when the strength of the anima is scattered about among the limbs, and in part has been cast out abroad and gone its way, and in part has been pushed back and passed inward deeper within the body. For then indeed the limbs are loosened and droop. For there is no doubt that this sense exists in us, thanks to the anima; and when sleep hinders it from being, then we must suppose that the anima is disturbed and cast out abroad: yet not all of it; for then the body would lie bathed in the eternal chill of death. For indeed, when no part of the anima stayed behind hidden in the limbs, as fire is hidden when choked beneath much ashes, whence could sense on a sudden be kindled again throughout the limbs, as flame can rise again from a secret fire?

929 But by what means this new state of things is brought about, and whence the anima can be disturbed and the body grow slack, I will unfold: be it your care that I do not scatter my words to the winds.

932 First of all it must needs be that the body on the outer side, since it is touched close at hand by the breezes of air, is thumped and buffeted by its oft-repeated blows, and for this cause it is that wellnigh all things are covered either by a hide, or else by shells, or by a hard skin, or by bark. Further, as creatures breathe, the air at the same time smites on the inner side, when it is drawn in and breathed out again. Wherefore, since the body is buffeted on both sides alike, and since the blows pass on through the tiny pores to the first parts and first particles of our body, little by little there comes to be, as it were, a falling asunder throughout our limbs. For the positions of the primary particles of body and mind are disordered. Then it comes to pass that a portion of the anima is cast out abroad, and part retreats and hides within; part too, torn asunder through the limbs, cannot be united in itself, nor by motion act and react; for nature bars its meetings and chokes the ways; and so, when the motions are changed, sense withdraws deep within. And since there is nothing which can, as it were, support the limbs, the body grows feeble, and all the limbs are slackened; arms and eyelids droop, and the hams, even as you lie down, often give way, and relax their strength. Again, sleep follows after food, because food brings about just what air does, while it is being spread into all the veins, and the slumber which you take when full or weary, is much heavier because then more bodies than ever are disordered, bruised with the great effort. In the same manner the anima comes to be in part thrust deeper within; it is also more abundantly driven out abroad, and is more divided and torn asunder in itself within.

962 And for the most part to whatever pursuit each man clings and cleaves, or on whatever things we have before spent much time, so that the mind was more strained in the task than is its wont, in our sleep we seem mostly to traffic in the same things. Lawyers think that they plead their cases and confront law with law. Generals that they fight and engage in battles. Sailors that they pass a life of conflict waged with winds. And we, that we pursue our task and seek for the nature of things forever, and set it forth, when it is found, in writings in our country's tongue.

971 Thus for the most part all other pursuits and arts seem to hold the minds of men in delusion during their sleep. And if ever men have for many days in succession given interest unflagging to the games, we see for the most part, that even when they have ceased to apprehend them with their senses, yet there remain open passages in their minds, whereby the same images of things may enter in. And so for many days the same sights pass before their eyes, so that even wide awake they think they see men dancing and moving their supple limbs, and drink in with their ears the clear-toned chant of the lyre, and its speaking strings, and behold the same assembly and at the same time the diverse glories of the stage all bright before them. So exceeding great is the import of zeal and pleasure, and the task wherein not only men are wont to spend their efforts, but even every living animal.

987 In truth you will see strong horses, when their limbs are lain to rest, yet sweat in their sleep, and pant for ever, and strain every nerve as though for victory, or else as though the barriers were opened [struggle to start]. And hunters' dogs often in their soft sleep yet suddenly toss their legs, and all at once give tongue, and again and again snuff the air with their nostrils, as if they had found and were following the tracks of wild beasts. Yes, roused from slumber they often pursue empty images of stags, as though they saw them in eager flight, until they shake off the delusion and return to themselves. But the fawning brood of pups brought up in the house, in a moment shake their body and lift it from the ground, just as if they beheld unknown forms and faces. And the wilder any breed may be, the more must it needs rage in its sleep. But the diverse tribes of birds fly off, and on a sudden in the night time trouble the peace of the groves of the gods, if in their gentle sleep they have seen hawks, flying in pursuit, offer fight and battle.

1011 Moreover, the minds of men, which with mighty movement perform mighty tasks, often in sleep do and dare just the same. Kings storm towns, are captured, join battle, raise a loud cry, as though being murdered – all without moving. Many men fight hard, and utter groans through their pain, and, as though they were bitten by the teeth of a panther or savage lion, fill all around them with their loud cries. Many in their sleep discourse of high affairs, and very often have been witness to their own guilt. Many meet death. Many, as though they were falling headlong with all their body from high mountains to the earth, are besides themselves with fear, and, as though bereft of reason, scarcely recover themselves from sleep, quivering with the turmoil of their body. Likewise a thirsty man sits down besides a stream or a pleasant spring, and gulps almost the whole river down his throat.

1026[72] Perfectly clean children, if deeply asleep, often think they are lifting their clothes at a latrine or a shallow pot, and pour forth the filtered liquid from their whole body, and the Babylonian coverlets of rich beauty are soaked. Later on, to boys, into the channel of whose life the vital seed is passing for the first time, when the ripeness of time has created it in their limbs, there come from without images, from other bodies, promising an exquisite face or a fair complexion. These excite and rouse their members swelling with much seed, and often, as though all were consummated, they pour forth great waves of fluid and mark their clothes.

SEX AND ITS TROUBLES,[73] 1037–287

1037 That seed is stirred in us, whereof we spoke before, when the age of manhood first strengthens our limbs. For one cause

---

[72] In lines 1026–57 and 1103–14 neither Bailey's 1921 translation nor his mildly revised version of 1947 comfortably embrace Lucretius' natural and relaxed language. The present Editor must therefore be held largely responsible for the wording here, and again in VI, 1207.

[73] Book IV, from line 1037 to the conclusion, is often interpreted as the writing of a man satiated with sex, or thwarted in love, or otherwise made bitter and almost unbalanced about sexual relations. This view may be partly the source of, and partly caused by, the unsupported anecdote of St Jerome (c. 342–420) that Lucretius died as a result of a love potion, having composed his poem in lucid intervals between periods of madness. But look closely at lines 1192–209 and the conclusion from line 1278 onwards (and see also V, 854). In the first passage Lucretius contrasts the fraught and violent selfishness of the excessive passion earlier described with what is kind and normal and mutually pleasing in human relationships. In the second passage there is a most touching gentleness and compassion towards what is ordinary, regular and domestic (see also III, 894–6). Violent love destroys; Epicurean friendship – gentle, considerate and constant – even when it properly involves sexual love, makes a long life glad. This is exactly what we would expect Lucretius to argue as an Epicurean, and the vividness of his picture of sexual misery is, I would suggest, more

moves and rouses one thing, a different cause another. From the human body only the influence of a human body stirs seed. And as soon as it issues, roused from its abode, it makes its way from out the whole body through the limbs and frame, coming together into fixed places, and straightway rouses at last the genital parts of the body. These places are stimulated and swell with seed, and there arises the desire to expel the seed towards the object to which fierce passion is moved, and the body seeks that body, by which the mind is smitten with love. For as a rule all men fall towards the wound, and the blood spirts out in that direction, whence we are struck by the blow, and, if it is near at hand, the red stream reaches our foe. Thus, then, he who receives a blow from the darts of Venus, be it a boy with feminine limbs who smites him, or a woman darting love from her whole body, inclines to that whereby he is smitten, and strives to join with it and cast the fluid drawn from his body into the other. For an unspeakable desire foretells the pleasure to come.

1058 This pleasure is Venus for us; from it comes Cupid [desire], our name for love, from it first of all that drop of Venus' sweetness has trickled into our heart and chilly care has followed after. For if the object of your love is away, yet images of her are at hand, her loved name is present to your ears. But it is best to flee those images, and scare away from you what feeds your love, and to turn your mind some other way, and vent your passion on other objects, and not to keep it, set once for all on the love of one, and thereby store up for yourself care and certain pain. For the sore gains strength and festers by feeding, and day by day the madness grows, and the misery becomes heavier, unless you can dissipate the first wounds by new strokes and heal them while still fresh by dallying after easy sex, or else can turn the movements of the mind elsewhere.

the vividness of a great writer than the personal outpourings of an unbalanced personality. As Shelley remarks in his 'A Defence of Poetry' (1812): ' A man . . . must imagine intensely and comprehensively; he must put himself in the place of another and of many others; the pains and pleasures of his species must become his own.'

1073 Nor is he who shuns love bereft of the fruits of Venus, but rather he chooses those joys which bring no pain. For surely the pleasure from these things is more untainted for the heart-whole than for the love-sick; for in the very moment of possession the passion of lovers ebbs and flows with undetermined current, nor are they sure what first to enjoy with eyes or hands. What they have grasped, they closely press and cause pain to the body, and often fasten their teeth in the lips, and dash mouth against mouth in kissing, because their pleasure is not straightforward, and there are secret stings which spur them to hurt even the very thing, be it what it may, whence arise those germs of madness.

1084 But Venus lightly breaks the force of these pains in love, and found pleasure mingled with them sets a curb upon their teeth. For therein there is hope that from the same body, whence comes the source of their flame, the fire may in turn be quenched. Yet nature protests that all this happens just the other way; and this is the one thing, whereof the more and more we have, the more does our heart burn with the cursed desire. For meat and drink are taken within the limbs; and since they are able to take up their abode in certain parts, thereby the desire for water and bread is easily sated. But from the face and beauteous bloom of man nothing passes into the body to be enjoyed save delicate images; and often his love-sick hope scatters them to the winds. Just as when in a dream a thirsty man seeks to drink and no liquid is granted him, which could allay the fire in his limbs, but he seeks after images of water, and struggles in vain, and is still thirsty, though he drinks amid the torrent stream, even so in love Venus mocks the lovers with images, nor can they sate their body, though they gaze on the loved body with all their eyes. Nor can they tear off anything from the tender limbs, as they wander with uncertain hands over all the body.

1105 Even at last with limbs entwined, when lovers taste the flower of their years, when the body has a forestate of its joy, and Venus is on the point of sowing the woman's furrows, eagerly they clasp and mingle the slaver of their mouths, and pressing lip on lip breathe deeply. Yet all is for nothing, since they cannot take anything away, nor enter in and dissolve, merging the whole body in the other's body. For at times they

seem to strive and struggle to do this, so eagerly are they locked
in the fetters of love, while their limbs are loosed and slackened
by the force of their delight. And at length when the gathering
desire has burst from their limbs, then for a while comes a little
respite in their furious passion. Then the same madness returns,
the old frenzy is back upon them, when they yearn to find out
what in truth they desire to attain, nor can they discover what
device may conquer their disease; in such deep doubt they waste
beneath their secret wound.

1121 Remember too that they waste their stength and are worn
away with effort, remember that their life is passed beneath
another's sway. Meanwhile their substance slips away, and is
turned to Babylonian coverlets, their duties grow slack, and
their fair name totters and sickens: while on the mistress's feet
sandals laugh, and lovely Sicyonian slippers; yes, and huge
emeralds with their green flash are set in gold, and the sea-dark
dress is for ever being frayed, and roughly used it drinks in
sweat. The well-gotten wealth of their fathers becomes hair-
ribbons and diadems; sometimes it is turned to Greek robes and
stuffs of Elis and Ceos. With gorgeous napery and delicacies
feasts are set out, and games and countless cups, perfumes, and
wreaths and garlands; all in vain, since from the heart of this
fountain of delights wells up some bitter taste to choke them
even amid the flowers – either when the conscience-stricken
mind feels the bite of remorse that life is being spent in sloth,
and is passing to ruin in wantonness, or because she has thrown
out some idle word and left its sense in doubt, and it is planted
deep in the passionate heart, and becomes alive like a flame, or
because he thinks she casts her eyes around too freely, and looks
upon some other, or sees in her face some trace of laughter.

1141 And these ills are found in love that is true and fully
prosperous. But when love is crossed and hopeless there are ills,
which you might detect even with closed eyes, ills without
number. So it is better to be on the watch beforehand, even as I
have taught you, and to beware that you be not entrapped. For
to avoid being drawn into the meshes of love, is not so hard a
task as when caught amid the toils to issue out and break
through the strong bonds of Venus. And yet even when tram-

melled and fettered you might escape the snare, unless you still stand in your own way, and at first overlook all the blemishes of mind and body in her, whom you seek and woo.

1153 For of the most part men act blinded by passion, and assign to women excellencies which are not truly theirs. And so we see those in many ways deformed and ugly dearly loved, yes even prospering in high favour. And one man laughs at another, and urges him to appease Venus, since he is wallowing in a base passion. Yet often, poor wretch, he cannot see his own ills, far greater than the rest.

1159 A black love is called 'honey-dark', the foul and filthy 'unadorned', the green-eyed 'Athena's image', the wiry and wooden 'a gazelle', the squat and dwarfish 'one of the graces', 'all pure delight', the lumpy and ungainly 'a wonder', and 'full of majesty'. She stammers and cannot speak, 'she has a lisp'; the dumb is 'modest'; the fiery, spiteful gossip is 'a burning torch'. One becomes a 'slender darling', when she can scarce live from consumption; another half dead with cough is 'frail'. Then the fat and full-bosomed is 'Ceres' self with Bacchus at breast'; the snub-nosed is 'sister to Silenus, or a Satyr'; the thick-lipped is 'a living kiss'. More of this sort it were tedious for me to try to tell.

1171 But yet let her be fair of face as you will, and from her every limb let the power of Venus issue forth: yet surely there are others like her? Surely we have lived without her before? Surely she does just the same in all things, and we know it, as an ugly woman? And of herself, poor wretch, she reeks of noisome smells, and her maids flee far from her and giggle in secret. But the tearful lover, denied entry, often smothers the threshold with flowers and garlands, and anoints the haughty door-posts with marjoram, and plants his kisses, poor wretch, upon the doors. Yet if, admitted at last, one single breath should meet him as he comes, he would seek some honest pretext to be gone, and the deep-drawn lament long-planned would fall idle, and then and there he would curse his folly, because he sees that he has assigned more to her than it is right to grant to any mortal.

1185 Nor is all this unknown to our Venuses, and that is why they are at pains to hide all behind the scenes from those whom they wish to keep fettered in love; all for naught, since you can even so by thought bring it all to light and seek the cause of all this laughter, and if she is of a fair mind, and not spiteful, overlook faults in your turn, and pardon human weaknesses.

1192 Nor does the woman sigh always with feigned love, when clasping her lover she unites her limbs with his and clings to him, as she sucks his lips and showers wet kisses. For often she does it from the heart, and yearning for mutual joys she woos him to reach the goal of love. And in no other way would birds, cattle, wild beasts, the flocks, and mares be able to submit to the males, except because their nature too is afire, and is burning to overflow, and greets the passion of the male with reluctant joy. Do you not see too how those whom mutual pleasure has bound, are often tortured in their common bonds? For dogs often at the cross-roads, longing to part, eagerly pull different ways with all their might, yet all the while they are locked in the strong fetters of love. This they could never do, unless they knew mutual joys, which could lure them to their hurt, and hold them fast in chains. Wherefore, again and again, as I say, the pleasure is common.

1209 And often when in the mingling of sex the woman perchance by sudden force has mastered the man's might and seized on it with her own, then children are born like the mother, thanks to the mother's seed, just as the father's seed may make them like the father. But those whom you see with the form of both, mingling side by side the features of both parents, spring alike from the father's body and the mother's blood, when mutual passion breathing in consort, has dashed together the seeds roused throughout the limbs by the goads of love, and neither has overcome or been overcome. It comes to pass too sometimes that they can be created like their grandparents, and often recall the form of their grandparents' parents, for the reason that many first-beginnings in many ways are often mingled and concealed in the body of their parents, which, starting from the stock of the race, father hands on to father; therefrom Venus unfolds forms with varying chance, and recalls the look, the voice, the hair of ancestors; since indeed these things are none the more created from a seed determined than are our faces and bodies and limbs. Again the female sex may spring from the father's seed, and males come forth formed from the mother's body. For every offspring is fashioned of the two seeds, and whichever of the two that which is created more resembles, of that parent it has more than an equal share; as you can yourself discern, whether it be a male offspring or a female birth.

1233 Nor do powers divine deny to any man a fruitful sowing of seed, that he may never be called father by sweet children, but must live out his years in barren wedlock; as men believe for the most part, and sorrowing sprinkle the altars with streams of blood and fire the high places with their gifts, that they may make their wives pregnant with bounteous seed. Yet all in vain they weary the majesty of the gods and their sacred lots.

1240 For some men are barren through seed overthick, and again overliquid and thin in turn. The thin seed, because it cannot fix its fastenings, suddenly trickles away and retracing its path departs abortively. Further since for others seed too thick is emitted, either it does not shoot forward with such far-reaching blow, or else it cannot equally penetrate to vital spots, of having penetrated it mingles ill with the woman's seed. For the couplings in wedlock are seen to be very diverse. Some men cause some women to conceive more easily; some women from some men more readily receive their burden and grow pregnant. And many women have been barren in several wedlocks before, yet at length have found a mate from whom they might conceive children, and grow rich with sweet offspring. And often too there have been men whose fertile wives had been unable to bear them children, but a well-matched partner has been found, so that they might fortify their old age with children. Of so great import is it that the one seed should be able to mingle with the other in a manner suited for generation, and that thick should unite with liquid and liquid with thick. And herein it is of import on what diet life is sustained; for on some food seeds swell within the limbs and on others they are thinned away and grow weak instead.

1263 And in what way even the enticing act of love is performed, that too is of great import; since for the most part it is thought that women conceive best after the fashion of beasts and in the manner of quadrupeds, because the seeds can thus take up their position, when the breast is below and the loins are raised. Nor have wives any need at all for lascivious movements. For the woman prevents herself from conceiving and fights against it, if despite her joy she withdraws from the man's organ with her buttocks, and receives the seminal fluid with her breast all relaxed. For thus she drives the furrow of the plough from the true direction of the path, and turns aside the blow of seed from the vital parts. Such motions whores are wont to make for their own sake, that they be not filled with seed and lie pregnant, and also that the act of love may be more seductive to men. But nought of this is seen to be needful for our wives.

1278 Sometimes it is by no divine act or through the shafts of Venus that a woman of form less fair is loved. For at times a woman may bring it about by her own doing, by her yielding ways, and the neat adornment of her body, that she accustoms you easily to live your life with her. Nay more, habit alone can win love; for that which is struck ever and again by a blow, however light, is yet mastered in long lapse of time, and gives way. Do you not see too how drops of water falling upon rocks in long lapse of time drill through the rocks?

BOOK V

The Natural Origins
Of The World, Life And Society

Synopsis

1–54   Address to Epicurus [verse translation by Charles Foxley, 1933].

55–75   Review of subjects past and to come.

76–90   We must appreciate that laws of nature, not divine intervention, account for events.

The Nature of Gods and the Natural History of this World System, 91–508

91–109   The ultimate destiny of this world is total dissolution.

110–45   The world is not an immortal divine being: stones, water and the sun's fire are not minds or intelligent gods.

146–55   The nature of the gods precludes them from doing anything in the world.

156–94   The gods had no need to create the world for uncreated beings like men who could know no need for their own creation.

195–234   Anyway, flaws in the world show it was not fashioned for us by divine grace.

235–415   The whole nature of the world, and all apparently permanent things, are subject to a beginning, development, decay and dissolution. Illustrations of this.

416–31   Primordia do not assemble in order with foreseeing mind, but sometimes happen to combine in ways which begin the development of a world.

432–48   In the beginning the world [*mundus*, approximately 'our galaxy'] was a fresh-formed storm of primordial particles.

449–508   Out of which the earth [*tellus*], sun, moon, stars and all the natural features of this earth slowly formed.

The Nature and Movement of Celestial Bodies, 509–779

509–33   Conjectural account of astral motions.

534–63   Relation between the earth and the world.

564–771   Of the size of the sun and moon, and the possible explanations of their relative powers, of the seasons and of eclipses.

The Beginnings of Life and the Origin of Man, 772–1010

772–820   First came herbage from the earth, then birds and animals.

821–36   But the earth, like all things, moves on to less productive old age.

837–77   The earth also produces deformities that cannot survive or procreate along with the well-adapted.

878–924   Monsters, the amalgam of two genera of living things, were never possible.

925–1010   The race of man was in its beginning like other wild animals: without laws or religious fears; without organized killing in wars, or navigation or artifacts.

The Development of Civil Society, 1011–457

1011–27   How communities of human beings developed.

1028–90   The natural development of language.

1091–104   Men acquired fire from lightning or friction.

1105–135   Property, and the evolution of self-destroying ambition for power, came next.

1136–60   But universal disorder is constrained by law, fear of punishment and a compact to keep the peace.

1161–240   The natural origins of religion and the source of fear of gods.

1241–296   Discovery of metals and their use in war.

1297–349   The harnessing of horses and the use of wild animals in war.

1350–60   Fabric and clothing.

1361–78   Agriculture and horticulture.

1379–1411   Music.

1412–35   The damaging growth of toil after possessions: we need so little, but seek so much that wars are let loose.

1436–57   The seasons give a profounder order than the histories of wars, and little by little civilization progresses.

Book V

Can genius burn with so intense a beam
Can human eloquence be framed so strong
That words may match the grandeur of the theme,
And these discov'ries hail in worthy song,
Nor do the name of Epicurus wrong,
Who left us fruits from inborn wisdom sprung
And prizes of research pursued so long?
For ever must his glories be unsung,
If I should be the judge, by bards of mortal tongue.

For if we given him his due meed of fame,
And recognize all that the majesty
Of his achievements may most justly claim,
A god, great Memmius, yea a god was he,
The pioneer of true philosophy,
That reasoned plan of life so named aright,
Who by his skill achieved our liberty
From such rough waves and from so black a night
To so serene a calm, so fair and clear a light.

Take the old stories of each godlike gift.
From Ceres corn, from Bacchus we derive
Our wine. Without them we could still make shift;
Some nations lack them both and yet survive.
But foul of heart, who lives is not alive.
Diviner honours then shall crown the head
Of him who taught us how our lives may thrive.
From him through mighty peoples yet are spread
Heart-joys whereby our lives are soothed and comforted.

But if thou plead the word of Hercules,
Away from truth thou driftest all the more.
Can that great lion's jaws disturb our ease,
Which gaping wide through Nemea's woods did roar?
Crete's gruesome bull? Arcadia's bristly boar?
Though fenced with pois'nous fangs of many a snake,

What wrath on us could hideous hydra pour,
  The hundred-headed pest of Lerna's lake?
What toll could monstrous force of triple Geryon take?

  Our danger's not Stymphalian birds unblest,
  Fire-breathing steeds of Diomed in Thrace,
  Gold-gleaming apples of the maids o' th' West;
  What though grisly serpent, fierce of face,
  Round the tree-trunk had coiled his huge embrace
  Beside th' Atlantic shore and Ocean rude,
  No home of ours nor haunt of barb'rous race?
  The slain of Hercules, the whole weird brood,
What worse were we if these were living unsubdued?

  No whit, say I; This Earth doth so abound
  E'en now with savage beasts and quivering fear
  In groves and mountains vast and woods profound;
  To such our duty seldom calls us near.
  But, if the heart's uncleansed, what battles here
  Await us, and what perils make their way
  Unbidden to the mind, a forest drear
  Infested by fierce lusts that rend and slay
With life devouring care and horrible dismay!

  Of sloth, of luxury's deceitful charms,
  Of petulance, impurity and pride
  The ravages how great! By words, not arms,
  These monsters of the mind being swept aside,
  'Tis meet their conq'ror should be deified,
  The more that he was wont, in words of gold,
  Of gods, who in immortal bliss abide,
  Divinely to discourse, and to unfold
The whole of Nature's work for mortals to behold.

55 In his footsteps I tread, and while I follow his reasonings
and set out in my discourse, by what law all things are created,
and how they must needs abide by it, nor can they break
through the firm ordinances of their being. First of all, the nature
of the mind has been found to be formed and created above
other things but with a body that has birth, and to be unable to

endure unharmed through the long ages. However, in sleep images are wont to deceive the mind, when we seem to behold one whom life has left.

64 For what remains, the train of my reasoning has now brought me to this point, that I must give account how the world is made of mortal body and also came to birth; and in what ways that gathering of matter established earth, sky, sea, stars, sun, and the ball of the moon. Then what living creatures sprang from the earth, and which have never been born at any time; and in what manner the race of men began to use ever-varying speech one to another by naming things; and in what ways that fear of the gods found its way into their breasts, which throughout the circle of the world keeps revered shrines, lakes, groves, altars, and images of the gods.

76 Moreover, I will unfold by what power nature, the helmsman, steers the courses of the sun and the wanderings of the moon; lest by chance we should think that they of their own will between earth and sky fulfil their courses from year to year, with kindly favour to the increase of earth's fruits and living creatures, or should suppose that they roll on by any forethought of the gods. For those who have learnt aright that the gods lead a life free from care, if from time to time they wonder by what means all things can be carried on, above all among those things which are descried above our head in the coasts of heaven, they are yet borne back again into the old beliefs of religion, and adopt stern overlords, whom in their misery they believe have all the power, knowing not what can be and what cannot, yea and in what way each thing has its power limited, and its deep-set boundary-stone.

THE NATURE OF GODS AND THE NATURAL HISTORY OF THIS WORLD SYSTEM, 91–508

91 For the rest, that I delay you no more with promises, first of all look upon seas, and lands, and sky; their threefold nature, their three bodies, Memmius, their three forms so diverse, their three textures so vast, one single day shall hurl all to ruin; and the massive form and fabric of the world, held up for many years, shall fall headlong. Nor does it escape me in my mind,

how strangely and wonderfully this strikes upon the understanding, the destruction of heaven and earth that is to be, and how
hard it is for me to prove it with certainty in my discourse; even
as it always happens, when you bring to men's ears something
unknown before, and yet you cannot place it before the sight of
their eyes, nor lay hands upon it. For by this way the paved path
of belief leads straightest into the heart of man and the quarters
of his mind. Yet still I will speak out. Maybe the fact itself will
give credence to my words, that earthquakes will arise and
within a little you will behold all things shaken in mighty shock.
But may fortune at the helm steer this far away from us, and
may reasoning rather than a mere instance make us believe that
all things can fall with a hideous rending crash.

110 Yet before I begin to utter my oracles on this matter, with
reasoning far more sure than the Pythian priestess who speaks
out from the tripod and laurel of Phoebus, I will unfold many a
solace for you in wise words; lest by chance, restrained by
religion, you should think that earth and sun, and sky, sea, stars,
and moon must needs abide for everlasting, because of their
divine body, and therefore should suppose it right that after the
manner of the giants[74] all should pay penalty for their monstrous
crime, who by their reasoning shake the walls of the world, and
would fain quench the glorious sun in heaven, branding things
immortal with mortal names.

122 Yet these are things so far separate from divine power,
and are so unworthy to be reckoned among gods, that rather
they are able to give us the concept of what it is to be far
removed from vital motion and sense. For indeed it cannot be
that we should suppose that the nature of mind and understanding can be linked with every bodily thing; even as a tree cannot
exist in the sky, nor clouds in the salt waters, nor can fishes live
in the fields, nor blood be present in wood nor sap in stones. It
is determined and ordained where each thing can grow and have
its place. So the nature of mind cannot come to birth alone
without body, nor exist far apart from sinews and blood. But if

---

[74] The giants were a mythical race, hideous in appearance and of great strength.
After an unsuccessful war with the Olympian gods they were entombed beneath
volcanoes in Greece and Italy.

this could be, far sooner might the force of mind itself exist in head or shoulders, or right down in the heels, and be wont to be born in any part you will, but at least remain in the same man or the same vessel. But since even within our body it is determined and seen to be ordained where anima and mind can dwell apart and grow, all the more must we deny that outside the whole body and the living creature's form, it could last on in the crumbling sods of earth or in the fire of the sun or in water or in the high coasts of heaven. They are not then created endowed with divine feeling, inasmuch as they cannot be quickened with the sense of life.

146 This, too, it cannot be that you should believe, that there are holy abodes of the gods in any parts of the world. For the fine nature of the gods, far sundered from our senses, is scarcely seen by the understanding of the mind. And since it lies far beneath all touch or blow from our hands, it cannot indeed touch anything which can be touched by us. For nothing can touch which may not itself be touched. Therefore even their abodes too must needs be unlike our abodes, fine even as are their bodies; all which I will hereafter prove to you with plenteous argument.[75]

156 Further, to say that for man's sake they were willing to fashion the glorious nature of the world, and for that reason it is fitting to praise the work of the gods, which is worthy to be praised, and to believe that it will be everlasting and immortal, and that it is sin ever to stir from its seats by any force what was established for the races of men for all time by the ancient wisdom of gods, or to assail it with argument, and to overthrow it from top to bottom; to imagine and to add all else of this sort, Memmius, is but foolishness.

165 For what profit could our thanks bestow on the immortal and blessed ones, that they should essay to do anything for our sakes? Or what new thing could have enticed them so long after, when they were aforetime at rest, to desire to change their former life? For it is clear that he must take joy in new things,

[75] But he does not, at least in the poem as it has come down to us. See note 97 at the end of Book VI.

to whom the old are painful. But for him, whom no sorrow has befallen in the time gone by, when he led a life of happiness, for such a one, what could have kindled a passion for new things? Or what ill had it been to us never to have been made? Did our life, indeed, lie wallowing in darkness and grief, until the first creation of things dawned upon us?

177 For whosoever has been born must needs wish to abide in life, so long as enticing pleasure shall hold him. But for him, who has never tasted the love of life, and was never in the ranks of the living, what harm is it never to have been made?

181 Further, how was there first implanted in the gods a pattern for the begetting of things, yes, and the concept of man, so that they might know and see in their mind what they wished to do? Or in what way was the power of primary particles ever learnt, or what they could do when they shifted their order one with the other, if nature did not herself give a model of creation? For so many primordia of things in many ways, driven on by blows from time everlasting until now, and moved by their own weight, have been wont to be borne on, and to unite in every way, and essay everything that they might create, meeting one with another, that it is no wonder if they have fallen also into such arrangements, and have passed into such movements, as those whereby this present sum of things is carried on, ever and again replenished.

195 But even if I knew not what are the primary particles of things, yet this I would dare to affirm from the very workings of heaven, and to prove from many other things as well; that by no means has the nature of things been fashioned for us by divine grace: so great are the flaws with which it stands beset.

200 First, of all that the huge expanse of heaven covers, half thereof mountains and forests of wild beasts have greedily seized; rocks possess it, and waste pools and the sea, which holds far apart the shores of the lands. Besides, about two thirds of it burning heat and the ceaseless fall of frost steal from mortals. Of all the field-land that remains, yet nature would by her force cover it up with thorns, were it not that the force of man resisted her, ever wont for his livelihood to groan over the strong mattock and to furrow the earth with the deep-pressed plough. But that by turning the fertile clods with the plough

share, and subduing the soil of the earth we summon them to birth, of their own accord the crops could not spring up into the liquid air, and even now sometimes, when won by great toil, things grow leafy throughout the land, and are all in flower, either the sun in heaven burns them with too much heat, or sudden rains destroy them and chill frosts, and the blasts of the winds harry them with headstrong hurricane.

218 Moreover, why does nature foster and increase the awesome tribe of wild beasts to do harm to the race of man by land and sea? Why do the seasons of the year bring maladies? Why does death stalk abroad before her time? Then again, the child, like a sailor tossed ashore by the cruel waves, lies naked on the ground, dumb, lacking all help for life, when first nature has cast him forth by travail from his mother's womb into the coasts of light, and he fills the place with woeful wailing, as is but right for one for whom it remains in life to pass through so much trouble.

228 But the diverse flocks and herds grow up and the wild beasts, nor have they need of rattles, nor must be spoken to any of them the fond and broken prattle of the fostering nurse, nor do they seek diverse garments to suit the season of heaven, nay, and they have no need of weapons or lofty walls, whereby to protect their own, since for all of them the earth itself brings forth all things bounteously, and nature, the quaint artificer of things.

235 First of all, since the body of earth and moisture, and the light breath of the winds and burning heat, of which this sum of things is seen to be made up, are all created of a body that has birth and death, of such, too, must we think that the whole nature of the world is fashioned. For indeed, things whose parts and limbs we see to be of a body that has birth and of mortal shapes, themselves too we perceive always to have death and birth likewise. Wherefore, when we see the mighty members and parts of the world consumed away and brought to birth again, we may know that sky too likewise and earth had some time of first-beginning, and will suffer destruction.

247 Now in case you should think that I have snatched at this proof for myself, because I have assumed that earth and fire are mortal things, nor have hesitated to say that moisture and

breezes perish, and have maintained that they too are born again
and increase, first of all [consider this]. Some part of earth, when
baked by ceaseless suns, trodden by the force of many feet, gives
off a mist and flying clouds of dust, which stormy winds scatter
through all the air. Part too of its sods is returned to swamp by
the rains, and streams graze and gnaw their banks. Moreover,
whatever the earth nourishes and increases, is, in its own
proportion, restored. And since without doubt the parent of all
is seen herself to be the universal tomb of things, therefore you
may see that the earth is eaten away, and again increases and
grows.

261 For the rest, that sea, streams, and springs are ever filling
with new moisture, and that waters are ceaselessly oozing forth,
there is no need of words to prove. The great downrush of
waters on every side shows this clearly. But the water which is
foremost is ever taken away, and so it comes to pass that there
is never overmuch moisture in the sum, partly because the strong
winds as they sweep the seas, diminish it, and so does the sun in
heaven, as he unravels their fabric with his rays, partly because
it is sent hither and thither under every land. For the brine is
strained through, and the substance of the moisture oozes back,
and all streams together at the fountain-head of rivers, and
thence comes back over the lands with freshened current, where
the channel once cleft has brought down the waters in their
liquid march.

273 Next then I will speak of air, which changes in its whole
body in countless ways each single hour. For always, whatever
flows off from things, is all carried into the great sea of air. And
unless in turn it were to give back bodies to things, and replenish
them as they flow away, all things would by now have been
dissolved and turned into air. Air then ceases not to be created
from things, and to pass back into things, since it is sure that all
things are constantly flowing away.

281 Likewise that bounteous source of liquid light, the sun
in heaven, ceaselessly floods the sky with fresh brightness, and
at once supplied the place of light with new light. For that which
is foremost of its brightness, ever perishes, on whatever spot it
falls. This you may learn from what follows. As soon as clouds
have begun for an instant to pass beneath the sun, and, as it
were, to break off the rays of light, straightway all the part of

the rays beneath perishes, and the earth is overshadowed, wherever the clouds are carried. Thus you may learn that things ever have need of fresh brilliance, and that the foremost shaft of light ever perishes, nor in any other way can things be seen in the sunlight, except that the very fountain-head of light gives supply for ever.

294 Nay more, lights and night, which are on the earth, hanging lamps and oily torches, bright with their flashing fires and thick smoke, in like manner hasten by aid of their heat to supply new light. They are quick to flicker with their fires, yes quick, nor is the light, as it were, broken off, nor does it quit the spot. In such eager haste is its destruction hidden by the quick birth of flame from all the fires. So then we must think that sun, moon, and stars throw out their light from new supplies, rising again and again, and lose ever what is foremost of their flames; lest you should by chance believe that they are strong with a strength inexhaustible.

306 Again, do you not behold stones too vanquished by time, high towers falling in ruins, and rocks crumbling away, shrines and images of the gods growing weary and worn, while the sacred presence cannot prolong the boundaries of fate nor struggles against the laws of nature? Again, do we not see the monuments of men fallen to bits, and thus asking: whether you believe that they grow old. And stones torn up from high mountains rushing headlong, unable to brook or bear the stern strength of a limited time? For indeed they would not be suddenly torn up and fall headlong, if from time everlasting they had held out against all the siege of age without breaking.

318 Now once again gaze on this sky, which above and all around holds the whole earth in its embrace: if it begets all things out of itself, as some tell, and receives them again when they perish, it is made altogether of a body that has birth and death. For whatsoever increases and nourishes other things out of itself, must needs be lessened, and replenished when it receives things back.

324 Moreover, if there was no birth and beginning of the earth and sky, and they were always from everlasting, why beyond the Theban war and the doom of Troy have not other poets sung of other happenings as well? Whither have so many deeds of men so often passed away? Why are they nowhere

enshrined in glory in the everlasting memorials of fame? But
indeed, I believe our whole world is in its youth, and quite new
is the nature of the firmament, nor long ago did it receive its
first-beginnings. Wherefore even now certain arts are being
perfected, even now are growing; much now has been added to
ships, but a while ago musicians gave birth to tuneful harmonies.
Again, this nature of things, this philosophy, is but lately
dicovered, and I myself was found the very first of all who could
turn it into the speech of my country. But if by chance you think
that all these same things were aforetime, but that the generations of men perished in burning heat, or that cities have fallen
in some great upheaval of the world, or that from ceaseless rains
ravening rivers have issued over the lands and swallowed up
cities, all the more must you be vanquished and confess that
here will come to pass a perishing of earth and sky as well. For
when things were assailed by such great maladies and dangers,
then if a more fatal cause had pressed upon them, far and wide
would they have spread their destruction and mighty ruin. Nor
in any other way do we see one another to be mortal; except
that we fall sick of the same diseases as those whom nature has
sundered from life.

357 Moreover, if ever things abide[76] for everlasting, it must
needs be *either* that, because they are of solid body, they beat
back assaults, nor suffer anything to come within them, which
might unloose the close-locked parts within, such as are the
bodies of matter, whose nature we have declared before; *or* that
they are able to continue through all time, because they are
exempt from blows, as is the void, which abides untouched nor
suffers a whit from assault; *or else because* there is no supply of
room all around, into which things might part asunder and be
broken up – even as the sum of sums is eternal – nor is there
any room without into which they may leap apart, nor are there
bodies which might fall upon them and break them up with
stout blow. But neither, as I have shown, is the nature of the
world endowed with solid body, since there is void mingled in
things; nor yet is it as the void, nor indeed are bodies lacking,
which might by chance gather together out of infinite space and
overwhelm this sum of things with headstrong hurricane, or

[76] Lines 351–61 are repeated with a few variations from III, 806–18.

bear down on it some other form of dangerous destruction; nor
again is there nature of room or space in the deep wanting, into
which the walls of the world might be scattered forth; or else
they may be pounded and perish by any other force you will.
The gate of death then is not shut on sky or sun or earth or the
deep waters of the sea, but it stands open facing them with huge
vast gaping maw. Wherefore, again, you must needs confess
that these same things have a birth; for indeed, things that are
of mortal body could not from limitless time up till now have
been able to set at defiance the stern strength of immeasurable
age.

380 Again, since the mighty members[77] of the world so
furiously fight one against the other, stirred up in most unhallowed warfare, do you not see that some end may be set to their
long contest? Either when the sun and every kind of heat have
drunk up all the moisture and won the day: which they are
struggling to do, but as yet they have not accomplished their
effort: so great a supply do the rivers bring and threaten to go
beyond their bounds, and deluge all things from out the deep
abyss of ocean — all in vain, since the winds as they sweep the
seas, diminish them, and so does the sun in heaven, as he
unravels their fabric with his rays, and they boast that they can
dry up all things, ere moisture can reach the end of its task. So
vast a war do they breathe out in equal contest, as they struggle
and strive one with another for mighty issues. Yet once in this
fight fire gained the upper hand, and once, as the story goes,
moisture reigned supreme on the plains. For fire won its way
and burnt up many things, all-devouring, when the resistless
might of the horses of the sun went astray and carried Phaëthon
amain through the whole heavens and over all lands. But,
thereupon, the almighty father, thrilled with keen anger, with
sudden stroke of his thunder dashed ambitious Phaëthon from
his chariot to earth, and the sun, meeting him as he fell, caught
the everlasting lamp of the world, and tamed the scattered
horses, and yoked them trembling, and so guiding them along
their own path, replenished all things. So indeed sang the old
poets of the Greeks. But it is exceeding far removed from true
reasoning. For fire can only prevail when more bodies of its

[77] Earth, air, fire and water.

matter have risen up out of infinite space. After that its strength fails, vanquished in some way, or else things perish, burnt up by its fiery breath.

411 Water likewise, once gathered together and began to prevail, as the story goes, when it overwhelmed living men with its waves. Thereafter, when its force was by some means turned aside and went its way, even all that had gathered together from infinite space, the rains ceased, and the strength of the rivers was brought low.

416 But by what means that gathering together of matter established earth and sky and the depths of ocean, and the courses of sun and moon, I will set forth in order. For in very truth not by design did the primordia of things place themselves each in their order with foreseeing mind, nor indeed did they make compact what movements each should start. But because many primary particles of things in many ways, driven on by blows from time everlasting until now, and moved by their own weight, have been wont to be borne on, and to unite in every way and essay everything that they might create, meeting one with another, therefore it comes to pass that scattered abroad through a great age, as they try meetings and motions of every kind, at last those come together, which, suddenly cast together, become often the beginnings of great things, of earth, sea and sky, and the race of living things.

432 Then, when things were so, neither could the sun's orb be seen, flying on high with its bounteous light, nor the stars of the great world, nor sea nor sky, nay nor earth nor air, nor anything at all like to the things we know, but only a sort of fresh-formed storm, a mass gathered together of primordia of every kind, whose discord was waging war and confounding interspaces, paths, interlacings, weights, blows, meetings, and motions, because owing to their unlike forms and diverse shapes, all things were unable to remain in union, as they do now, and to give and receive harmonious motions. From this mass parts began to fly off hither and thither, and like things to unite with like, and so to unfold a world, and to sunder its members and dispose its great parts, that is, to mark off the high heaven from the earth, and the sea by itself, so that it might spread out with

its moisture kept apart, and likewise the fires of the sky by themselves, unmixed and kept apart.

449 In plain truth first of all the several bodies of earth, because they were heavy and interlaced, met together in the middle, and all took up the lowest places; and the more they met and interlaced, the more did they squeeze out those which were to make sea, stars, sun, and moon, and the walls of the great world. For all these are of smoother and rounder seeds, and of much smaller particles than earth. And so, bursting out from the quarter of the earth through its loose-knit openings, first of all the fiery ether rose up and, being so light, carried off with it many fires, in not far different wise than often we see now, when first the golden morning light of the radiant sun reddens over the grass bejewelled with dew, and the pools and ever-running streams give off a mist, yea, even as the earth from time to time is seen to steam: and when all these are gathered together as they move upwards, clouds with body now formed weave a web beneath the sky on high. Thus then at that time the light and spreading ether, with body now formed, was set all around and curved on every side, and spreading wide towards every part on all sides, thus fenced in all else in its greedy embrace.

471 There followed then the beginnings of sun and moon, whose spheres turn in air midway betwixt earth and ether; for neither earth nor the great ether claimed them for itself, because they were neither heavy enough to sink and settle down, nor light enough to be able to glide along the topmost coasts, yet they are so set between the two that they can move along their living bodies, and are parts of the whole world; even as in our bodies some limbs may abide in their place, while yet there are others moving.

480 So when these things were withdrawn, at once the earth sank down, where now the vast blue belt of ocean stretches, and flooded the furrows with salt surge. And day by day, the more the tide of ether and the rays of the sun with constant blows along its outer edges constrained the earth into closer texture, so that thus smitten it condensed and drew together round its centre, the more did the salt sweat, squeezed out from its body, go to increase the sea and the swimming plains, as it trickled

forth. Yes, and the more did those many bodies of heat and air
slip forth and fly abroad, and far away from earth condense the
high glowing quarters of the sky. Plains sank down, lofty
mountains grew in height; for indeed the rocks could not settle
down, nor could all parts subside equally in the same degree.

495 So then the weight of earth, with body now formed,
sank to its place, and, as it were, all the slime of the world slid
heavily to the bottom, and sank right down like dregs; then the
sea and then the air and then the fiery ether itself were all left
unmixed with their liquid bodies; they are lighter each than the
next beneath, and ether, most liquid and lightest of all, floats
above the breezes of air, nor does it mingle its liquid body with
the boisterous breezes of air; it suffers all our air below to be
churned by headstrong hurricanes, if suffers it to brawl with
shifting storms, but itself bears on its fires as it glides in
changeless advance. For that the ether can follow on quietly and
with one constant effort, the Pontos [the Black Sea] proves, the
sea which flows on with changeless tide, preserving ever the one
constant rhythm of its gliding.

THE NATURE AND MOVEMENT OF CELESTIAL BODIES, 509-779.

509 Now let us sing what is the cause of the motions of the
stars.[78] First of all, if the great globe of the sky turns round, we
must say that the air presses on the pole at either end, and holds
it outside and closes it in at both ends; and that then another
current of air flows above, straining on to the same goal,
towards which the twinkling stars of the everlasting world roll
on; or else that there is another current beneath, to drive up the
sphere reversely, as we see streams moving round wheels with
their scoops.

517 It may be also that the whole sky can abide in its place,
while yet the shining signs are carried on; *either* because swift
currents of ether are shut within them, and seeking a way out

---

[78] Lucretius is beginning a long series of accounts of celestial and terrestrial
phenomena with the same restrictions that marked Epicurus' efforts in the 'Letter to
Pythocles': namely that in the absence of further evidence, more than one hypothesis
may account for the given phenomena, some phenomena are produced by more than
one type of cause, and some conjectural explanations are merely possible.

are turned round and round, and so roll on the fires this way and that through the nightly quarters of the sky; *or else* an air streaming from some other quarter without turns and drives the fires; *or else* they can themselves creep on, whither its own food invites and summons each as they move on, feeding their flaming bodies everywhere throughout the sky.

526 For it is hard to declare for certain which of these causes holds in this world. But what can happen and does happen throughout the universe in diverse worlds, fashioned on diverse plans, that is what I teach, and I shall go on to set forth many causes for the motions of the stars, which may exist throughout the universe; and of these it must needs be one which in our world too gives strength to the motions of the heavenly signs; but to affirm which of them it is, is in no wise the task of one treading forward step by step.

534 Now so that the earth may rest quiet in the mid region of the world, it is natural that its mass should gradually thin out and grow less, and that it should have another nature underneath from the beginning of its being, linked and closely bound in one with those airy parts of the world amid which it has its place and life. For this cause it is no burden, nor does it weigh down the air; even as for every man his own limbs are no weight, nor is the head a burden to the neck,[79] nor do we feel that the whole weight of the body is resting on the feet; but all weights which come from without and are laid upon us, hurt us, though often they are many times smaller. Of such great matter is it, what is the power of each thing. So then the earth is not suddenly brought in as some alien body, nor cast from elsewhere on alien air, but it has been begotten along with it from the first beginning of the world, a determined part of it, as our limbs are seen to be of us.

550 Moreover, the earth, when shaken suddenly by violent thunder, shakes with its motion all that is above it; which it could not by any means do, were it not bound up with the airy parts of the world and with the sky. For they cling one to the other with common roots, linked and closely bound in one from the beginning of their being.

[79] Surely a remark that proves the youth of the poet.

556 Do you not see too how great is the weight of our body, which the force of the anima though exceeding fine, supports, just because it is so nearly linked and closely bound in one with it? And again, what can lift the body in a nimble leap save the force of the anima, which steers the limbs? Do you not see now how great can be the power of a fine nature, when it is linked with a heavy body, even as the air is linked with earth, and the force of the mind with us?

564 Nor can the sun's blazing wheel be much greater or less, than it is seen to be by our senses.[80] For from whatsoever distances fires can throw us their light and breathe their warm heat upon our limbs, they lose nothing of the body of their flames because of the interspaces, their fire is no whit shrunken to the sight. Even so, since the heat of the sun and the light he sheds, arrive at our senses and cheer the spots on which they fall, the form and bulk of the sun as well must needs be seen truly from earth, so that you could alter it almost nothing to greater or less.

575 The moon, too, whether she illumines places with a borrowed light as she moves along, or throws out her own rays from her own body, however that may be, moves on with a shape no whit greater than seems that shape, with which we perceive her with our eyes. For all things which we behold far sundered from us through much air, are seen to grow confused in shape, ere their outline is lessened. Wherefore it must needs be that the moon, inasmuch as she shows a clear-marked shape and an outline well defined, is seen by us from earth in the heights, just as she is, clear-cut all along her outer edges, and just the size she is.

585 Lastly, all the fires of heaven that you see from earth; inasmuch as all fires that we see on earth, so long as their twinkling light is clear, so long as their blaze is perceived, are seen to change their size only in some very small degree from time to time to greater or less, the further they are away: so we may know that the heavenly fires can only be a very minute degree smaller or larger by a little tiny piece.

592 This too is unremarkable, how the sun, small as it is, can

[80] A pure but quaint Epicurean doctrine. See the 'Letter to Pythocles' and note 10.

send out so great light, to fill seas and all lands and sky with its flood, and to bathe all things in its warm heat. For it may be that from this spot the one well of light for the whole world is opened up and teems with bounteous stream, and shoots out its rays, because the particles of heat from all the world gather together on every side, and their assembled mass flows together in such a way, that here, from a single fountain-head, their blazing light streams forth. Do you not see too how widely a tiny spring of water sometimes moistens the fields, and floods out over the plains.

604 Or again, it may be that from the sun's fire, though it be not great, blazing light seizes on the air with its burning heat, if by chance there is air ready to hand and rightly suited to be kindled when smitten by tiny rays of heat; even as sometimes we see crops or straw caught in widespread fire from one single spark.

610 Perhaps, too, the sun, shining on high with its rosy torch, has at his command much fire with hidden heat all around him, fire which is never marked by any radiance, so that it is only laden with heat and increases the stroke of the sun's rays.

614 Nor is there any single and straightforward account of the sun, to show how from the summer regions he draws near the winter turning-point of Capricorn, and how turning back thence, he betakes himself to the solstice-goal of Cancer; and how the moon is seen in single months to traverse that course, on which the sun spends the period of a year as he runs. There is not, I say, any single cause assigned for these things.

621 For, first and foremost, it is clear that it may come to pass, as the judgement of that venerable man, Democritus, sets before us, that the nearer the several stars are to earth, the less can they be borne on with the whirl of heaven. For its swift keen strength passes away and is lessened beneath, and so little by little the sun is left behind with the hindmost signs, because it is much lower than the burning signs.[81] And even more the moon: the lower her course, the further it is from the sky and nearer to earth, the less can she strain on her course level with the signs.

---

[81] Note that here and elsewhere Lucretius accepts the conventional view (challenged in antiquity by the Alexandrian astronomer Aristarchus of Samos) that the earth is still and in the middle of our world which is itself conceived as a sphere surrounded by ether.

Moreover the weaker the whirl with which she is borne along, being lower than the sun, the more do all the signs catch her up all around and pass her. Therefore, it comes to pass that she seems to turn back more speedily to each several sign, because the signs come back to her. It may be too that from quarters of the world athwart his path two airs may stream alternately, each at a fixed season, one such as to push the sun away from the summer signs right to the winter turning-places and their icy frost, and the other to hurl him back from the icy shades of cold right to the heat-laden quarters and the burning signs. And in like manner must we think that the moon and those stars which roll through the great years in great orbits, can be moved by airs from the opposite quarters in turn. Do you not see how by contrary winds the lower clouds too are moved in directions contrary to those above? Why should those stars be less able to be borne on by currents contrary one to the other through the great orbits in the heaven?

650 But night shrouds the earth in thick darkness, either when after his long journey the sun has trodden the farthest parts of heaven, and fainting has breathed out his fires shaken by the journey and made weak by much air, or because the same force, which carried on his orb above the earth, constrains him to turn his course back beneath the earth.

656 Likewise at a fixed time Matuta[82] sends abroad the rosy dawn through the coasts of heaven, and spreads the light, either because the same sun, returning again beneath the earth, seizes the sky in advance with his rays, fain to kindle it, or because the fires come together and many seeds of heat are wont to stream together at a fixed time, which each day cause the light of a new sun to come to birth. Even so story tells that from the high mountains of Ida scattered fires are seen as the light rises, and then they gather as if into a single ball, and make up the orb. Nor again ought this to be cause of wonder herein, that these seeds of fire can stream together at so fixed a time and renew the brightness of the sun. For we see many events, which come to pass at a fixed time in all things. Trees blossom at a fixed time, and at a fixed time lose their flower. Even so at a fixed

---

[82] Matuta was an ancient Roman deity of the first light of morning, sometimes identified with Aurora.

time age bids the teeth fall, and the hairless youth grow hairy with soft down and let a soft beard flow alike from either cheek. Lastly, thunder, snow, rains, clouds, winds come to pass at seasons of the year more or less fixed. For since the first-beginnings of causes were ever thus and things have so fallen out from the first outset of the world, one after the other they come round even now in fixed order.

680 And likewise it may be that days grow longer and nights wane, and again daylight grows less, when nights take increase; either because the same sun, as he fulfils his course in unequal arcs below the earth and above, parts the coasts of heaven, and divides his circuit into unequal portions; and whatever he has taken away from the one part, so much the more he replaces, as he goes round, in the part opposite it, until he arrives at that sign in the sky, where the node of the year makes the shades of night equal to the daylight. For in the mid-course of the blast of the north wind and of the south wind, the sky holds his turning-points apart at a distance then made equal, on account of the position of the whole starry orbit, in which the sun covers the space of a year in his winding course, as he lights earth and heaven with his slanting rays: as is shown by the plans of those who have marked out all the quarters of the sky, adorned with their signs in due order.

696 Or else, because the air is thicker in certain regions, and therefore the trembling ray of his fire is delayed beneath the earth, nor can it easily pierce through and burst out to its rising. Therefore in winter time the long nights lag on, until the radiant ensign of day comes forth.

701 Or else again, because in the same way in alternate parts of the year the fires, which cause the sun to rise from a fixed quarter, are wont to stream together now more slowly, now more quickly, therefore it is that those seem to speak the truth [who say that a new sun is born every day].

705 The moon may shine when struck by the sun's rays, and day by day turn that light more straightly to our sight, the more she retires from the sun's orb, until opposite him she has glowed with quite full light and, as she rises, towering on high, has seen his setting; then little by little she must needs retire back again, and, as it were, hide her light, the nearer she glides now to the sun's fire from the opposite quarter through the orbit of the

signs; as those have it, who picture that the moon is like a ball, and keeps to the path of her course below the sun.

715 There is also a way by which she can roll on with her own light, and yet show changing phases of brightness. For there may be another body, which is borne on and glides together with her, in every way obstructing and obscuring her; yet it cannot be seen, because it is borne on without light.

720 Or she may turn round, just like, if it so chance, the sphere of a ball, tinged over half its surface with gleaming light, and so by turning round the sphere produce changing phases, until she turns to our sight and open eyes that side, whichever it be, that is endowed with fires; and then little by little she twists back again and carries away from us the light-giving part of the round mass of the ball; as the Babylonian teaching of the Chaldaeans, denying the science of the astronomers, essays to prove in opposition; just as if what each of them fights for may not be the truth, or there were any cause why you should venture to adopt the one less than the other.

731 Or again, why a fresh moon could not be created every day with fixed succession of phases and fixed shapes, so that each several day the moon created would pass away, and another be supplied in its room and place, it is difficult to teach by reasoning or prove by words, since so many things can be created in fixed order. Spring goes on her way with Venus, and before them treads Venus's winged harbinger [Cupid]; and following close on the steps of Zephyrus, mother Flora strews and fills all the way before them with glorious colours and scents. Next after follows parching heat, and as companion at her side dusty Ceres and the etesian blasts of the north winds. Then autumn advances, and step by step with her Euhius Euan [Bacchus]. Then follow the other seasons and their winds, Volturnus, thundering on high, and the south wind, whose strength is the lightning. Last of all the year's end brings snow, and winter renews numbing frost. It is followed by cold, with chattering teeth. Wherefore it is less wonderful if the moon is born at a fixed time, and again at a fixed time is blotted out, since so many things can come to pass at fixed times.

751 Likewise also the eclipses of the sun and the hidings of the moon, you must suppose to be brought about by several possible causes. For why should the moon be able to shut out

the earth from the sun's light, and thrust her head high before him in the line of earth, throwing her dark orb before his glorious rays; and at the same time it should not be thought that another body could do this, which glides on ever without light. And besides, why should not the sun be able at a fixed time to faint and lose his fires, and again renew his light, when, in his journey through the air, he has passed by places hostile to his flames, which cause his fires to be put out and perish? And why should the earth be able in turn to rob the moon of light, and herself on high to keep the sun hidden beneath, while the moon in her monthly journey glides through the sharp-drawn shadows of the cone; and at the same time another body be unable to run beneath the moon or glide above the sun's orb, to break off his rays and streaming light? And indeed, if the moon shines with her own light, why should she not be able to grow faint in a certain region of the world, while she passes out through spots unfriendly to her own light?

THE BEGINNINGS OF LIFE AND THE ORIGIN OF MAN, 772–1010

772 For the rest, since I have unfolded in what manner each thing could take place throughout the blue vault of the great world, so that we might learn what force and what cause started the diverse courses of the sun, and the journeyings of the moon, and in what way they might go hiding with their light obscured, and shroud the unexpecting earth in darkness, when, as it were, they wink and once again open their eye and look upon all places shining with their clear rays: Now I return to the youth of the world, and the soft fields of earth, and what first with new power of creation they resolved to raise into the coasts of light and entrust to the wayward winds.

783 In the beginning the earth gave birth to the tribes of herbage and bright verdure all around the hills and over all the plains, the flowering fields gleamed in their green hue, and thereafter the diverse trees were started with loose rein on their great race of growing through the air. Even as down and hair and bristles are first formed on the limbs of four-footed beasts and the body of fowls strong of wing, so then the newborn earth raised up herbage and shrubs first, and thereafter produced the

races of mortal things, many races born in many ways by diverse means. For neither can living animals have fallen from the sky nor the beasts of earth have issued forth from the salt pools.

795 It remains that rightly has the earth won the name of mother, since out of earth all things are produced. And even now many animals spring forth from the earth, formed by the rains and the warm heat of the sun; wherefore we may wonder the less, if then more animals and greater were born, reaching their full growth when earth and air were fresh.

801 First of all the tribe of winged fowls and the diverse birds left their eggs, hatched out in the spring season, as now in the summer the grasshoppers of their own will leave their smooth shells, seeking life and livelihood. Then it was that the earth first gave birth to the race of mortal things. For much heat and moisture abounded then in the fields; thereby, wherever a suitable spot or place was afforded, there grew up wombs,[83] clinging to the earth by their roots; and when in the fullness of time the age of the little ones, fleeing moisture and eager for air, had opened them, nature would turn to that place the pores in the earth and constrain them to give forth from their opened veins a sap, most like to milk; even as now every woman, when she has brought forth, is filled with sweet milk, because all the current of her nourishment is turned towards her paps. The earth furnished food for the young, the warmth raiment, the grass a couch rich in much soft down. But the youth of the world called not into being hard frosts nor exceeding heat nor winds of mighty violence: for all things grow and come to their strength in like degrees.

821 Wherefore, again and again, rightly has the earth won, rightly does she keep the name of mother, since she herself formed the race of men, and almost at a fixed time brought forth every animal which ranges everywhere on the mighty mountains, and with them the fowls of the air with their diverse forms.

---

[83] A most curious device to try to emphasize the *natural* motherhood of the earth rather than the earth as a living goddess. It also helps to bridge the gap between vegetable and animal life. As Bailey observes, Lucretius 'seems to be a little conscious of its improbability and is careful just after (line 813) to supply an analogy for this apparently gratuitous act of kindness on the part of the earth.'

826 But because she must needs come to some end of child-bearing, she ceased, like a woman worn with the lapse of age. For time changes the nature of the whole world, and one state after another must needs overtake all things, nor does anything abide like itself: all things change their abode, nature alters all things and constrains them to turn. For one thing rots away and grows faint and feeble with age, thereon another grows up and issues from its place of scorn. So then time changes the nature of the whole world, and one state after another overtakes the earth, so that it cannot bear what it did, but can bear what it did not of old.[84]

837 And many monsters the earth then tried to create, born with strange faces and strange limbs, the man-woman, between the two, yet not either, sundered from both sexes; some things bereft of feet, or in turn robbed of hands, things too found dumb without mouths, or blind without eyes, or locked through the whole body by the clinging of the limbs, so that they could not do anything or move towards any side or avoid calamity or take what they needed. All other monsters and prodigies of this sort she would create; all in vain, since nature forbade their increase, nor could they reach the coveted bloom of age nor find food nor join in the work of Venus. For we see that many happenings must be united for things, that they may be able to beget and propagate their races; first that they may have food, and then a way whereby birth-giving seeds may pass through their frames, and issue from their slackened limbs; and that woman may be joined with man, they must needs each have means whereby they can interchange mutual joys.

855 And it must needs be that many races of living things then perished and could not beget and propagate their offspring. For whatever animals you see feeding on the breath of life, either their craft or bravery, aye or their swiftness has protected and

[84] That one thing grows by the loss of another, that the world is ever moving on, and that even for man there is a fitness in this, are themes which weave their way right through the poem: see, for example, I, 262–4; II, 962–5; and the most memorable simile in II, 77–9, 'Thus the sum of things is ever being replenished and mortals live one and all by give and take. Some races wax and others wane, and in a short space the tribes of living things are changed and like runners hand on the torch of life.'

preserved their kind from the beginning of their being. And many there are, which by their usefulness are commended to us, and so abide, trusted to our tutelage.

862 First of all the fierce race of lions, that savage stock, their bravery has protected, foxes their cunning, and deer their fleet foot. But the lightly sleeping minds of dogs with their loyal heart, and all the race which is born of the seed of beasts of burden, and withal the fleecy flocks and the horned herds, are all trusted to the tutelage of men, Memmius. For eagerly did they flee the wild beasts and ensue peace and bounteous fodder gained without toil of theirs, which we grant them as a reward because of their usefulness.

871 But those to whom nature granted none of these things, neither that they might live on by themselves of their own might, nor do us any useful service, for which we might suffer their kind to feed and be kept safe under our defence, you may know that these fell a prey and spoil to others, all entangled in the fateful trammels of their own being, until nature brought their kind to destruction.

878 But Centaurs never existed either, nor at any time can there be animals of twofold nature and double body, put together of limbs of alien birth, so that the power and strength of each, derived from this parent and that, could be equal. That this is so we may learn, however dull be our understanding, from what follows.

883 First of all, when three years have come round, the horse is in the prime of vigour, but the child by no means so; for often even now in his sleep he will clutch for the milky paps of his mother's breasts. Afterwards, when the stout strength and limbs of horses fail through old age and droop, as life flees from them, then at last youth sets in in the prime of boyish years, and clothes the cheeks with soft down; that you may not by chance believe that Centaurs can be created or exist, formed of a man and the load-laden breed of horses, or Scyllas either, with bodies half of sea-monsters, girt about with ravening dogs, or any other beasts of their kind, whose limbs we see cannot agree one with another; for they neither reach prime together nor gain the full strength of their bodies nor let it fall away in old age, nor are they fired with a like love, nor do they agree in a single character,

nor are the same things pleasant to them throughout their frame. Indeed, we may see the bearded goats often grow fat on hemlock, which to man is rank poison.

901 Since moreover flame is wont to scorch and burn the tawny bodies of lions just as much as every kind of flesh and blood that exists on the earth, how could it have come to pass that the Chimaera, one in her threefold body, in front a lion, in the rear a dragon, in the middle, as her name shows, a goat should breathe out at her mouth fierce flame from her body?

907 Wherefore again, he who supposes that when the earth was young and the sky new-born, such animals could have been begotten, trusting only in this one empty plea of the world's youth, may blurt out many things in like manner from his lips; he may say that then streams of gold flowed everywhere over the lands, and that trees were wont to blossom with jewels, or that a man was born with such expanse of limbs, that he could plant his footsteps right across the deep seas, and with his hands twist the whole sky about him. For because there were in the earth many seeds of things at the time when first the land brought forth animals, yet that is no proof that beasts of mingled breed could have been born, or the limbs of living creatures put together in one; because the races of herbage and the crops and fruitful trees, which even now spring forth abundantly from the earth, yet cannot be created intertwined one with another, but each of these things comes forth after its own manner, and all preserve their separate marks by a fixed law of nature.

925 But the race of man was much hardier then in the fields, as was seemly for a race born of the hard earth. It was built up on larger and more solid bones within, fastened with strong sinews traversing the flesh; not easily to be harmed by heat or cold or strange food or any taint of the body. And during many lustres of the sun rolling through the sky they passed their lives after the roving manner of wild beasts. Nor was there any sturdy guide of the bent plough, nor any one who knew how to work the fields with iron, or to plant young shoots in the earth, or cut down the old branches of high trees with knives. What sun and rains had brought to birth, what earth had created unasked, such gift was enough to appease their hearts. Among oaks laden with acorns they would refresh their bodies for the most part;

and the arbute-berries, which now you see ripening in winter-time with scarlet hue, the earth bore then in abundance, yes and larger than now. And besides these, the flowering youth of the world then bare much other rough food, enough and to spare for miserable mortals. But to slake their thirst streams and springs summoned them, even as now the downrush of water from the great mountains calls clear far and wide to the thirsting tribes of wild beasts. Or again they dwelt in the woodland haunts of the nymphs, which they had learnt in their wander-ings, from which they knew that gliding streams of water washed the wet rocks with bounteous flood, yea washed the wet rocks, as they dripped down over the green moss, and here and there welled up and burst forth over the level plain.

953 Not as yet did they know how to serve their purposes with fire, nor to use skins and clothe their body in the spoils of wild beasts, but dwelt in woods and the caves on mountains and forests, and amid brushwood would hide their rough limbs, when constrained to shun the shock of winds and the rain-showers. Nor could they look to the common good, nor had they knowledge to make mutual use of any customs or laws. Whatever booty chance had offered to each, he bore it off; for each was taught at his own will to live and thrive for himself alone.

962 And Venus would unite lovers in the woods; for each woman was wooed either by mutual passion, or by the man's fierce force and reckless lust, or by a price, acorns and arbute-berries or choice pears. And trusting in their strange strength of hand and foot they would hunt the woodland tribes of wild beasts with stones to hurl or clubs of huge weight. Many they would vanquish, a few they would avoid in hiding; and like bristly boars these woodland men would lay their limbs naked on the ground, when overtaken by nighttime, wrapping them-selves up around with leaves and foliage.

973 Nor did they look for daylight and the sun with loud wailing, wandering fearful through the fields in the darkness of night, but silent and buried in sleep waited mindful, until the sun with rosy torch should bring the light into the sky. For, because they had been wont ever from childhood to behold darkness and light born, turn by turn, it could not come to pass that they should ever wonder, or feel mistrust lest the light of

the sun should be withdrawn for ever, and never-ending night possess the earth. But much greater was another care, inasmuch as the tribes of wild beasts often made rest dangerous for wretched men. Driven from their home they would flee from their rocky roof at the coming of a foaming boar or a mighty lion, and in the dead of night in terror they would yield their couches spread with leaves to their cruel guests.

988 Nor then much more than now would the races of men leave the sweet light of life with lamentation. For then more often would some one of them be caught and furnish living food to the wild beasts, devoured by their teeth, and would fill woods and mountains and forests with his groaning, as he looked on his living flesh being buried in a living tomb. And those whom flight had saved with mangled body, thereafter, holding trembling hands over their hideous injuries, would summon Orcus with terrible cries, until savage griping pains had robbed them of life, all helpless and knowing not what wounds wanted.

999 Yet never were many thousands of men led beneath the standards and done to death in a single day, nor did the stormy waters of ocean dash ships and men upon the rocks. Then rashly, idly, in vain would the sea often arise and rage, and lightly lay aside its empty threatenings, nor could the treacherous wiles of the windless waves lure any man to destruction with smiling waters; then the wanton art of sailing lay as yet unknown. Then, too, want of food would give over their drooping limbs to death. But in contrast now it is surfeit of good things that brings them low. They all unwitting would often pour out poison for themselves. Now, with more skill, they give it to others.

THE DEVELOPMENT OF CIVIL SOCIETY, 1011–457

1011 Then after they got themselves huts and skins and fire, and woman yoked with man retired to a single [home, and the laws of marriage] were learnt, and they saw children sprung from them, then first the race of man began to soften. For fire brought it about that their chilly limbs could not now so well bear cold under the roof of heaven, and Venus lessened their strength, and children, by their winning ways, easily broke down the haughty will of their parents. Then, too, neighbours began eagerly to form friendship one with another, not to hurt or be harmed,[85] and they commended to mercy children and the race of women, when with cries and gestures they taught by broken words that is right for all men to have pity on the weak. Yet not in all ways could unity be begotten, but a good part, the larger part, would keep their compacts loyally; or else the human race would even then have been all destroyed, nor could breeding have prolonged the generations until now.

1028 But the diverse sounds of the tongue nature constrained men to utter, and use shaped the names of things, in a manner not far other than the very speechlessness of their tongue is seen to lead children on to gesture, when it makes them point out with the finger the things that are before their eyes. For every one feels to what purpose he can use his own powers. Before the horns of a calf appear and sprout from his forehead, he butts with them when angry, and pushes passionately. But the whelps of panthers and lion-cubs already fight with claws and feet and biting, when their teeth and claws are scarce yet formed. Further, we see all the tribe of winged fowls trusting to their wings, and seeking an unsteady aid from their pinions.

1041 Therefore to think that any one then parcelled out names to things, and that from him men learnt their first words, is mere folly. For why should he be able to mark off all things by words, and to utter the diverse sounds of the tongue, and at the same time others be thought unable to do this? Moreover, if others too had not used words to one another, whence was implanted in him the concept of their use? Whence was he given the first power to know and see in his mind what he wanted to do? Likewise one man could not avail to constrain many, and vanquish them to his will, that they should be willing to learn all *his* names for things; nor indeed is it easy in any way to teach and persuade the deaf what is needful to do; for they would not endure it, nor in any way suffer the sounds of words unheard before to batter on their ears any more to no purpose. Lastly, what is there so marvellous in this, if the human race, with strong voice and tongue, should mark off things with diverse sounds for diverse feelings? When the dumb cattle, yes and the races of wild beasts are wont to give forth diverse unlike sounds,

---

[85] Cf. Epicurus, 'Principal Doctrines' 31.

when they are in fear or pain, or again when their joys grow strong. Yes, indeed, we may learn this from things clear to see.

1063 When the large loose lips of Molossian dogs start to snarl in anger, baring their hard teeth, thus drawn back in rage, they threaten with a noise far other than when they bark and fill all around with their clamour. Yet when they attempt fondly to lick their cubs with their tongue, or when they toss them with their feet, and making for them with open mouth, feign gently to swallow them, checking their closing teeth, they fondle them with growling voice in a way far other than when left alone in the house they bay, or when whining they shrink from a beating with cringing body.

1073 Again, is not neighing seen to differ likewise, when a young stallion in the flower of his years rages among the mares, pricked by the spur of winged love, and from spreading nostrils snorts for the fray, and when, it may be, at other times he whinnies with trembling limbs?

1078 Lastly, the tribe of winged fowls and the diverse birds, hawks and ospreys and gulls amid the sea-waves, seeking in the salt waters for life and livelihood, utter at other times cries far other than when they are struggling for their food and fighting for their prey. And some of them change their harsh notes with the weather, as the long-lived tribes of crows and flocks of rooks, when they are said to cry for water and rains, and anon to summon the winds and breezes.

1087 And so, if diverse feelings constrain animals, though they are dumb, to utter diverse sounds, how much more likely is it that mortals should then have been able to mark off things unlike with one sound and another.

1091 Herein, lest by chance you should ask a silent question, it was lightning that first of all brought fire to earth for mortals, and from it all the heat of flames is spread abroad. For we see many things flare up, kindled with flames from heaven, when a stroke from the sky has brought the gift of heat. Yet again, when a branching tree is lashed by the winds and sways to and fro, reeling and pressing on the branches of another tree, fire is struck out by the strong force of the rubbing, anon the fiery heat of flame sparkles out, while branches and trunks rub each against each other. Either of these happenings may have given fire to mortals. And then the sun taught them to cook food and soften it by the heat of flame, since they saw many things among the fields grow mellow, vanquished by the lashing of his rays and by the heat.

1105 And day by day those who excelled in understanding and were strong in mind showed them more and more how to change their former life and livelihood for new habits and for fire. Kings began to build cities and to found a citadel, to be for themselves a stronghold and a refuge; and they parcelled out and gave flocks and fields to each man for his beauty or his strength or understanding; for beauty was then of much avail, and strength stood high. Thereafter property was invented and gold found, which easily robbed the strong and beautiful of honour; for, of the most part, however strong men are born, however beautiful their body, they follow the lead of the richer man.

1117 Yet if a man would steer his life by true reasoning, it is great riches to a man to live thriftily with calm mind; for never can he lack for a little. But men wished to be famous and powerful, that their fortune might rest on a sure foundation, and they might in wealth lead a peaceful life; all in vain, since struggling to rise to the heights of honour, they made the path of their journey beset with danger, and yet from the top, like lightning, envy smites them and casts them down anon in scorn to a loathsome Hell; since by envy, as by lightning, the topmost heights are most often set ablaze, and all places that rise high above others; so that it is far better to obey in peace than to long to rule the world with kingly power and to sway kingdoms.

1131 Wherefore let them sweat out their life-blood, worn away to no purpose, battling their way along the narrow path of ambition; inasmuch as their wisdom is but from the lips of others, and they seek things rather through hearsay than from their own feelings, and that is of no more avail now nor shall be hereafter than it was of old.

1136 And so the kings were put to death, and the ancient majesty of thrones and proud sceptres was overthrown and lay in ruins, and the glorious emblem on the head of kings was stained with blood, and beneath the feet of the mob mourned the loss of its high honour; for once dreaded overmuch, eagerly now it is trampled. And so things would pass to the utmost dregs of disorder, when every man sought for himself the power and the headship. Then some of them taught men to appoint magistrates and establish laws that they might consent to obey ordinances.

1145 For the race of men, worn out with leading a life of violence, lay faint from its feuds; wherefore the more easily of its own will it gave in to ordinances and the close mesh of laws. For since each man set out to avenge himself more fiercely in his passion than is now suffered by equal laws, for this cause men were weary of leading a life of violence. Thence fear of punishment taints the prizes of life. For violence and hurt tangle every man in their toils, and for the most part fall on the head of him from whom they had their rise, nor is it easy for one who by his act breaks the common pact of peace to lead a calm and quiet life.

1156 For though he be unnoticed of the race of gods and men, yet he must needs mistrust that his secret will be kept for ever; nay indeed, many by speaking in their sleep or raving in fever have often, so it is said, betrayed themselves, and brought to light misdeeds long hidden.

1161 Next, what cause spread abroad the divine powers of the gods among great nations, and filled cities with altars, and taught men to undertake sacred rites at yearly festivals, rites which are honoured to-day in great empires and at great places; whence even now there is implanted in mortals a shuddering dread, which raises new shrines of the gods over all the world, and constrains men to throng them on the holy days; of all this it is not hard to give account in words.

1169 For indeed already the races of mortals used to perceive the glorious shapes of the gods with waking mind, and all the more in sleep with wondrous bulk of body. To these then they would assign sense because they were seen to move their limbs, and to utter haughty sounds befitting their noble mien and ample strength. And they gave them everlasting life because their images came in constant stream and the form remained unchanged, but above all because they thought that those endowed with such strength could not readily be vanquished by any force. They thought that they far excelled in happiness, because the fear of death never harassed any of them, and at the same time because in sleep they saw them accomplish many marvels, yet themselves not undergo any toil.

1183 Moreover, they beheld the workings of the sky in due order, and the diverse seasons of the year come round, nor could they learn by what causes that was brought about. And so they made it their refuge to lay all to the charge of the gods, and to suppose that all was guided by their will. And they placed the abodes and quarters of the gods in the sky, because through the night sky and the moon are seen to roll on their way, moon, day and night, and the stern signs of night, and the torches of heaven that rove through the night, and the flying flames, clouds, sunlight, rain, snow, winds, lightning, hail, and the rapid roar and mighty murmurings of heaven's threats.

1194 Ah! unhappy race of men, when it has assigned such acts to the gods and joined therewith bitter anger! What groaning did they then beget for themselves, what sores for us, what tears for our children to come! Nor is it piety at all to be seen often with veiled head turning towards a stone and drawing near to every altar, no, nor to lie prostrate on the ground with outstretched palms before the shrines of the gods, nor to sprinkle the altars with the streaming blood of beasts, nor to link vow to vow, but rather to be able to contemplate all things with a mind at rest.

1204 For indeed when we look up at the heavenly quarters of the great world, and the firm-set ether above the twinkling stars, and it comes to our mind to think of the journeyings of sun and moon, then into our hearts weighed down with other ills, this misgiving too begins to raise up its wakened head, that there may be perchance some immeasurable power of the gods over us, which whirls on the bright stars in their diverse motions. For lack of reasoning assails our mind with doubt, whether there was any creation and beginning of the world, and again whether there is an end, until which the walls of the world may be able to endure this weariness of restless motion, or whether gifted by the gods' will with an everlasting groove of time, and set at naught the mighty strength of measureless time.[86]

---

[86] Lines 1204–17 are a striking reversal of the typical religious feeling characterized by, for example, Psalm 19 'The heavens are telling the glory of God; and the firmament proclaims his handiwork'. For Lucretius such a feeling is not only based on false reasoning, but also one that leads to unnecessary fears.

1217 Moreover, whose heart does not shrink with terror of the gods, whose limbs do not crouch in fear, when the parched earth trembles beneath the awful stroke of lightning and rumblings run across the great sky? Do not the peoples and nations tremble, and proud kings shrink in every limb, thrilled with the fear of the gods, lest for some foul crime or haughty word the heavy time of retribution be ripe? Or again, when the fiercest force of furious wind at sea sweeps the commander of a fleet over the waters with his strong legions and his elephants, all in like case, does he not seek with vows the peace of the gods, and fearfully crave in prayer a calm from wind and favouring breezes; all in vain, since often when caught in the headstrong hurricane he is borne for all his prayers to the shallow waters of death? So greatly does some secret force grind beneath its heel the greatness of men, and it is seen to tread down and make sport for itself of the glorious rods and relentless axes.[87]

1236 Again, when the whole earth rocks beneath men's feet, and cities are shaken to their fall or threaten doubtful of their doom, what wonder if the races of mortal men despise themselves and leave room in the world for the mighty power and marvellous strength of the gods, to guide all things?

1241 For the rest, copper and gold and iron were discovered, and with them the weight of silver and the usefulness of lead, when a fire had burnt down vast forests with its heat on mighty mountains, either when heaven's lightning was hurled upon it, or because waging a forest-war with one another men had carried fire among the foe to rouse panic, or else because allured by the richness of the land they desired to clear the fat fields, and make the countryside into pasture, or else to put the wild beasts to death, and enrich themselves with prey. For hunting with pit and fire arose first before fencing the grove with nets and scaring the beasts with dogs. However, that may be, for whatever cause the flaming heat had eaten up the forests from their deep roots with terrible crackling, and had baked the earth with fire, the streams of silver and gold, and likewise of copper and lead, gathered together and trickled from the boiling veins into hollow places in the ground. And when they saw them

[87] The insignia of Roman magistrates.

afterwards hardened and shining on the ground with brilliant hue, they picked them up, charmed by their smooth bright beauty, and saw that they were shaped with outline like that of the several prints of the hollows. Then it came home to them that these metals might be melted by heat, and would run into the form and figure of anything, and indeed might be hammered out and shaped into points and tips, however sharp and fine, so that they might fashion weapons for themselves, and be able to cut down forests and hew timber and plane beams smooth, yea, and to bore and punch and drill holes. And, first of all, they set forth to do this no less with silver and gold than with the resistless strength of stout copper; all in vain, since their power was vanquished and yielded, nor could they like the others endure the cruel strain. For copper was of more value, and gold was despised for its uselessness, so soon blunted with its dull edge. Now copper is despised, gold has risen to the height of honour. So rolling time changes the seasons of things. What was of value, becomes in turn of no worth; and then another thing rises up and leaves its place of scorn, and is sought more and more each day, and when found blossoms into fame, and is of wondrous honour among men.

1281 Now, in what manner the nature of iron was found, it is easy for you to learn for yourself, Memmius. Their arms of old were hands, nails, teeth, and stones, and likewise branches torn from the forests, and flame and fires, when once they were known. Thereafter the strength of iron and bronze was discovered. And the use of bronze was learnt before that of iron, inasmuch as its nature is more tractable, and it is found in greater stores. With bronze they would work the soil of the earth, and with bronze mingle in billowy warfare, and deal wasting wounds and seize upon flocks and fields. For all things naked and unarmed would readily give in to them equipped with arms. Then, little by little, the iron sword made its way, and the form of the bronze sickle was made a thing of scorn, and with iron they began to plough up the soil of earth; and the contests of war, now hovering in doubt, were made equal.

1297 It was their way to climb armed on to the back of a horse, to guide it with reins, and do doughty deeds with the right hand, before they learnt to essay the dangers of war in a two-horsed chariot. And the yoking of two horses came before yoking four, and climbing up armed into chariots set with scythes. Then it was the Carthaginians who taught the Lucanian kine, [elephants] with towered body, grim beasts with snaky hands, to bear the wounds of warfare and work havoc among the hosts of Mars. So did gloomy discord beget one thing after another, to bring panic into the races of men in warfare, and day by day gave increase to the terrors of war.

1308 They tried bulls, too, in the service of war, and attempted to send savage boars against the foe. And some sent on before them mighty lions with armed trainers and cruel masters, who might be able to control them, and hold them in chains; all in vain, since in the heat of the mellay of slaughter they grew savage, and made havoc of the hosts, both sides alike, tossing everywhere the fearful manes upon their heads, nor could the horsemen soothe the hearts of their horses, alarmed at the roaring, and turn them with their bridles against the foe. The lionesses launched their furious bodies in a leap on every side, and made for the faces of those that came against them, or tore them down in the rear when off their guard, and twining round them hurled them to the ground foredone with the wound, fastening on them with their strong bite and crooked claws. The bulls tossed their own friends and trampled them with their feet, and with their horns gashed the flanks and bellies of the horses underneath, and ploughed up the ground with threatening purpose. And the boars gored their masters with their strong tusks, savagely splashing with their own blood the weapons broken in them, and threw to the ground horsemen and footmen in one heap. For the horses would swerve aside to avoid the fierce onset of a tusk, or rear and beat the air with their feet; all in vain, since you would see them tumble with tendons severed, and strew the ground in their heavy fall. If ever they thought they had been tamed enough at home before the fight, they saw them burst into fury, when it came to conflict, maddened by the wounds, shouting, flying, panic, and confusion, nor could they rally any part of them; for all the diverse kinds of wild beasts would scatter hither and thither; even as now often the Lucanian kine cruelly mangled by the steel, scatter abroad, when they have dealt many deadly deeds to their own friends. If indeed they ever acted thus. But scarce can I be brought to believe that, before this dire disaster befell both sides alike, they could not foresee and perceive in mind what would come to pass. And you could more readily maintain that this was done somewhere in the universe, in the diverse worlds fashioned in diverse fashion, than on any one determined earth. But indeed they wished to do it not so much in the hope of victory, as to give the foemen cause to moan, resolved to perish themselves, since they mistrusted their numbers and lacked arms.

1350 A garment tied together came before woven raiment. Woven fabric comes after iron, for by iron the loom is fashioned, nor in any other way can such smooth treadles be made, or spindles or shuttles and ringing rods. And nature constrained men to work wool before the race of women; for all the race of men far excels in skill and is much more cunning; until the sturdy husbandman made scorn of it, so that they were glad to leave it to women's hands, and themselves share in enduring hard toil, and in hard work to harden limbs and hands.

1361 But nature herself, creatress of things, was first a pattern for sowing and the beginning of grafting, since berries and acorns fallen from the trees in due time put forth swarms of shoots beneath; from nature, too, they learnt to insert grafts into branches, and to plant young saplings in the ground over the fields. Then one after another they tried ways of tilling their smiling plot, and saw the earth tame wild fruits with tender care and fond tilling. And day by day they would constrain the woods more and more to retire up the mountains, and to give up the land beneath to tilth, that on hills, and plains they might have meadows, pools, streams, crops, and glad vineyards, and the grey belt of olives might run between with its clear line, spreading over hillocks and hollows and plains; even as now you see all the land clear marked with diverse beauties, where men make it bright by planting it here and there with sweet fruit-trees, and fence it by planting it all round with fruitful shrubs.

1379 But imitating with the mouth the liquid notes of birds came long before men were able to sing in melody right through smooth songs and please the ear. And the whistling of the zephyr through the hollows of reeds first taught the men of the countryside to breathe into hollowed hemlock-stalks. Then little by little they learned the sweet lament, which the pipe pours forth, stopped by the players' fingers, the pipe invented amid the pathless woods and forests and glades, among the desolate haunts of shepherds, and the divine places of their rest.

1390 These tunes would soothe their minds and please them when sated with food; for then all things win the heart. And so often, lying in friendly groups on the soft grass near some stream of water under the branches of a tall tree, at no great cost they would give pleasure to their bodies, above all when the weather smiled and the season of the year painted the green grass with flowers. Then were there wont to be jests, and talk, and merry laughter. For then the rustic muse was at its best; then glad mirth would prompt to wreathe head and shoulders with garlands twined of flowers and foliage, and to dance all out of step, moving their limbs heavily, and with heavy foot to strike mother earth; whence arose smiles and merry laughter, for all these things then were strong in freshness and wonder. And hence came to the wakeful a solace for lost sleep, to guide their voices through many notes, and follow the windings of a song, and to run over the reeds with curling lip; whence even now the watchmen preserve these traditions, and have learnt to keep to the rhythm of the song, nor yet for all that do they gain a whit greater enjoyment from the pleasure, than the woodland race of earthborn men of old.

1412 For what is here at hand, unless we have learnt anything sweeter before, pleases us above all, and is thought to excel, but for the most part the better thing found later on destroys or changes our feeling for all the old things. So hatred for their acorns set in, and the old couches strewn with grass and piled with leaves were deserted. Likewise the garment of wild beasts' skin fell into contempt; yet I suppose that of old it was so envied when found, that he who first wore it was waylaid and put to death, though after all it was torn to pieces among them, and was spoiled with much blood, and could be turned to no profit.

1423 It was skins then in those days, and now gold and purple that vex men's life with cares and weary them out with war; and for this, I think, the greater fault lies with us. For cold used to torture the earth-born, as they lay naked without skins; but it does us no hurt to go without our purple robes, set with gold and massy figures, if only there be some common garment to protect us. And so the race of men toils fruitlessly and in vain for ever, and wastes its life in idle cares, because, we may be sure, it has not learned what are the limits of possession, nor at all how far true pleasure can increase. And this, little by little, has advanced life to its high plane, and has stirred up from the lowest depths the great seething tide of war.

1436 But sun and moon, like watchmen, traversing with their light all round the great turning vault of the world, taught men that the seasons of the year come round, and that the work goes on after a sure plan and a sure order.

   1440 Now fenced in with strong towers they would live their life, and the land was parcelled out and marked off: then the sea was gay with the flying sails of ships: now treaties were drawn up, and they had auxiliaries and allies, when poets first began to hand down men's deeds in songs; yet not much before that were letters discovered. Therefore our age cannot look back to see what was done before, unless in any way reason points out traces.

   1448 Ships and the tilling of the land, walls, laws, weapons, roads, dress, and all things of this kind, all the prizes, and the luxuries of life, one and all, songs and pictures, and the polishing of quaintly wrought statues, practice and therewith the experience of the eager mind taught them litle by little, as they went forward step by step. So, little by little, time brings out each several thing into view, and reason raises it up into the coasts of light. For they saw one thing after another grow clear in their mind, until by their arts they reached the topmost pinnacle.

Erratic Atmosphere And Terrestrial Events

Synopsis

1–42   In praise of Epicurus [verse translation by Charles Foxley, 1933].

43–95   The programme is to understand natural events so that we do not attribute them to the gods.

Atmospheric Phenomena, 96–534

96–159   Thunder.

160–218   Lightning: the speed of light is much greater than the speed of sound.

219–378   Thunderbolts have numerous natural explanations.

379–422   And this is the way to see them, not as the anger of Jupiter.

423–50   Waterspouts.

451–94   Clouds.

495–526   Rain.

527–34   And other phenomena of climate and weather: all have understandable explanations.

Terrestrial Phenomena, 535–1137

535–607   Earthquakes.

608–38   Evaporation causes the sea to be always the same size.

639–702   Volcanoes.

703–11   Some events have many natural causes.

712–37   The summer flooding of the Nile.

738–68   There are lakes and other places with the natural capacity to kill birds or be otherwise pestilential.

769–839   Why this is so.

840–905   Strange wells, springs and fountains.

906–20   How the magnet works requires a long explanation.

921–1089   The explanation given.

Epidemics and the Great Plague at Athens, 1090–286

1090–137   The causes of plagues in general.

1138–44   The source of the plague at Athens [in 430 BC].

1145–229   Detailed description of its symptoms and outcome [compare Thucydides, II, 47–54].

1230–51   The psychological effects of the plague.

1252–71   The vast numbers of dead bodies.

1272–7   The gods did nothing even in their own temples, and were 'not counted for much'.

1278–86   Even the sacred rites of burial were overwhelmed by the scale of the disaster.

Book VI

The first that made the fruitful grain to grow
And spread the boon to many a needy nation
Was glorious Athens. Athens long ago
By ordered law made life a new creation.
And Athens gave us life's dear consolation,
Brought forth the sage who nothing spake but sooth,
The new-found prophet of his generation.
He passed long since, that seer of godlike truth,
But heav'nward soars his fame; its age is fresh as youth.

For seeing almost all things plenteously
Provided now for mortal man's content,
With life made safe (so safe as well may be),
And seeing men illustrious, affluent,
In children's honest fame pre-eminent,
Nor less their hearts disquieted by taint
Of cares, unwelcome strangers, which torment
Men's thought-life ceaselessly with harsh constraint
Till sore bestead they rage with fierce and angry plaint,

He found the vessel's own defects to blame;
The stores within were tainted by the jar,
Whate'er the quarter whence those comforts came.
Too leaky, frail and faulty ware by far,
Our minds, he noted, ne'er replenished are.
A rank ill-savor he perceived thereto,
Which all within them did befoul and mar.
He therefore scoured the heart with doctrine true,
And stayed th' excess of lust and fear with limits due.

That highest good, for which we all are bound,
He did define for us, and demonstrate
Before our eyes the way whereby 'tis found.
Though small the track, press on! it leads you straight.
He showed what evils threaten man's estate
By chance or force, not providence or art,

Explained what foe to strike at from which gate,
And showed how vainly man for the most part
Doth roll the gloomy waves of care around his heart.

So, weaving in my words right hopefully,
On tow'rd the finished web I'll work my way.
As children shudder in the dark, and see
Naught, but fear all, so we in light of day
Dread much that's no more dreadful than when they
All quaking, look for what they cannot tell.
It is a night, this spiritual dismay,
Nor sun nor day's bright arrows may dispel,
But Nature must be seen and known, and all is well.

This terror then, this darkness of the mind, must needs be scattered not by the rays and the gleaming shafts of day, but by the outer view and the inner law of nature. Wherefore I will hasten the more to weave the thread of my task in my discourse.

43 And now that I have shown that the quarters of the firmament are mortal, and that the heaven is fashioned of a body that has birth, and have unravelled wellnigh all that happens therein, and must needs happen, listen still to what remains; forasmuch as once [I have ventured to climb the glorious chariot of the Muses, I will explain how the tempests][88] of the winds arise, and are appeased, and all that once was raging is changed again, when its fury is appeased; and all else which mortals see coming to pass on earth and in the sky, when often they are in suspense with panic-stricken mind — things which bring their hearts low through dread of the gods, and bow them down grovelling to earth, because their ignorance of true causes constrains them to assign things to the ordinance of the gods, and to admit their domination. For if from time to time those who have learnt aright that the gods lead a life free from care, yet wonder by what means all things can be carried on (above all among those things which are descried above our heads in the coasts of heaven) then they are borne back again into the old beliefs of religion. They adopt stern

[88] About two lines seem to be missing here.

overlords, whom in their misery they believe have all power, knowing not what can be and what cannot, yes, and in what way each thing has its power limited, and its deepset boundary-stone. Therefore all the more they stray, borne on by a blind reasoning.

68 And unless you spew out all this from your mind and banish far away thoughts unworthy of the gods and alien to their peace, the holy powers of the gods, degraded by your thought, will often do you harm. Not because the high majesty of the gods can be polluted by you, so that in wrath they should wish to seek sharp retribution, but because you yourself will imagine that those tranquil beings in their placid peace set tossing the great billows of wrath. Nor with quiet breast will you approach the shrines of the gods, nor will you have strength to drink in with tranquil peace of mind the images which are borne from their holy body to herald their divine form to the minds of men.[89] And therefore what manner of life will follow, you may perceive.

80 And in order that truest reasoning may drive this far from us, although much has already gone forth from me, yet much remains to be adorned with polished verse. We must grasp the outer view and inner law of the sky. We must sing of storms and flashing lightnings, of how they act and by what cause they are severally carried along; that you may not mark out the quarters of the sky, and ask in frenzied anxiety, whence came this winged flash, or to what quarter it departed hence, in what manner it won its way through walled places, and how after tyrant deeds it brought itself forth again. The causes of these workings they can by no means see, and think that a divine power brings them about.

92 Do you, as I speed towards the white line of the final goal, mark out the track before me, Calliope, muse of knowledge, thou who art rest to men and pleasure to the gods, that with thee to guide I may win the wreath with praise conspicuous.

---

[89] In simplistic terms, for the Epicureans gods were known by images or concepts experienced directly in the mind, not sensed. But the story is very complex. For a good analytic discussion see A. A. Long and D. N. Sidley, *The Hellenistic Philosophers* (Cambridge, 1987), vol. I, pp. 144–9. See also above, pp. xxxii–iv.

ATMOSPHERIC PHENOMENA,[90] 96–534

96 First of all the blue of the sky is shaken by thunder because the clouds in high heaven, scudding aloft, clash together when the winds are fighting in combat. For the sound comes not from a clear quarter of the sky, but whatever the clouds are massed in denser host, from there more often comes the roar and its loud rumbling. Moreover, the clouds cannot be of so dense a body as are sticks and stones, nor yet so thin as are mists and flying smoke. For either they were bound to fall dragged down by their dead weight, as do stones, or like smoke they could not hold together or keep within them chill snow and showers of hail.

108 Again, they give forth a sound over the levels of the spreading firmament, as often an awning stretched over a great theatre gives a crack, as it tosses among the posts and beams; sometimes, too, it rages madly, rent by the boisterous breezes, and imitates the rending noise of sheets of paper – for that kind of sound too you may recognize in the thunder – or else a sound as when the winds buffet with their blows and beat through the air a hanging garment or flying papers. For indeed it also comes to pass at times that the clouds cannot so much clash together face to face, but rather pass along the flank, moving from diverse quarters, and slowly grazing body against body; and then the dry sound brushes upon the ears, and is drawn out long, until they have issued from their close quarters.

121 In this way, too, all things seem often to tremble with heavy thunder, and the great walls of the containing world to be torn apart suddenly and leap asunder, when all at once a gathered storm of mighty wind has twisted its way into the clouds, and, shut up there with its whirling eddy, constrains the cloud more and more on all sides to hollow itself out with body thickening all around; and then, when the force and fierce onslaught of the wind have weakened it, it splits and makes a rending crash with a frightful cracking sound. Nor is that strange, when a little bladder full of air often likewise gives forth a little noise, if suddenly burst.

---

[90] Lucretius is particularly concerned with overtly terrifying and erratically occurring phenomena such as thunderbolts and earthquakes because it is in precisely these things that human beings most readily see the actions of God or gods.

132 There is also another way, when winds blow through clouds, whereby they may make a noise. For often we see clouds borne along, branching in many ways, and rough-edged; even as, we may be sure, when the blasts of the north-west blow through a dense forest, the leaves give out a noise and the branches a rending crash.

137 It comes to pass, too, sometimes, that the force of a mighty wind rushing on tears through the cloud and breaks it asunder with a front attack. For what the blast can do there is shown by things clear to see here on earth, where the wind is gentler and yet it tears out and sucks up tall trees from their lowest roots.

142 There are, too, waves moving through the clouds, which as it were make a heavy roar in breaking; just as it comes to pass in deep rivers and the great sea, when the tide breaks.

145 This happens too, when the fiery force of the thunderbolt falls from cloud to cloud; if by chance the cloud has received the flame in deep moisture, it straightway slays it with a great noise; just as often iron white-hot from the fiery furnaces hisses, when we have plunged it quickly into cold water.

150 Or again, if a drier cloud receives the flame, it is at once fired, and burns with a vast noise; just as if among the laurel-leafed mountains flame were to roam abroad beneath the eddying of the winds, burning them up in its mighty onset; nor is there any other thing which is burnt up by the crackling flame with sound so terrible as the Delphic laurel of Phoebus.

156 Again, often the great cracking of ice and the falling of hail makes a noise in the mighty clouds on high. For when the wind packs them tight, the mountains of storm-clouds, frozen close and mingled with hail, break up.

160 It lightnings likewise, when the clouds at their clashing have struck out many seeds of fire; just as if stone should strike on stone or on iron; for then, too, a flash leaps out and scatters abroad bright sparks of fire.

164 But it comes to pass that we receive the thunder in our ears after our eyes perceive the lightning, because things always move more slowly to the ears than things which stir the eyes. That you may learn from this too; if you see some one far off cutting down a giant tree with double-edged axe,

it comes to pass that you see the stroke before the blow resounds in your ear; even so we see the lightning too before we hear the thunder, which is sent abroad at the same moment with the flash, from a like cause, yes, born indeed from the same collision.

173 In this manner, too, the clouds colour places with leaping light, and the storm lightens with quivering dart. When wind has come within a cloud, and moving there has, as I have shown before, made the hollow cloud grow thick, it grows hot with its own swift movement; even as you see all things become hot and catch fire through motion, yes, even a ball of lead too, whirling in a long course, will melt. And so when this heated wind has torn through the black cloud, it scatters abroad seeds of fire, as though struck out all at once by force, and they make the pulsing flashes of flame; thereafter follows the sound, which reaches our ears more slowly than things which come to the light of our eyes. This, we must know, comes to pass in thick clouds, which are also piled up high one on the other in wondrous slope; lest you be deceived because we below see how broad they are rather than to what a height they stand piled up. For do but look, when next the winds carry athwart the air clouds in the semblance of mountains, or when you see them heaped along a mighty mountain-range one above the other, pressing down from above, at rest in their appointed place, when the winds on all sides are in their graves. Then you will be able to mark their mighty mass, and to see their caverns built up, as it were, of hanging rocks: and when the storm has risen and the winds have filled them, with loud roar they chafe prisoned in the clouds, and threaten like wild beasts in cages; now from this side, now from that they send forth their roaring through the clouds, and seeking an outlet they move round and round, and roll together the seeds of fire from out the clouds, and so drive many into a mass and set the flame whirling within the hollow furnaces, until they have rent asunder the cloud and flashed blazing out.

204 For this cause, too, it comes to pass that this swift golden tinge of liquid fire flies down to earth, because it must needs be that the clouds have in themselves very many seeds of fire; for indeed when they are without any moisture, they have for the most part a bright and flaming colour. For verily it must needs

be that they catch many such from the sun's light, so that with reason they are red, and pour forth their fires. When then the wind as it drives them has pushed and packed and compelled them into one spot, they squeeze out and pour forth the seeds which make the colours of flame to flash.

214 It lightnings likewise, also when the clouds of heaven grow thin. For when the wind lightly draws them asunder as they move, and breaks them up, it must needs be that those seeds, which make the flash, fall out unbidden. Then it lightnings without hideous alarm, without noise, and with no uproar.

219 For the rest, with what kind of nature thunderbolts are endowed, is shown by the blows and the burned markings of their heat and the brands which breathe out vile vapours of sulphur. For these are marks of fire, not of wind or rain. Moreover, often too they set the roofs of dwellings on fire, and with swiftly moving flame play the tyrant even within the houses. This fire, you must know, nature has fashioned most subtle of all subtle fires, of tiny swift-moving bodies – a flame to which nothing at all can be a barrier. For the strong thunderbolt can pass through the walls of houses, even as shouts and cries, can pass through rocks, through things of bronze, and in a moment of time can melt bronze and gold. Likewise it causes wine in an instant to flee away, though the vessels be untouched, because, we may be sure, its heat as it comes easily loosens all around and makes rarefied the porcelain of the vessel, and finding its way right into the wine, with quick motion dissolves and scatters the primordia of the wine. Yet this the heat of the sun is seen to be unable to bring about in a long age, though it has such exceeding strength in its flashing blaze. So much swifter and more masterful is this force of the thunderbolt.

239 Now in what manner they are fashioned and made with such force that they can with their blow burst open towers, overthrow houses, pluck up beams and joists, and upset and destroy the monuments of men, take the life from men, lay low the flocks on every side; by what force they are able to do all other things of this sort, I will set forth, nor keep you longer waiting on my promise.

246 We must suppose that thunderbolts are produced from thick clouds, piled up on high; for none are ever hurled abroad

from the clear sky or from clouds of slight thickness. For without doubt clear-seen facts show that this comes to pass. At such times clouds grow into a mass throughout all the air, so that on all sides we might think that all darkness has left Acheron and filled the great vault of the sky; so terribly, when the noisome night of clouds has gathered together, do the shapes of black fear hang over us on high, when the storm begins to forge its thunderbolts.

256 Moreover, very often a black storm-cloud over the sea, like a stream of pitch shot from the sky, falls upon the waters, laden with darkness afar off, and draws on a black storm big with thunderbolts and hurricanes, itself more than all filled full with fires and winds in such wise that even on land men shudder and seek for shelter. Thus then above our head must we suppose the storm is raised high. For indeed they would not shroud the earth in such thick gloom, unless there were many clouds built up aloft on many others, shutting out all sunlight; nor when they come could they drown it in such heavy rain, as to make the rivers overflow and the fields swim, unless the ether were filled with clouds piled up on high.

269 Here, then, all is full of winds and fires; for this cause all around come crashings and lightnings. For truly I have shown before now that the hollow clouds possess very many seeds of heat, and many they must needs catch from the sun's rays and their blaze. Therefore, when the same wind, which drives them together, as it chances, into some one place, has squeezed out many seeds of heat, and at the same time has mingled itself with this fire, an eddy finds its way in there and whirls round in a narrow space and sharpens the thunderbolt in the hot furnaces within. For it is kindled in two ways, both when it grows hot with its own swift motion, and from contact with the fire. Next, when the force of the wind has grown exceeding hot, and the fierce onset of the fire has entered in, then the thunderbolt, full-forged, as it were, suddenly rends through the cloud, and shot out is borne on flooding all places with its blazing light. In its train follows a heavy crash, so that the quarters of the sky above seem to be burst asunder on a sudden and crush us. Then a trembling thrills violently through the earth, and rumblings race over the high heaven; for then all the storm is shaken into trembling and roarings move abroad. And from this shock

follows rain, heavy and abundant, so that all the air seems to be turned into rain, and thus falling headlong to summon earth back to deluge: so great a shower is shot forth with the rending of the cloud and the hurricane of wind, when the thunderclap flies forth with its burning blow.

295 At times, too, the rushing force of wind falls from without upon the cloud hot with its new-forged thunderbolt; and when it has rent the cloud, straightway there falls out that fiery eddy which we call by the name our fathers gave it, the thunderbolt. The same thing happens in other directions, wherever its force has carried it.

300 It comes to pass, too, sometimes that the force of the wind, starting without fire, yet catches fire on its course and its long wandering, as it loses in its journey, while it is approaching, certain large bodies, which cannot like the others make their way through the air; and gathering other small bodies from the air itself it carries them along, and they mingling with it make fire in their flight; in no other way than often a ball [i.e., bullet, as from a sling] of lead grows hot in its course, when dropping many bodies of stiff cold it catches fire in the air.

309 It comes to pass, too, that the force of the very blow rouses fire, when the force of the wind, starting cold without fire, has struck its stroke; because, we may be sure, when it has hit with violent blow, particles of heat can stream together out of the wind itself, and at the same time from the thing which then receives the blow; just as, when we strike a stone with iron, fire flies out, nor do the seeds of blazing heat rush together any more slowly at its blow, because the force of the iron is cold. Thus then a thing is bound to be kindled by the thunderbolt too, if by chance it is made fit and suitable for flame. Nor must we rashly think that the force of the wind can be wholly and utterly cold, when it has been discharged with such force on high; rather, if it is not beforehand on its journey kindled with fire, yet it arrives warmed and mingled with heat.

323 But the great speed of the thunderbolt and its heavy blow comes to pass, yea, the thunderbolts always run their course with swift descent, because their force unaided is first of all set in motion in each case, and gathers itself within the clouds, and conceives a great effort for starting; and then, when the cloud has not been able to contain the growing strength of

its onset, its force is squeezed out, and so flies with wondrous
impulse even as the missiles which are borne on, when shot from
engines of war.

330 Remember, too, that it is made of small and smooth
particles, nor is it easy for anything to withstand such a nature:
for it flies in between and pierces through the hollow passages,
and so it is not clogged and delayed by many obstacles, and
therefore it flies on falling with swift impulse.

335 Again, because all weights by nature always press downwards, but when a blow is given as well, their swiftness is
doubled and the impulse grows stronger, so that the more
violently and quickly does it scatter with its blows all that
impedes it, and continues on its journey.

340 Once again, because it comes from far with great
momentum, it is bound to gather speed ever more and more,
which grows as it moves, and increases its strong might and
strengthens its stroke. For it brings it about that the seeds of the
thunderbolt are one and all carried in a straight line, as it were
towards one spot, driving them all as they fly into the same
course. It may chance too that as it goes it picks up certain
bodies even from the air, which kindle its momentum by their
blows.

348 And it passes through things without harming them, and
goes right through many things, and leaves them whole, because
the liquid fire flies through the pores. And it pierces through
many things, since the very bodies of the thunderbolt have fallen
on the bodies of things just where they are interlaced and held
together. Moreover, it easily melts bronze and in an instant
makes gold to boil, because its force is fashioned delicately of
tiny bodies and of smooth particles, which easily force a way
within, and being there at once loose all the knots and slacken
the bonds.

357 And most in autumn is the house of heaven, set with
shining stars, shaken on all sides and all the earth, and again
when the flowery season of spring spreads itself abroad. For in
the cold, fires are lacking; and in the heat, winds fail, nor are
clouds of so dense a body. And so when the seasons of heaven
stand midway between the two, then all the diverse causes of
the thunderbolt meet together. For the narrow channels of the
year [i.e. spring and autumn] mingle cold and heat – of both of

which the cloud has need for the forging of thunderbolts – so that there is a wrangling among things, and with great uproar the air rages and tosses with fires and winds. For the first part of the heat is the last of the stiff cold, that is the spring season: wherefore it must needs be that different elements, mingled with one another, make battle and turmoil. And again, when the last heat rolls on mingled with the first cold – the season which is called by the name of autumn – then, too, keen winters do battle with summers. For this cause these seasons must be called the narrow channels of the year, nor is it strange, if at that time thunderbolts come most often, and a turbulent tempest is gathered in the sky, since from either side is roused the turmoil of doubtful battle, on the one side with flames, on the other with mingled wind and wet.

379 This is the way to see into the true nature of the thunder-bolt, and to perceive by what force it does each thing, and not by unrolling vainly the Tyrrhenian prophecies and seeking out tokens of the hidden purpose of the gods, marking whence came the winged flash, or to what quarter it departed hence, in what manner it won its way through walled places, and how after tyrant deeds it brought itself forth again, or what harm the stroke of the thunderbolt from heaven can do.

387 But if Jupiter and the other gods shake the shining quarters of heaven with awe-inspiring crash and hurl the fire to whatever point each may will, why do they not bring it about that those who have not guarded against some sin from which men hide their face, are struck and reek of the flames of lightning, with their breast pierced through, a sharp lesson to mortals? Why rather is one conscious of no foul guilt wrapt and entangled, all innocent, in the flames, caught up in a moment in the fiery whirlwind of heaven? Why again do they aim at waste places and spend their strength for naught? Are they then practising their arms and strengthening their muscles? And why do they suffer the father's weapon to be blunted on the earth? Why does he himself endure it and not spare it for his foes? Again, why does Jupiter never hurl his thunderbolt to earth and pour forth his thunders when the heaven is clear on all sides? Or, as soon as the clouds have come up, does he himself then come down into them, so that from them he may direct the

blow of his weapon from close at hand? Again, with what purpose does he throw into the sea? What charge has he against the waves, the mass of water and the floating fields? Moreover, if he wishes us to beware of the thunderbolt's stroke, why is he reluctant to let us be able to see its cast? But if he wishes to overwhelm us with the fire when off our guard, why does he thunder from that quarter, so that we can shun it? Why does he gather darkness beforehand and rumblings and roarings? And how can you believe that he hurls his bolts at once to many sides? Or would you dare to argue that this has never come to pass, that several strokes were made at one time? Nay, but very often has it happened and must needs happen, that as it rains, and showers fall in many regions, so many thunderbolts are fashioned at one time. Lastly, why does he smite asunder the sacred shrines of the gods and his own glorious dwelling-places with hostile bolt? Why does he destroy the fair-fashioned simulacra of the gods and take away their beauty from his images with his furious wound? And why does he aim mostly at lofty spots, so that we see most traces of his fire on mountain-tops?

423 Next after this, it is easy to learn from these things in what way there come into the sea, shot from on high, what the Greeks from their nature have named fiery presters [water spouts]. For it comes to pass sometimes that as it were a column let down descends from the sky into the sea, around which the surges boil, violently stirred by breathing blasts, and all ships that are then caught in that turmoil, are harried and come into great danger.

431 This comes to pass sometimes when the force of the wind set in motion cannot burst the cloud it starts to burst, but presses it down, so that it is weighed down like a column from sky to sea, little by little, as though something were being thrust down and stretched out into the waves by a fist and the pushing of an arm above; and when it has rent this cloud asunder, the force of the wind bursts forth thence into the sea and brings to pass a wondrous seething in the waters. For a whirling eddy descends and brings down along with it that cloud of pliant body; and as soon as it has forced it down pregnant on to the levels of ocean, the eddy on a sudden plunges its whole self into

the water, and stirs up all the sea with a great roar, constraining it to seethe.

447 It comes to pass also that an eddy of wind by itself wraps itself in clouds, gathering together seeds of cloud from the air and, as it were, imitates the prester let down from the sky. When this eddy has let itself down to earth and broken up, it vomits forth a furious force of whirlwind and storm. But because this happens but rarely at all, and mountains must needs bar it on land, it is seen more often on a wide prospect of sea, and in an open stretch of sky.

451 Clouds gather up, when many bodies as they fly in this upper expanse of the sky have all at once come together – bodies of rougher kind, such as can, though they be but intertwined with slight links, yet grasp and cling to one another. These first of all cause little clouds to form; then these grip hold of one another and flock together, and uniting they grow and are borne on by the winds, until at last a furious tempest has gathered together.

459 It comes to pass, too, that mountain-tops, the closer they are to the sky, the more at that height do they smoke continually with the thick darkness of a murky cloud, because, when first the clouds form, still thin, before the eyes can see them, the winds carry them and drive them together to the topmost peaks of the mountain. There it comes to pass at last that, gathered now in a greater throng and thickened, they can be seen, and at once they seem to rise into the open sky from the very summit of the mountain. For clear fact and our sense, when we climb high mountains, proclaim that windy regions stretch above.

470 Moreover, that nature lifts up many such bodies all over the sea is shown by clothes hung out on the shore, when they take in a clinging moisture. Wherefore it is all the more seen that many bodies too can rise to swell the clouds from the salt tossing ocean; for in all their nature these two moistures are akin.

476 Moreover, we see clouds and vapour rising from all rivers, and likewise from the very earth which, like a breath, are forced out hence and carried upwards, and curtain the heaven with their darkness, and little by little, as they meet, build up the clouds on high. For the vapour of the starry ether above

presses down on them too, and, as it were by thickening, weaves
a web of storm-cloud beneath the blue.

483 It happens, too, that there come into our sky those
bodies from without which make clouds and flying storms. For
I have shown that their number is innumerable, and the sum of
the deep measureless, and I have set forth with what speed the
bodies fly, and how in a moment they are wont to traverse
through space that none can tell. So it is not strange if often in a
short time storm and darkness cover up sea and land with such
great storm-clouds, brooding above, inasmuch as on all sides
through all the pores of the ether, and, as it were, through the
breathing-holes of the great world all around there is furnished
for the particles exit and entrance.

495 Come now, in what manner the rainy moisture gathers
together in the high clouds, and how the shower falls shot down
upon the earth, I will unfold.

497 First of all it will be granted me that already many seeds
of water rise up with the clouds themselves from out of all
things, and that both alike grow in this manner, both clouds
and all water that is in the clouds, just as our body grows along
with its blood, and likewise sweat and all the moisture too that
is within the limbs. Also clouds often take in much moisture
from the sea, just like hanging fleeces of wool, when the winds
carry the clouds over the great sea. In like manner moisture
from all streams is raised to the clouds. And when many seeds
of waters in many ways have duly come together there, increased
from all quarters, the packed clouds are eager to shoot out the
moisture for a double cause; for the force of the wind pushes it
on and the very mass of the clouds, driven together in greater
throng, presses on it and weighs it down from above, and makes
the showers stream out. Moreover, when the clouds, too, are
thinned by the winds or broken up, smitten by the sun's heat
above, they send out the rainy moisture and drip, even as wax
over a hot fire melts and flows in a thick stream.

517 But a violent downpour comes to pass, when the clouds
are violently pressed by either force, their own mass and the
impulse of the wind. Yes, and the rains are wont to hold on long
and make a great stay, when many seeds of water are gathered,
and clouds piled upon clouds and streaming storms above them

are borne on from every quarter, and when the whole earth smoking, breathes out its moisture.

524 When at such time the sun amid the dark tempest, has shone out with its rays full against the spray of the storm-clouds, then among the black clouds stand out the hues of the rainbow.

527 All other things which grow above and are brought to being above, and which gather together in the clouds, all, yea all of them, snow, winds, hail, chill hoar-frosts, and the great force of ice, that great hardener of waters, the curb which everywhere reins in the eager streams, it is yet right easy to find these out, and to see in the mind in what manner they all come to be and in what way they are brought to being, when you have duly learned the powers which belong to the elements.

TERRESTRIAL PHENOMENA, 535–1137

535 Come now and learn what is the law of earthquakes. And first of all let yourself suppose that the earth is below, just as above, full on all sides of windy caverns; and you must think it bears in its bosom many lakes and many pools and cliffs and sheer rocks; and that many rivers hidden beneath the back of the earth roll on amain their waves and submerged stones. For clear fact demands that it should be everywhere like itself.

543 When these things then are placed and linked together beneath it, the earth above trembles, shaken by great falling masses, when beneath time has caused huge caverns to fall in; nay, indeed, whole mountains fall, and at the great and sudden shock tremblings creep abroad thence far and wide. And with good reason, since whole houses by the roadside tremble when shaken by a wagon of no great weight, and rock none the less, whenever a stone in the road jolts on the iron circles of the wheels on either side. It comes to pass too, when a vast mass of soil, loosened by age from the earth, rolls down into huge wide pools of water, that the earth too tosses and sways beneath the wave of water; even as a vessel sometimes cannot stand still, unless the liquid within has ceased to toss with unsteady wave.

557 Moreover, when the wind (gathering throughout the cavernous places of the earth) blows strong from one point, and with all its weight presses on the lofty caves with mighty

strength, the earth leans over to where the swooping force of the wind presses it. Then the houses that are built up upon the earth, yes, the more they are each one raised towards the sky, bend over in suspense, tottering towards the same quarter, and the timbers driven forward hang out ready to fall. And yet men fear to believe that a time of destruction and ruin awaits the nature of the great world, even when they see so great a mass of earth bowing to its fall. Why, unless the winds breathed in again, no force could put a curb on things or avail to pull them back from destruction as they fell. As it is, because turn by turn they breathe in and then grow violent, because, as it were, they rally and charge again and then are driven back and give ground, for this reason the earth more often threatens a fall than brings it to pass; for it leans over and then sways back again, and after falling forward recovers its position to a steady poise. In this way, then, the whole building rocks, the top more than the middle, the middle more than the bottom, the bottom but a very little.

577 There is this cause, too, of that same great shaking, when suddenly wind and some exceeding great force of air, gathering either from without or within the earth itself, have hurled themselves into the hollow places of the earth, and there first rage among the great caves in turmoil, and rise, carried on in a whirl; and when afterwards the moving force driven forth bursts out and at the same time cleaves the earth and causes a huge chasm. Even as it came to pass at Sidon in Syria, and was the case at Aegium in Peloponnese, cities are overthrown by this issue of air and the quaking of the earth which arose. And besides many walled towns have fallen through great movements on land, and many cities have sunk down deep into the sea, inhabitants and all.

591 And even if it does not burst forth, yet the very impulse of the air and the fierce force of the wind are spread, like a fit of shivering, throughout the riddling passages of the earth, and thereby induce a trembling: even as cold, when it comes deep into our members, shakes them against their will and constrains them to tremble and to move. So men quiver with anxious terror throughout the cities, they fear the houses above, they dread the hollow places beneath, lest the nature of the earth should break them open all at once, and lest torn asunder she should open

wide her maw, and, tumbled all together, desire to fill it with her own falling ruins.

601 Let them then believe as they will that heaven and earth will be indestructible, entrusted to some everlasting protection; and yet from time to time the very present force of danger applies on some side or other this goad of fear, lest the earth, snatched away suddenly from beneath their feet be carried into the abyss, and the sum of things, left utterly without foundation, follow on, and there be a tumbling wreck of the whole world.

608 First of all they wonder why nature does not make the sea bigger, since there comes into it so great a downpour of water, yes, all the streams from every quarter. Add, if you will, the shifting showers and the scudding storms, which bespatter and drench all seas and lands; add too its own springs; yet compared to the sum of the sea all these things will scarce be equal to the increase of a single drop; therefore it is the less strange that the great sea does not increase.

616 Moreover, the sun draws off a great part by his heat. For verily we see the sun with its blazing rays dry clothes wringing with moisture; and yet we see many oceans spread wide beneath earth's level. Therefore, although from each single place the sun sucks up but a small part of moisture from the level sea; yet in so great a space it will draw largely from the waves.

623 Then again, the winds too can lift a great part of moisture as they sweep the level seas, since very often we see roads dried by the wind in a single night, and the soft mud harden into crusts.

627 Moreover, I have shown that the clouds too lift up much moisture taken in from the great level of ocean, and scatter it broadcast over all the circle of lands, when it rains on the earth and the winds carry on the clouds.

631 Lastly, since the earth is formed of porous body, and is continuous, surrounding on all sides the shores of the sea, it must needs be that, just as the moisture of water passes into the sea from the lands, it likewise filters through into the land from the salt sea levels. For the brine is strained through, and the substance of moisture oozes back and all streams together at the fountain-head of rivers, and thence comes back over the lands

with freshened current, where the channel once cleft has brought down the waters in their liquid march.

639 Now what is the reason that through the jaws of Mount Etna flames sometimes breathe forth in so great a hurricane, I will unfold. For indeed the flaming storm gathered with no ordinary force of destruction, and ruled supreme through the fields of the Sicilians and turned to itself the gaze of neighbouring nations. They saw all the quarters of the heavens smoke and sparkle, and filled their hearts with shuddering fear for what new and universal change nature might be working.

647 Herein you must look far and deep and take a wide view to every quarter, that you may remember that the sum of things is unfathomable, and see how small, how infinitely small a part of the totality of things is one single sky – not so large a part, as is a single man of the whole earth. And if you have this duly before you and look clearly at it and see it clearly, you would cease to wonder at many things.

655 For does any of us wonder, if a man has caught in his limbs a fever gathering with burning heat, or any other painful disease in his members? For a foot will swell suddenly, often a sharp pain seizes on the teeth or makes its way right into the eyes; the accursed fire [erysipelas] breaks out and creeping about in the body burns any part which it has seized, and crawls through the limbs, because, as we may be sure, there are seeds of many things, and this earth and heaven has enough disease and malady, from which the force of measureless disease might avail to spread abroad.

665 So then we must suppose that out of the infinite all things are supplied to the whole heaven and earth in number enough that on a sudden the earth might be shaken and moved, a tearing hurricane course over sea and land, the fire of Etna well forth, and the heaven be aflame. For that too comes to pass, and the quarters of heaven blaze, and there are rainstorms gathering in heavier mass, when by chance the seeds of the waters have so arranged themselves.

673 'Nay, but the stormy blaze of this fire is exceeding gigantic.' So, too, be sure, is the river which is the greatest seen by a man, who has never before seen any greater: so a tree or a man may seem gigantic, and in every kind of thing, the greatest that each man has seen, he always imagines gigantic, and yet all

of them together, yes, with heaven and earth and sea besides, are nothing to the whole sum of the universal all.

680 But now in what ways that flame is suddenly excited and breathes abroad from out the vast furnaces of Etna, I will unfold.

682 First of all the nature of the whole mountain is hollow beneath, resting everywhere on caverns of basalt. Moreover, in all the caves there is wind and air. For air becomes wind, when it is set in motion and aroused. When it has grown hot, and as it rages has heated all the rocks and the earth around wherever it touches them, and has struck out from them a fire hot with swift flames, it rises up and so drives itself forth on high straight through the mountain's jaws. And so it carries its heat far, and afar it scatters the ash and rolls on a smoke with thick murky darkness, and all the while hurls out rocks of marvellous weight; for you must not doubt that this is the stormy force of air.

694 Moreover, in great part the sea makes its waves break and sucks in its tide at the roots of that mountain. From this sea caves stretch underneath right to the deep jaws of the mountain. By this path we must admit that [water] passes in, and the fact compels us [to believe that wind is mingled with it] and pierces deep in from the open sea, and then breathes out, and so lifts up the flame and casts up rocks and raises clouds of dust. For on the topmost peak are craters, as the inhabitants name them; what we call jaws or mouths.

703 Some things there are, too, not a few, for which to tell one cause is not enough; we must give more, one of which is yet the actual cause; just as if you yourself were to see the lifeless body of a man lying before you, it would be right that you should name all causes of death, in order that the one cause of that man's death might be told. For you could not prove that he had perished by the sword or of cold, or by disease or perchance by poison. But we know that it was something of this sort which happened to him. Likewise, we can say the same in many cases.

712 The Nile, the river of all Egypt, alone in the world rises, as summer comes, and overflows the plains.

714 It waters Egypt often amid the hot season, either because

in summer the north winds, which at that time are said to be the etesian winds, are dead against its mouths; blowing against its stream they check it, and driving the waters upwards fill the channel and make it stop. For without doubt these blasts, which are started from the chill constellations of the pole are driven full against the stream. The river comes from the south out of the quarter where heat is born, rising among the black races of men of sunburnt colour far inland in the region of mid-day.

724 It may be too that a great heaping up of sand may choke up the mouths as a bar against the opposing waves, when the sea, troubled by the winds, drives the sand within; and in this manner it comes to pass that the river has less free issue, and the waves likewise a less easy downward flow.

729 It is also possible that rains occur more at its source at that season, because the etesian blasts of the north winds then drive all the clouds together into those quarters. And, we may suppose, when they have come together driven towards the region of mid-day, there at last the clouds, thrust together upon the high mountains, are massed and violently pressed.

735 Perchance it swells from deep among the high mountains of the Ethiopians, where the sun, traversing all with his melting rays, forces the white snows to run down into the plains.

738 Come now, I will unfold to you with what nature are endowed all Avernian places and lakes. First of all they are called by the name Avernian[91] because they are harmful to all birds, in that, when they have come right over those spots in their flight, forgetting the oarage of their wings, they slack their sails, and fall headlong, drooping with languid neck to earth, if by chance the nature of the spots so determines it, or into the water, if by chance the lake of Avernus spreads beneath them. That spot is by Cumae, where mountains smoke, choked with biting sulphur and enriched with hot springs.

[91] Lake Avernus, near Cumae in southern Italy, was, from the noxious vapours that were reputed to kill birds and its setting amid dark woods and mountains, regarded as a place of entrance to the underworld. The name 'Avernus' was connected by the ancients with the Greek *aornos* 'birdless' (see Virgil, *Aeneid*, VI, 239–42). Thus Lucretius gives the name 'Avernian' to all places fatal to birds.

749 There is too[92] a spot within the walls of Athens, on the very summit of the citadel, by the temple of Pallas Tritonis, the life-giver, whither croaking crows never steer their bodies on the wing, not even when the altars smoke with offerings. So surely do they fly, not in truth from the fierce wrath of Pallas, because of their vigil, as the poets of the Greeks have sung, but the nature of the spot of its own force accomplishes the task.

756 In Syria, too, it is said that there is likewise a spot to be seen, where, as soon as even four-footed beasts have set foot, its natural force constrains them to fall heavily, as though they were on a sudden slaughtered to the gods of the dead.

760 Yet all these things are brought about by a natural law, and it is clearly seen from what causes to begin with they come to be; lest by chance the gateway of Orcus should be thought to be in these regions; and thereafter we should by chance believe that the gods of the dead lead the souls below from this spot to the shores of Acheron; even as stags of winged feet are often thought by their scent to drag from their lairs the races of crawling serpents. And how far removed this is from true reason, now learn; for now I will try to tell of the true fact.

769 First of all I say, what I have often said before as well, that in the earth there are shapes of things of every kind; many which are good for food, helpful to life, and many which can induce diseases and hasten death. And that for different animals different things are suited for the purpose of life, I have shown before, because their nature and texture and the shapes of their primary particles are unlike, the one to the other. Many things which are harmful pass through the ears, many which are dangerous and rough to draw in find their way even through the nostrils, nor are there a few which should be avoided by the touch, yes, and shunned by the sight, or else are bitter to the taste.

781 Next we may see how many things are for man of a sensation keenly harmful, and are nauseous and noxious.

783 First, certain trees are endowed with a shade so exceed-

[92] The story (told by Ovid, *Metamorphoses*, II, 542–65) was that the crow brought some very unwelcome news to Pallas Athena and in a fury about it she banished him permanently from the Acropolis: a classic case of attacking the reporter because one is outraged at the news.

ing noxious, that often they cause an aching of the head, if one has lain beneath them, stretched upon the grass. There is, too, a tree on the great mountains of Helicon, which is wont to kill a man with the noisome scent of its flower. We may be sure that these things all grow in this way from the earth, because the earth contains in itself many seeds of many things, mingled in many ways, and gives them forth singled out. Again, a light but newly extinguished at night, when it meets the nostrils with its pungent smell, at once puts to sleep a man who is wont through disease to fall down and foam at the mouth. And a woman will fall back asleep with the heavy scent of castor, and her gay-coloured work slips from her delicate hands, if she has smelt it at the time when she has her monthly discharge. And many other things also slacken the drooping members throughout the frame, and make the anima totter within its abode.

799 Once again, if you dally in the hot bath when you are too full, how easily it comes to pass often that you fall down, as you sit on the stool in the middle of the boiling water. And how easily the noxious force and smell of charcoal finds its way into the brain, unless we have taken water beforehand. And when the burning fever has seized and subdued the limbs, 'then the smell of wine is like a slaughtering blow. Do you not see, too, sulphur produced in the very earth, and pitch harden into crusts of a noisome scent? And again, when men are following up the veins of gold and silver, probing with the pick deep into the hidden parts of earth, what stenches Scaptensula[93] breathes out underground? And what poison gold mines may exhale! How strange they make men's faces, how they change their colour! Have you not seen or heard how they are wont to die in a short time and how the powers of life fail those, whom the strong force of necessity imprisons in such work? All these effluences then earth sends steaming forth, and breathes them out into the open and the clear spaces of heaven.

818 So these Avernian places must also send up some fume deadly to the birds, which rises from the earth into the air, so that it poisons the expanse of heaven in a certain quarter. And at the very moment when the bird is carried thither on its wings, it is checked there, seized by the secret poison, so that it tumbles

---

[93] A town in Thrace near to which many mines were located.

straight down on the spot, where the effluence has its course. And when it has fallen into it, there the same force of the effluence takes away the remnant of life out of all its limbs. For truly first of all it causes a kind of dizzy seething in the birds. Afterwards it comes to pass that, when they have fallen right into the sources of the poison, there they must needs vomit forth their life as well, because there is great store of poison all around them.

830 It may happen, too, sometimes that this force and effluence of Avernus dispels all the air that is situated between the birds and the ground, so that there is left here an almost empty space. And when the birds in their flight have come straight over this place, on a sudden the lifting force of their pinions is crippled and useless, and all the effort of their wings fails on either side. And then, when they cannot support themselves or rest upon their wings, of course nature constrains them to sink by their weight to the ground, and lying in death in what is now almost empty void, they scatter abroad their anima through all the pores of their body.

840 Moreover, the water in wells becomes colder in summer, because the earth grows porous with the heat, and if by chance it has any seeds of heat of its own, it sends them abroad into the air. The more then earth is exhausted of its heat, the colder too becomes the moisture which is hidden in the earth. Moreover, when all the earth is hard pressed with cold, and contracts and, as it were, congeals, of course it comes to pass that, as it contracts, it squeezes out into the wells any heat it bears in itself.

848 There is said to be near the shrine of Ammon[94] a fountain, cold in the daylight and warm in the night time. At this fountain men marvel overmuch, and think that it is made to boil in haste by the fierceness of the sun beneath the earth, when night has shrouded earth in dreadful darkness. But this is exceeding far removed from true reasoning. For verily, when the sun, touching the uncovered body of the water, could not make

[94] The shrine of Jupiter-Ammon in the Libyan desert about 300 miles west of the Nile. Lucretius' conjectures in 840–78 are in many cases seeking to explain experiences resulting from different *comparative* temperatures rather than from what he treats as actual temperature changes. Thermometers were not invented until the seventeenth century.

it warm on the upper side, though its light in the upper air enjoys heat so great, how could it beneath the earth with its body so dense boil the water and fill it with warm heat? and that when it can scarcely with its blazing rays make its hot effluence pierce through the walls of houses. What then is the reason? We may be sure, because the ground is rarer and warmer around the fountain than the rest of the earth, and there are many seeds of fire near the body of the water. Therefore, when night covers the earth with the shadows that bring the dew, straightway the earth grows cold deep within and contracts. By this means it comes to pass that, as though it were pressed by the hand, it squeezes out into the fountain all the seeds of fire it has, which make warm the touch and vapour of the water. Then when the rising sun has parted asunder the ground with his rays, and has made it rarer, as his warm heat grows stronger, the first-beginnings of fire pass back again into their old abode, and all the heat of the water retires into the earth. For this cause the fountain becomes cold in the light of day. Moreover, the moisture of the water is buffeted by the sun's rays, and in the light grows rarer through the throbbing heat; therefore it comes to pass that it loses all the seeds of fire that it has; just as often it gives out the frost that it contains in itself, and melts the ice and loosens its bindings.

879 There is also a cold spring, over which if tow be held, it often straightway catches fire and casts out a flame, and a torch in like manner is kindled and shines over the waters, wherever, as it floats, it is driven by the breezes. Because, we may be sure, there are in the water very many seeds of heat, and it must needs be that from the very earth at the bottom bodies of fire rise up through the whole spring, and at the same time are breathed forth and issue into the air, yet not so many of them that the spring can be made hot. Moreover, a force constrains them suddenly to burst forth through the water scattered singly, and then to enter into union up above. Even as there is a spring within the sea at Aradus,[95] which bubbles up with fresh water and parts the salt waters asunder all around it; and in many other spots too the level sea affords a welcome help to thirsty sailors, because amid the salt it vomits forth fresh water. So then

---

[95] An important island off the north coast of Phoenicia.

those seeds are able to burst out through that spring, and to bubble out into the tow; and when they gather together or cling to the body of the torch, readily they blaze out all at once, because the tow and torches too have many seeds of hidden fire in themselves.

900 Do you not see too, when you move a wick just extinguished near a night-lamp, that it is kindled before it has touched the flame, and a torch in like manner? And many other things as well are touched first by the mere heat and blaze out at a distance, before the fire soaks them close at hand. This then we must suppose comes to pass in that spring too.

906 For what follows, I will essay to tell by what law of nature it comes to pass that iron can be attracted by the stone which the Greeks call the magnet, from the name of its native place, because it has its origin within the boundaries of its native country, the land of the Magnetes. At this stone men marvel; indeed, it often makes a chain of rings all hanging to itself. For sometimes you may see five or more in a hanging chain, and swaying in the light breezes, when one hangs on to the other, clinging to it beneath, and each from the next comes to feel the binding force of the stone: in such penetrating fashion does its force prevail.

917 In things of this kind much must be made certain before you can give account of the thing itself, and you must approach by a circuit exceeding long: therefore all the more I ask for attentive ears and mind.

921 First of all from all things, whatsoever we can see, it must needs be that there stream off, shot out and scattered abroad, bodies such as to strike the eyes and awake our vision. And from certain things scents stream off unceasingly; even as cold streams from rivers, heat from the sun, spray from the waves of the sea, which gnaws away the walls by the seashore. Nor do diverse sounds cease to ooze through the air. Again, moisture of a salt savour often comes into our mouth, when we walk by the sea, and on the other hand, when we behold wormwood being diluted and mixed, a bitter taste touches it. So surely from all things each several thing is carried off in a stream, and is sent abroad to every quarter on all sides, nor is any delay or respite

granted in this flux, since we perceive unceasingly, and we are suffered always to descry and smell all things, and to hear them sound.

936 Now I will tell over again of how rarefied a body all things are; which is clearly shown in the beginning of my poem. For in truth, although it is of great matter to learn this for many things, it is above all necessary for this very thing, about which I am attempting to discourse, to make it sure that there is nothing perceptible except body mingled with void.

942 First of all it comes to pass that in caves the upper rocks sweat with moisture and drip with trickling drops. Likewise sweat oozes out from all our body, the beard grows and hairs over all our limbs and members, food is spread abroad into all the veins, yes, it increases and nourishes even the extreme parts of the body, and the tiny nails. We feel cold likewise pass through bronze and warm heat, we feel it likewise pass through gold and through silver, when we hold full cups in our hands. Again voices fly through stone partitions in houses, smell penetrates and cold and the heat of fire, which is wont to pierce too through the strength of iron. Again, where the breastplate of the sky closes in the world all around [the bodies of clouds and the seeds of storms enter in], and with them the force of disease, when it finds its way in from without; and tempests, gathering from earth and heaven, hasten naturally to remote parts of heaven and earth; since there is nothing but has a rare texture of body.

959 There is this besides, that not all bodies, which are thrown off severally from things, are endowed with the same effect of sense, nor suited in the same way to all things. First of all the sun bakes the ground and parches it, but ice it thaws and causes the snows piled high on the high mountains to melt beneath its rays. Again, wax becomes liquid when placed in the sun's heat. Fire likewise makes bronze liquid and fuses gold, but skins and flesh it shrivels and draws all together. Moreover, the moisture of water hardens iron fresh from the fire, but skins and flesh it softens, when hardened in the heat. The wild olive as much delights the bearded she-goats, as though it breathed out a flavour steeped in ambrosia and real nectar; and yet for a man there is no leafy plant more bitter than this for food. Again, the pig shuns marjoram, and fears every kind of ointment; for to bristling pigs it is deadly poison, though to us it sometimes seems almost to give new life. But on the other hand, though to us mud is the foulest filth, this very thing is seen to be pleasant to pigs, so that they wallow all over in it and never have enough.

979 This too remains, which it is clear should be said, before I start to speak of the thing itself. Since many pores are assigned to diverse things, they must needs be endowed with a nature differing from one another, and have each their own nature and passages. For in truth there are diverse senses in living creatures, each of which in its own way takes in its own object within itself. For we see that sounds pass into one place and the taste from savours into another, and to another the scent of smells. Moreover, one thing is seen to pierce through rocks, another through wood, and another to pass through gold, and yet another to make its way out from silver and glass. For through the one vision is seen to stream, though the other heat to travel, and one thing is seen to force its way along the same path quicker than others. We may know that the nature of the passages causes this to come to pass, since it varies in many ways, as we have shown a little before on account of the unlike nature and texture of things.

998 When therefore all these things have been surely established and settled for us, laid down in advance and ready for use, for what remains, from them we shall easily give account, and the whole cause will be laid bare, which attracts the force of iron.

1002 First of all it must be that there stream off this stone very many seeds or an effluence, which, with its blows, parts asunder all the air which has its place between the stone and the iron. When this space is emptied and much room in the middle becomes void, straightway primordia of the iron start forward and fall into the void, all joined together. It comes to pass that the ring itself follows and advances in this way, with its whole body. Nor is anything so closely interlaced in its first particles, all clinging linked together, as the nature of strong iron and its cold roughness. Therefore it is the less strange, since it is led on by its particles, that it is impossible for many bodies, springing together from the iron, to pass into the void, but that the ring itself follows. And this it does, and follows on, until it has now reached the very stone and clung to it with hidden fastenings.

This same thing takes place in every direction. On whichever side room becomes void, whether athwart or above, the neighbouring bodies are carried at once into the void. For indeed they are set in motion by blows from the other side, nor can they themselves of their own accord rise upwards into the air.

1022 To this there is added, that it may the more be able to come to pass, this further thing as an aid, yes, the motion is helped, because, as soon as the air in front of the ring is made rarer, and the place becomes more empty and void, it straightway comes to pass that all the air which has its place behind, drives, as it were, and pushes the ring forward. For the air which is set all around is for ever buffeting things; but it happens that at times like this it pushes the iron forward, because on one side there is empty space, which receives the ring into itself. This air, of which I am telling you, finds its way in subtly through the countless pores of the iron right to its tiny parts, and thrusts and drives it on, as wind drives ship and sails. Again, all things must have air in their body seeing that they are of porus body, and the air is placed round and set close against all things. This air then, which is hidden away deep within the iron, is ever tossed about with restless motion, and therefore without doubt it buffets the ring and stirs it within; the ring, we may be sure, is carried towards the same side to which it has once moved headlong, struggling hard towards the empty spot.

1040 Sometimes as well the nature of the iron retreats from this stone, and is wont to flee and follow turn by turn. Further, I have seen Samothracian iron rings even leap up, and at the same time iron filings move in a frenzy inside brass bowls, when this Magnesian stone was placed beneath: so eagerly is the iron seen to desire to flee from the stone. When the brass is placed between, so great a disturbance is brought about because, we may be sure, when the effluence of the brass has seized beforehand and occupied the open passages in the iron, afterwards comes the effluence of the stone, and finds all full in the iron, nor has it a path by which it may stream through as before. And so it is constrained to dash against it and beat with its wave upon the iron texture; and in this way it repels it from itself, and through the brass drives away that which without it it often sucks in.

1056 In this matter do not be surprised that the effluence from this stone has not the power to drive other things in the same way. For in part they stand still by the force of their own weight, as for instance, gold; and partly, because they are of such porus body, that the effluence flies through untouched, they cannot be driven anywhere; among this kind is seen to be the substance of wood. The nature of iron then has its place between the two, and when it has taken in certain tiny bodies of brass, then it comes to pass that the Magnesian stones drive it on with their stream.

1065 And yet these powers are not so alien to other things that I have only a small collection of things of this kind, of which I can tell – things fitted just for each other and for nothing besides. First you see that stones are stuck together only by mortar. Wood is united only by bulls' glue, so that the veins of boards more often gape than the bindings of the glue will loosen their hold. The juice born of the grape is willing to mingle with streams of water, though heavy pitch and light olive-oil refuse. And the purple tint of the shellfish is united only with the body of wool, yet so that it cannot be separated at all, no, not if you were to be at pains to restore it with Neptune's wave, no, nor if the whole sea should strive to wash it out with all its waves. Again, is not there one thing only that binds gold to gold? is it not true that brass is joined to brass only by white lead? How many other cases might we find! What then? You have no need at all of long rambling roads, nor is it fitting that I should spend so much pains on this, but it is best shortly in a few words to include many cases. Those things, whose textures fall so aptly one upon the other that hollows fit solids, each in the one and the other, make the best joining. Sometimes, too, they may be held linked with one another, as it were, fastened by rings and hooks; as is seen to be more the case with this stone and the iron.

EPIDEMICS AND THE GREAT PLAGUE AT ATHENS, 1090–286

1090 Now what is the law of plagues, and from what cause on a sudden the force of disease can arise and gather deadly destruction for the race of men and the herds of cattle, I will unfold. First I have shown before that there are seeds of many things which are helpful to our life, and on the other hand it must needs be that many fly about which cause disease and death. And when by chance they have happened to gather and distemper the sky, then the air becomes full of disease. And all that force of disease and pestilence either comes from without the world through the sky above, as do clouds and mists, or else often it gathers and rises up from the earth itself, when, full of moisture, it has contracted foulness, smitten by unseasonable rains or suns.

1103 Do you not see, too, that those who journey far from their home and country are assailed by the strangeness of the climate and the water, just because things are far different? For what a difference may we suppose there is between the climate the Britons know and that which is in Egypt, where the axis of the world slants crippled; what difference between the climate in Pontus and at Gades, and so right on to the black races of men with their sunburnt colour? And as we see these four climates at the four winds and quarters of the sky thus diverse one from the other, so the colour and face of the men are seen to vary greatly, and diseases too to attack the diverse races each after their kind. There is the elephant disease, which arises along the streams of the Nile in mid Egypt, and in no other place. In Attica the feet are assailed, and the eyes in the Achaean country. And so each place is harmful to different parts and limbs: the varying air is the cause.

1119 Wherefore, when an atmosphere, which chances to be noxious to us, sets itself in motion, and harmful air begins to creep forward, just as cloud and mist crawls on little by little and distempers all, wherever it advances, and brings about change, it comes to pass also, that when at last it comes to our sky, it corrupts it and makes it like itself, and noxious to us. And so this strange destruction and pestilence suddenly falls upon the waters or settles even on the crops or on other food of men or fodder of the flocks; or else this force remains poised in the air itself, and, when we draw in these mingled airs as we breathe, it must needs be that we suck in these plagues with them into our body. In like manner the pestilence falls too often on the cattle, and sickness also on the lazy bleating sheep. Nor does it matter whether we pass into spots hostile to us and change the vesture of the sky, or whether nature attacking us brings a corrupt sky upon us, or something which we are not accustomed to feel, which can assail us by its first coming.

1138 Such a cause of plague, such a deadly influence, once in the country of Cecrops filled the fields with dead and emptied the streets, draining the city of its citizens. For it arose deep within the country of Egypt, and came, traversing much sky and floating fields, and brooded at last over all the people of Pandion. Then troop by troop they were given over to disease and death.

1145 First of all they felt the head burning with heat, and both eyes red with a glare shot over them. The throat, too, blackened inside, would sweat with blood, and the path of the voice was blocked and choked with ulcers, and the tongue, the mind's spokesman, would ooze with blood weakened with pain, heavy in movement, rough to touch. Then, when through the throat the force of disease had filled the breast and had streamed on right into the pained heart of the sick, then indeed all the fastnesses of life were loosened. Their breath rolled out a foul smell from the mouth, like the stench of rotting carcasses thrown out of doors. And straightway all the strength of the mind and the whole body grew faint, as though now on the very threshold of death. And aching anguish went ever in the train of their unbearable suffering, and lamentation, mingled with sobbing. And a constant retching, ever and again, by night and day, would constrain them continually to spasms in sinews and limbs, and would utterly break them down, wearing them out, full weary before.

1163 And yet in none could you see the topmost skin on the surface of the body burning with exceeding heat, but rather the body offered a lukewarm touch to the hands and at the same time all was red as though with the scar of ulcers, as it is when the accursed fire spreads through the limbs. But the inward parts of the men were burning to the bones, a flame was burning within the stomach as in a furnace. There was nothing light or thin that you could apply to the limbs of any to do him good, but ever only wind and cold. Some would cast their limbs, burning with disease, into the icy streams, hurling their naked body into the waters. Many leapt headlong deep into the waters of wells, reaching the water with their very mouth agape: a parching thirst, that knew no slaking, soaking their bodies, made a great draught no better than a few drops.

1178 Nor was there any respite from suffering; their bodies lay there foredone. The healers' art muttered low in silent fear, when indeed again and again they would turn on them their eyes burning with disease and reft of sleep.

1182 And many more signs of death were afforded then: the understanding of the mind distraught with pain and panic, the gloomy brow, the fierce frenzied face, and the ears too plagued and beset with noises, the breath quickened or drawn rarely and very deep, and the wet sweat glistening dank over the neck, the spittle thin and tiny, tainted with a tinge of yellow and salt, scarcely brought up through the throat with a hoarse cough. Then in the hands the sinews ceased not to contract and the limbs to tremble, and cold to come up little by little from the feet. Likewise, even till the last moment, the nostrils were pinched, and the tip of the nose sharp and thin, the eyes hollowed, the temples sunk, the skin cold and hard, a grin on the set face, the forehead tense and swollen. And not long afterwards the limbs would lie stretched stiff in death. And usually on the eighth day of the shining sunlight, or else beneath his ninth torch, they would yield up their life.

1199 And if any of them even so had avoided the doom of death, yet afterwards wasting and death would await him with noisome ulcers, and a black discharge from the bowels, or else often with aching head a flow of tainted blood would pour from his choked nostrils: into this would stream all the strength and the body of the man. Or again, when a man had escaped this fierce outpouring of corrupt blood, yet the disease would make its way into his sinews and limbs, and even into the genital organs of his body. And some in heavy fear of the threshold of death would live on, bereft of these parts by the knife, and not a few lingered in life without hands or feet and some lost their eyes. So firmly had the sharp fear of death got hold on them. On some, too, forgetfulness of all things seized, so that they could not even know themselves.

1215 And although bodies piled on bodies lay in numbers unburied on the ground, yet the race of birds and wild beasts either would range far away, to escape the bitter stench, or, when they had tasted, would fall drooping in quick-coming death. And indeed in those days hardly would any bird appear at all, nor would the gloomy race of wild beasts issue from the woods. Full many would droop in disease and die. More than all the faithful strength of dogs, fighting hard, would lay down their lives, strewn about every street; for the power of disease would wrest the life from their limbs.

1225 Funerals deserted, unattended, were hurried on almost in rivalry. Nor was any sure kind of remedy afforded for all alike; for that which had granted to one strength to breathe in his mouth the life-giving breezes of air, and to gaze upon the quarters of the sky, was destruction to others, and made death ready for them.

1230 And herein was one thing pitiful and exceeding full of anguish, that as each man saw himself caught in the toils of the plague, so that he was condemned to death, losing courage he would lie with grieving heart; looking for death to come he would breathe out his spirit straightway. For indeed, at no time would the contagion of the greedy plague cease to lay hold on one after the other, as though they were woolly flocks or horned herds. And this above all heaped death on death. For all who shunned to visit their own sick, over-greedy of life and fearful of death, were punished a while afterwards by slaughtering neglect with a death hard and shameful, abandoned and reft of help. But those who had stayed near at hand would die by contagion and the toil, which shame would then constrain them to undergo, and the appealing voice of the weary, mingled with the voice of complaining. And so all the nobler among them suffered this manner of death . . .[96] and one upon others, as they vied in burying the crowd of their dead: worn out with weeping and wailing they would return; and the greater part would take to their bed from grief. Nor could one man be found, whom at this awful season neither disease touched nor death nor mourning.

1252 Moreover, by now the shepherd and every herdsman, and likewise the sturdy steersman of the curving plough, would fall drooping, and their bodies would lie thrust together into the recess of a hut, given over to death by poverty and disease. On lifeless children you might often have seen the lifeless bodies of parents, and again, children breathing out their life upon mothers and fathers.

1259 And in no small degree that affliction streamed from the

---

[96] Some lines of connection seem to be missing here.

fields into the city, brought by the drooping crowd of countrymen coming together diseased from every quarter. They would fill all places, all houses; and so all the more, packed in stifling heat, death piled them up in heaps. Many bodies, laid low by thirst and rolled forward through the streets, lay strewn at the fountains of water, the breath of life shut off from them by the exceeding delight of the water, and many in full view throughout the public places and the streets you might have seen, their limbs drooping on their half-dead body, filthy with stench and covered with rags, dying through the foulness of their body, only skin on bones, wellnigh buried already in noisome ulcers and dirt.

1272 Again, death had filled all the sacred shrines of the gods with lifeless bodies, and all the temples of the heavenly ones remained everywhere cumbered with carcasses; for these places the guardians had filled with guests.

1276 For indeed by now neither the religion of the gods nor their power was counted for much: the grief of the moment overwhelmed it all.

1278 Nor did the old rites of burial continue in the city, with which aforetime this people had ever been wont to be buried; for the whole people was disordered and in panic, and every man sorrowing buried his dead, laid out as best he could. And to many things the sudden calamity and filthy poverty prompted men. For with great clamouring they would place their own kin on the high-piled pyres of others, and set the torches to them, often wrangling with much bloodshed, rather than abandon the bodies.[97]

---

[97] Lucretius' account in lines 1138–286 of the great plague of Athens of 430 BC follows Thucydides' account (II, 47–52), but it is a strange way to end a vast work on the nature of the universe. Why does he do it? Perhaps in part to contrast the physical sickness of Athens with the psychological sickness cured by the Athenian Epicurus that is celebrated at the start of Book VI. But, as has often been observed, there are strong signs that Lucretius was interrupted – probably by death – when his poem was not quite completed. If this is so, then it is reasonable to suppose that Book VI is not entirely complete. What one misses is anything like the Epicurean remedy that accompanies the account of wretched sexual relations in Book IV. It would have been in keeping with Lucretius' overall intentions to have added that an Epicurean view of the nature of things will assist human beings to accept disaster; that blaming gods or expecting their help is futile and worrying, and that understanding nature will enable us to see how things happen and thus, perhaps, enable us to avoid some pain and suffering.

DIOGENES OF
OENOANDA

The Last Appeal

'Diogenes of Oenoanda's[98] Epitome on Sensation and Physics'

2 [... observing that most people suffer from false notions about things and do not listen to the body] when it brings important and just [accusations] against the soul, alleging that it is unwarrantably mauled and maltreated by the soul and dragged to things which are not necessary (in fact, the wants of the body are small and easy to obtain – and the soul too can live well by sharing in their enjoyment – , while those of the soul are both great and difficult to obtain and, besides being of no benefit to our nature, actually involve dangers). So (to reiterate what I was saying) observing that these people are in this predicament, I bewailed their behaviour and wept over the wasting of their lives, and I considered it the responsibility of a good man to give [benevolent] assistance, to the utmost of one's ability, to those of them who are well-constituted. [This] is [the first reason] for the inscription.

I declare that the [vain] fear of [death and that] of the [gods

---

[98] Oenoanda was a small Greek city, about thirty miles inland from the sea, in the south-western corner of Asia Minor. Diogenes was a (presumably) wealthy citizen. He was responsible for the most unusually constructed philosophical document in the history of the world. It took the form of an inscription – recently estimated to have been in the region of 25,000 words – cut on a stone colonnade of the city. For a long time it was thought to have been executed about AD 200, but more recent evidence seems to suggest the AD 120s or 130s. Possibly because its Epicurean message came to be regarded as sacrilegious by Christians, possibly from some more practical cause, the colonnade was dismantled, probably between 250 and 275, and its stones re-used in the city walls and other structures. From the ruins of these, since the first observation of fragments of Greek text on them in 1884, about 6,000 words of the original text have been reconstructed. What emerges is Epicurean essays on physics, ethics and old age, letters and other maxims. About one-third of the essays on physics and ethics have been retrieved.

The definitive modern work on this extraordinary matter is *The Epicurean Inscription* by Martin Ferguson Smith (Naples, 1993). I am greatly obliged to him for permission to reproduce his translation of fragments 2 and 3, part of the opening passages of the physics, the first in order of the essays. As Smith observes, much more of the inscription will be found if an excavation takes place. Meanwhile, the translation – necessarily fragmentary – in his book, pp. 367–426, should be consulted. Words in square brackets indicate conjectural reconstruction of damaged or missing fractions of stone. Fragment 1 is the title, here used, for the essay on physics.

grip many] of us, [and that] joy [of real value is generated not by theatres] and [. . . and] baths [and perfumes] and ointments, [which we] have left to [the] masses, [but by natural science . . .].

3 [And I wanted to refute those who accuse natural science of being unable to be of any benefit to us.] In this way, [citizens,] even though I am not engaging in public affairs, I say these things through the inscription just as if I were taking action, and in an endeavour to prove that what benefits our nature, namely freedom from disturbance, is identical for one and all.

And so, having described the second reason for the inscription, I now go on to mention my mission and to explain its character and nature.

Having already reached the sunset of my life (being almost on the verge of departure from the world on account of old age), I wanted, before being overtaken by death, to compose a [fine] anthem [to celebrate the] fullness [of pleasure] and so to help now those who are well-constituted. Now, if only one person or two or three or four or five or six or any larger number you choose, sir, provided that it is not very large, were in a bad predicament, I should address them individually and do all in my power to give them the best advice. But, as I have said before, the majority of people suffer from a common disease, as in a plague, with their false notions about things, and their number is increasing (for in mutual emulation they catch the disease from one another, like sheep); moreover, [it is] right to help [also] generations to come (for they too belong to us, though they are still unborn); and, besides, love of humanity prompts us to aid also the foreigners who come here. Now, since the remedies of the inscription reach a larger number of people, I wished to use this stoa to advertise publicly the [medicines] that bring salvation. These medicines we have put [fully] to the test; for we have dispelled the fears [that grip] us without justification, and, as for pains, those that are groundless we have completely excised, while those that are natural we have reduced to an absolute minimum, making their magnitude minute.

SUGGESTIONS FOR FURTHER READING

The text of Epicurus' own writings in the context in which they survive can best be seen in the Loeb edition of *Diogenes Laertius*, translated by R. D. Hicks (Cambridge, Mass., 1925). Epicurus' writings are in Book X. A full, scholarly and annotated edition of Epicurus' texts and fragments together with their translation into English can be found in Cyril Bailey, *Epicurus: The Extant Remains* (Oxford, 1926). But the most comprehensive edition of Epicurus, including the papyrus fragments from *On Nature* (not represented in the present volume) is G. Arrighetti, *Epicuro Opere* (Turin, 1960; 2nd edn., 1973).

Books on Epicurus' philosophy as such (as distinct from its exhumation and examination from a textual, historical and linguistic point of view) are not numerous. A. A. Long's *Hellenistic Philosophy* (London, 1974), pp. 14–74 remains an excellent survey and J. M. Rist's *Epicurus: an Introduction* (Cambridge, 1972) is interesting and more extensive. For detailed studies of important aspects of early Atomism and Epicureanism consult D. J. Furley, *Two Studies in the Greek Atomists* (Princeton, 1967) and *The Greek Cosmologists*, vol. I, *The Formation of the Atomic Theory and its Earliest Critics* (Cambridge, 1987); Julia Annas, *Hellenistic Philosophy of Mind* (Berkeley, 1992), chs. 6 to 8; E. Asmis, *Epicurus' Scientific Method* (Ithaca and London, 1984); B. Farrington, *The Faith of Epicurus* (London, 1967); Stephen Everson 'Epicurus on the Truth of the Senses' in *Epistemology*, ed. S. Everson (Cambridge, 1990); C. C. W. Taylor 'All Perceptions are True' in *Doubt and Dogmatism*, ed. M. Schofield et al. (Oxford, 1980).

The best annotated edition of Lucretius in English is Cyril Bailey, *De Rerum Natura*, three vols. (Oxford, 1947, re-issued 1986). A more moderately annotated text together with Introduction etc. is in the Loeb Classics' *Lucretius* (Cambridge, Mass., and London, 1924), translated by W. H. D. Rouse and revised by M. F. Smith. Commendable books on Lucretius include E. J. Kenny, *Lucretius* (Oxford, 1977); C. Segal, *Lucretius on Death and Anxiety* (Princeton, 1990); D. Clay, *Lucretius and Epicurus* (Ithaca and London, 1983); D. R. Dudley (ed.), *Lucretius* (London, 1965).

At the time of writing, Philodemus' reasonably extensive but very fragmentary extant works are in effect not available in English. A Loeb edition, perhaps coupled with Diogenes of Oenoanda, is urgently needed.

The progress of work on Diogenes of Oenoanda's uniquely constructed philosophical essays is recorded in C. W. Chilton, *Diogenes of Oenoanda – the Fragments* (Oxford, 1971). The most recent, exciting and complete version of the text and its translation is in M. F. Smith, *Diogenes of Oenoanda: The Epicurean Inscription* (Naples, 1992).

The Epicureans have been cast in so many characters – as philosophical drones, as the Antichrist, as founders of modern science, and as mere dilettante sensualists – that the history of their influence on ideas is fascinating. It is well told in Howard Jones, *The Epicurean Tradition* (London and New York, 1989).

A complete printing history of Lucretius can be found in C. A. Gordon, *A Bibliography of Lucretius* (London, 1962; 2nd edn., 1985).

ANCIENT CLASSICS
IN EVERYMAN

A SELECTION

The Republic
PLATO
The most important and enduring of
Plato's works **£5.99**

The Education of Cyrus
XENOPHON
A fascinating insight into the culture
and politics of ancient Greece **£6.99**

Juvenal's Satires with the
Satires of Persius
JUVENAL AND PERSIUS
Unique and acute observations of
contemporary Roman society **£5.99**

The Odyssey
HOMER
A classic translation of one of the
greatest adventures ever told **£5.99**

£5.99

History of the
Peloponnesian War
THUCYDIDES
The war that brought to an end a
golden age of democracy **£5.99**

The Histories
HERODOTUS
The earliest surviving work of
Greek prose literature **£7.99**

PHILOSOPHY AND RELIGIOUS WRITING IN EVERYMAN

A SELECTION

Ethics
SPINOZA
Spinoza's famous discourse on the power of understanding **£4.99**

Critique of Pure Reason
IMMANUEL KANT
The capacity of the human intellect examined **£6.99**

A Discourse on Method, Meditations, and Principles
RENÉ DESCARTES
Takes the theory of mind over matter into a new dimension **£4.99**

Philosophical Works including the Works on Vision
GEORGE BERKELEY
An eloquent defence of the power of the spirit in the physical world **£4.99**

Utilitarianism, On Liberty, Considerations on Representative Government
J. S. MILL
Three radical works which transformed political science **£5.99**

Utopia
THOMAS MORE
A critique of contemporary ills allied with a visionary ideal for society **£3.99**

An Essay Concerning Human Understanding
JOHN LOCKE
A central work in the development of modern philosophy **£5.99**

Hindu Scriptures
The most important ancient Hindu writings in one volume **£6.99**

Apologia Pro Vita Sua
JOHN HENRY NEWMAN
A moving and inspiring account of a Christian's spiritual journey **£5.99**

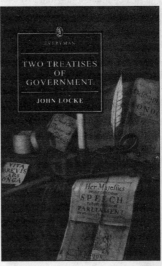

£3.99

AVAILABILITY

All books are available from your local bookshop or direct from
Littlehampton Book Services Cash Sales, 14 Eldon Way, Lineside Estate, Littlehampton, West Sussex BN17 7HE. PRICES ARE SUBJECT TO CHANGE.

To order any of the books, please enclose a cheque (in £ sterling) made payable to Littlehampton Book Services, or phone your order through with credit card details (Access, Visa or Mastercard) on 0903 721596 (24 hour answering service) stating card number and expiry date. Please add £1.25 for package and postage to the total value of your order.

In the USA, for further information and a complete catalogue call 1-800-526-2778.

SAGAS AND OLD ENGLISH LITERATURE IN EVERYMAN

A SELECTION

Egils saga

TRANSLATED BY
CHRISTINE FELL
A gripping story of Viking exploits
in Iceland, Norway and Britain **£4.99**

Edda

SNORRI STURLUSON
TRANSLATED BY
ANTHONY FAULKES
The first complete English transla-
tion **£5.99**

The Fljotsdale Saga and The Droplaugarsons

TRANSLATED BY
ELEANOR HAWORTH
AND JEAN YOUNG
A brilliant portrayal of life and
times in medieval Iceland **£3.99**

The Anglo-Saxon Chronicle

TRANSLATED BY
G. N. GARMONSWAY
A fascinating record of events in
ancient Britain **£4.99**

Anglo-Saxon Poetry

TRANSLATED BY
S. A. J. BRADLEY
A widely acclaimed collection **£6.99**

Fergus of Galloway: Knight of King Arthur

GUILLAUME LE CLERC
TRANSLATED BY
D. D. R. OWEN
Essential reading for students of
Arthurian romance **£3.99**

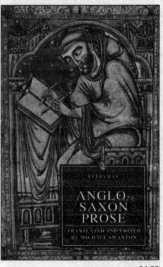

£4.99

AVAILABILITY

All books are available from your local bookshop or direct from
**Littlehampton Book Services Cash Sales, 14 Eldon Way, Lineside Estate,
Littlehampton, West Sussex BN17 7HE.** PRICES ARE SUBJECT TO CHANGE.

To order any of the books, please enclose a cheque (in £ sterling) made payable to
Littlehampton Book Services, or phone your order through with credit card details (Access,
Visa or Mastercard) on 0903 721596 (24 hour answering service) stating card number and
expiry date. Please add £1.25 for package and postage to the total value of your order.

In the USA, for further information and a complete catalogue call 1-800-526-2778.